# Creating a *Total Rewards* Strategy

# Creating a *Total Rewards* Strategy

## A TOOLKIT FOR DESIGNING BUSINESS-BASED PLANS

*Todd M. Manas and*
*Michael Dennis Graham*

AMACOM

**American Management Association**

New York • Atlanta • Brussels • Buenos Aires • Chicago • London • Mexico City
San Francisco • Shanghai • Tokyo • Toronto • Washington, D.C.

*This publication is designed to provide accurate and authoritative information in regard to the subject matter covered. It is sold with the understanding that the publisher is not engaged in rendering legal, accounting, or other professional service. If legal advice or other expert assistance is required, the services of a competent professional person should be sought.*

*Library of Congress Cataloging-in-Publication Data*

*Manas, Todd M., 1959–*
  *Creating a total rewards strategy : a toolkit for designing business-based plans / Todd M. Manas, Michael Dennis Graham.*
      *p.   cm.*
  *Includes bibliographical references and index.*
  *ISBN 0-8144-0722-6*
  *1. Incentive awards.   2. Performance awards.   I. Graham, Michael Dennis, 1952–   II. Title.*
  *HF5549.5.I5 M273   2002*
  *658.3'142—dc21*

                                        *2002007991*

*Printing number*

*10   9   8   7   6   5   4   3*

## Dedication

*To my wife, Fran, and my girls, Lillian and Sydney.*
*The true rewards of my world.—TMM*

*To Elizabeth, Rivendale, family, friends, clients, and associates.*
*All my learnings are from you.—MDG*

# Contents

**List of Figures**                                                    **xiii**
**Preface**                                                           **xvii**
**Acknowledgments**                                                   **xxix**

**Chapter 1:  Defining Total Rewards and a Rewards Strategy**            **1**

Total Rewards                                                            1
Noncash Rewards                                                          3
Total Rewards Strategy and Its Context                                   6
The Total Rewards Strategy Development Process                           8
Turnover and Employee Motivation Issues                                 10

**Chapter 2:  Planning the Total Rewards Development Process**          **13**

Total Rewards Strategy Process Owners                                   15
Reward Plan Development Business Case                                   18
   Issue Resolution (Why)                                21
   Objective (What)                                      21
   Diagnosis (Where)                                     22
   Timing (When)                                         22
   Involvement (Who)                                     22
   Project Scope (How)                                   24
   Cost/Benefit Modeling (How Much)                      24
Gap Analysis                                                            25
Composition of the Project Team                                         26
Project Planning                                                        30
The Transfer of Know-How                                               32

**Chapter 3:  Developing an Understanding of the Organization**        **39**

Defining What's Critical                                                39
External Environment                                                    42

Key Stakeholders                                                        45
Vision, Mission, and Values                                            47
Business Strategy                                                      48
Organization Capabilities                                             54
    The Balanced Scorecard as a Framework for Valuing
        Organization Capabilities                                     54
People Strategy                                                        65
    Organizational Structure                                          65
    Management Processes                                              66
    Organizational Culture                                            73
People Strategy Critical Success Factors                             82
Conclusion                                                            83

**Chapter 4:  Creating Linkage—Translating the Dimensions of
               Business into a Total Rewards Strategy            87**

Key Stakeholder Considerations in the External Environment           90
TRS Considerations and Vision, Mission, and Values                   95
    Key Messages                                                    100
    Money                                                           101
    Mix                                                             101
TRS Considerations and General Business Strategy                   102
    Key Messages                                                   102
    Money                                                          102
    Mix                                                            104
TRS Considerations and Organization Capabilities                   104
Value Chain Strategy–Based TRS Considerations                      105
    Examples of VCS-Based Strategies                               107
TRS Considerations and Specific Business Strategy                  109
    Examples of SBS                                                110
TRS Considerations and People Strategy                             112
    Structure                                                      113
    Process                                                        114
    Culture                                                        115
TRS Considerations and People Strategy Critical Success Factors    117
Priority Setting                                                    123

**Chapter 5:  Leveraging People—Creating the Total
               Rewards Architecture                              127**

Collecting Information for Analysis                                 128
    Document Review                                                128
    Stakeholder Input                                              130

Organizing the Information Collected 132
   Therefore Statements 134
Transferring Know-How: The Building Knowledge Phase 136
Making Business Strategy Operational 137
   Understanding the Level of Knowledge of
      Organization Strategy 139
   Value Proposition 142
   People Strategy Critical Success Factors 144
   Metrics 144
Knowing Your Strengths and Weaknesses, Opportunities
   and Threats 152
Linking TRS Mission and Objectives: Key Messages 155
   Key Messages Examples 157
   Because Statements 160
   Curly's "One Thing" (The Key Message) 161
Analyzing the Information Collected 162
   Gap Analysis 162
   Program Design SWOT Analysis 162
   Readiness for Change 166
   Reconsidering the Business Case 167
   Transfer of Know-How 167
Defining Reward Elements—Money 167
   Determining Which Elements to Include 168
   Determining People Markets 171
   Determining Competitive Levels 171
   Articulating a Mission and Objective for Each Reward Element 172
Determining the Appropriate Mix 174
Confirming Objectives 177
   Architecture Constituency Review 181
   Field Testing 182
Transferring Know-How: Leveraging People 183

**Chapter 6: Turning Architecture into Program Design 187**

Standard Reward Design Principles 187
Base Pay Design Principles 190
   Looking at Work 190
   Looking at People 197
   Delivering Pay 199
   Administration 203
Variable Rewards Design Principles 203
   Eligibility (Who) 205

Goals (What and How)                                        206
Line of Sight (Where)                                       208
Performance and Payout Relationship (Why)                   210
Amount (How Much)                                           212
Timing (When)                                               216
Administration                                              216
Long-Term Incentive Plans                                   218
Indirect Compensation Design Principles                     221
Perquisites                                                 225
Other Noncash Rewards                                       229
Where We Have Come From and Where We Are Going              235

**Chapter 7: Delivering the Desired Key Messages**          **239**

Impact Testing                                              241
Financial Analysis                                          242
Plan Objectives Testing                                     245
Barriers to Success/Easy Wins                               250
Implementation                                              253
Communication                                               253
Core Activities                                             256

**Chapter 8: Sustaining Plan Effectiveness**                **261**

Data Collection                                             268
Plan Design Assessment                                      269
Employee Commitment to Plan Design Principles               269
Fit with Business Strategy and Tactics                      272
Linkage and Leverage                                        274
The Need to Adjust and Communicate                          274
That's Not All, Folks                                       278

**Chapter 9: Approaches to Help Condense the Process**      **279**

The Conclave Approach to Total Rewards
    Strategy Development                                    281
Step One: Prework                                           282
Step Two: Day One                                           283
Step Three: Interim Work                                    285
Step Four: Day Two                                          286
Step Five: Finalize Money, Mix, and Messages                286
The Expert Panel/Ivory Tower Approach to Total Reward
    Strategy Development                                    288

The Upstream and Downstream Reward Strategy Audits          290
    Upstream Reward Strategy Audit                           290
    Downstream Reward Strategy Audit                         291

**Notes**                                                                 **293**
**Bibliography**                                                          **295**
**Index**                                                                 **297**
**About the Authors**                                                     **303**

# List of Figures

Figure P-1.   Link between business strategy, people,
              and rewards.                                           xx
Figure P-2.   Respondents' profile.                                 xxii
Figure 1-1.   Total rewards.                                          2
Figure 1-2.   Reward strategy and objectives.                        7
Figure 1-3.   Five phases of reward strategy development.            9
Figure 2-1.   The building know-how phase.                          14
Figure 2-2.   Employee involvement in Total Rewards
              Strategy design.                                       16
Figure 2-3.   Defining why-what-where-when-who-how-
              how much.                                              20
Figure 2-4.   The project team structure.                           23
Figure 2-5.   Project team roles and responsibilities.              27
Figure 2-6.   The breadth of communications.                        34
Figure 2-7.   Phased communication planning.                        36
Figure 3-1.   Factors influencing Total Rewards Strategy design.    40
Figure 3-2.   Vision: the compelling statement of how we
              see ourselves.                                         47
Figure 3-3.   The "how we are going to get there" mission.          48
Figure 3-4.   Forms of general business strategy (GBS).             50
Figure 3-5.   General business strategy (GBS).                      51
Figure 3-6.   Porter's value chain.                                 52
Figure 3-7.   Value chain strategy (VCS).                           53
Figure 3-8.   Specific business strategy (SBS).                     55
Figure 3-9.   The balanced scorecard as a strategic framework
              for action.                                           57
Figure 3-10.  Organization capabilities: customers.                 60

Figure 3-11.   Organization capabilities: products and services.        61
Figure 3-12.   Organization capabilities: management.                  62
Figure 3-13.   Organization capabilities: people.                      63
Figure 3-14.   Organization capabilities: technology.                  64
Figure 3-15.   Three components of organization
               structure concepts.                                     67
Figure 3-16.   Organization structure: number of layers.               68
Figure 3-17.   Organization structure: line/staff ratios.              69
Figure 3-18.   Organization structure: organizing themes.              70
Figure 3-19.   Management process framework.                           72
Figure 3-20.   Organizational processes: managing knowledge.           74
Figure 3-21.   Organizational processes: decision making.              75
Figure 3-22.   Organizational processes: contacts
               and communications.                                     76
Figure 3-23.   Organizational processes: supervision and
               people management.                                      77
Figure 3-24.   Organizational processes: change management.            78
Figure 3-25.   Characteristics of culture.                             81
Figure 3-26.   Key influences on reward designs.                       85
Figure 4-1.    Identifying Total Rewards Strategy
               alternatives.                                           89
Figure 4-2.    Ownership structure and its impact on TRS.              92
Figure 4-3.    Suppliers/customers and their impact on TRS.            94
Figure 4-4.    Government regulatory environment and its
               impact on TRS.                                          96
Figure 4-5.    Vision, mission, and values and their impact
               on TRS.                                                 97
Figure 4-6.    General business strategy and its impact
               on TRS.                                                 103
Figure 4-7.    Value chain strategy and its impact on TRS.             106
Figure 4-8.    The retail industry value chain.                        108
Figure 4-9.    Specific business strategy and its impact
               on TRS.                                                 111
Figure 4-10.   Organizational culture and its impact on TRS.           118
Figure 4-11.   Employee knowledge requirements and their
               impact on TRS.                                          119
Figure 4-12.   A balanced view of success.                             122
Figure 4-13.   Efficient frontiers.                                    124
Figure 5-1.    The fact/perception matrix.                             133
Figure 5-2.    Therefore statement tool.                               135

Figure 5-3.     Knowledge transfer timeline.                                 138
Figure 5-4.     Value chain behavioral analysis.                             141
Figure 5-5.     Customer/cost differentiation.                               143
Figure 5-6.     Value propositions and key metrics.                          145
Figure 5-7.     Brainstorm value proposition.                                146
Figure 5-8.     Define value propositions.                                   147
Figure 5-9.     Value proposition matrix.                                    148
Figure 5-10.    Determining the critical success factors.                    149
Figure 5-11.    People strategy critical success factors definitions.        150
Figure 5-12.    People strategy critical success factors matrix.             151
Figure 5-13.    Value proposition/PSCSF matrix.                              153
Figure 5-14.    Value proposition/ PSCSF measurement analysis.               154
Figure 5-15.    SWOT and the rewards strategy imperative.                    156
Figure 5-16.    Gap analysis.                                                163
Figure 5-17.    SWOT analysis.                                               164
Figure 5-18.    The money dimension.                                         169
Figure 5-19.    Feasibility matrix.                                          170
Figure 5-20.    Overall competitive level and people markets.                173
Figure 5-21.    Mix and the personality conundrum.                           175
Figure 5-22.    Future desired objectives.                                   178
Figure 6-1.     Consider rewards broadly.                                    188
Figure 6-2.     Total Reward elements.                                       189
Figure 6-3.     Base pay design principles.                                  191
Figure 6-4.     Work documentation.                                          192
Figure 6-5.     Job analysis.                                                194
Figure 6-6.     Job valuation.                                               195
Figure 6-7.     Organizing work.                                             196
Figure 6-8.     Short-term variable design principles.                       204
Figure 6-9.     Organizational level of measure: communists and
                cowboys example.                                             209
Figure 6-10.    Performance and payout relationships.                        211
Figure 6-11.    Distribution timing.                                         217
Figure 6-12.    Long-term variable design principles.                        220
Figure 6-13.    Indirect compensation design principles.                     226
Figure 6-14.    Perquisites design principles.                               228
Figure 6-15.    Other noncash rewards design principles.                     230
Figure 6-16.    Total Rewards and the business environment.                  236
Figure 6-17.    Field testing techniques.                                    238
Figure 7-1.     Implementation for superior performance.                     240
Figure 7-2.     The compounding impact of fixed compensation.                246

Figure 7-3.    Evaluating plan objectives.                          248
Figure 7-4.    Analyzing "because statements."                      249
Figure 7-5.    Surfing or sinking.                                  252
Figure 8-1.    Considering plan effectiveness.                      262
Figure 8-2.    Plans to reorganize.                                 263
Figure 8-3.    The increasing dimensions of business strategy,
               core capabilities, and cultural intensity.          264
Figure 8-4.    Reward program key messages.                         266
Figure 8-5.    Reward strategy change frequency.                    267
Figure 8-6.    Business factors for reconsideration.                270
Figure 8-7.    Measuring employee commitment                        271
Figure 8-8.    The balanced view of metrics.                        273

# Preface

MANY ORGANIZATIONS TODAY ARE OPERATING reward programs that are out of date, out of touch, and should be out of the question. These plans were developed for a labor force that has moved into retirement, leaving a new world in its wake. In the past two decades, the workforce has become more diverse, less likely to stay at the same organization for an extended period of time, and more sophisticated about compensation, rendering traditional pay plans ineffective at best and, in many cases, counterproductive. Despite these changes, fewer than one-half of U.S. companies have undertaken any systematic review of their reward plans in the last five years. Even more unsettling is the fact that the majority of organizations indicate that their Total Rewards Strategy fails to make a better-than-average connection to business or people strategies. When asked whether the reward strategy had met its objectives, fewer than one respondent in five (i.e., less than 20 percent) responded with an unqualified "Yes!"[1] These organizations are hesitant to change their policies because they are uncertain of how to go about doing it, they are afraid of change, they are too inflexible, or they are unable to respond fast enough to changes in the business.

The purpose of this book is to provide business leaders, human resources professionals, and reward plan designers with the framework necessary to measure the effectiveness of existing plans and, even more important, the *process* to design new ones. Bringing new plans to the table requires:

- Building a base of knowledge about what makes the company successful, and organizing that information in a way that can be communicated easily to the people who make it happen

- Transferring that knowledge to employees—that is, ensuring that they understand how what they do every day adds value to the company's customers and removing any cloak of secrecy
- Motivating people to accomplish business outcomes using human resources processes—and providing management tools to drive results
- Leveraging the power that is within the workforce by arming employees with the knowledge they need to understand their role and the business and to focus their efforts toward key outcomes—in short, engaging people in success by informing them, motivating them, and demonstrating their fit in the organization
- Sustaining that power through reward programs that provide the medium to transfer knowledge, motivate toward specified outcomes, engage people, and rejuvenate as business plans change

As your business changes so, too, must your rewards strategy and program to ensure you are rewarding the right kinds of behaviors. To get a sense of how much and how often you will need to update your rewards strategy, determine first how your business has changed and how quickly this change has taken place. Then, assess the extent to which that change will continue. Balance that change with the degree to which reward plans have changed. On a scale of one to ten—with one being no change and ten being no similarity—ask your business line leaders:

1. To what extent is the business environment the same as it was ten years ago? How different will it be ten years hence?
2. How similar is our means of competing in that environment? Are we positioned for continued change?
3. How different are our objectives and business plans? Will they continue to change at the current rate?
4. What is the degree of similarity of the demographics of our workforce from a decade ago? How similar will it be ten years from now, considering demographic predictions?
5. How similar are our reward plans to what they were ten years ago? How positioned are our plans to change to reflect the new business realities?

The first four sets of questions demonstrate the degree of change that companies have and will continue to experience. In our research, the answers to these questions tend to be in the range of seven to ten, suggesting fairly significant change. The two questions in the fifth set illustrate how compensation plans have and will keep pace. The answer to these questions is closer to three, suggesting minimal change, and that reward plan redesigns have not kept pace with the changing business environment. What is more, business leaders foresee significant change to their business, people, and strategy, but fail to realize how rewards will support that change. Other research in the area of Total Rewards Strategy illustrates a disappointingly low degree of linkage between business strategy, people, and rewards. When asked, "To what extent is your Total Rewards Strategy linked to your organization's business strategy?" nearly two-thirds of the respondents indicated a connection of only average or worse (see Figure P-1). At the same time, fewer than one-third of the respondents indicated a significant or greater connection when asked the question, "To what extent is your Total Rewards Strategy linked to your organization's people strategy?"

## The Data Behind the Process

The design of a Total Rewards Strategy, as set forth in this book, is the result of the authors' combined forty years of work spent, both together and individually, identifying how business and rewards are connected. It is also based on our work together recently, as we set out to prove or disprove those theories using a diagnostic tool—the *Business, People, and Total Reward Strategy Alignment Questionnaire*—with our clients. This groundbreaking research analyzed the main factors of reward program design and its influence on business outcomes. The data-based tool can help organizations in any business environment execute their business strategies by developing focused reward plans. It is referred to extensively throughout the text, and appears on the accompanying CD-ROM.

### Methodology

A questionnaire was used to determine the key influences on rewards. Senior human resources professionals were interviewed to collect several thousand data points about the participants. The questionnaire was divided into sections, including:

  ▪ *Environment and Organization Profile.* This section recorded factors reflecting the maturity of organizations and industries—for example, an organization's scope of operations, size, and fit within its industry sectors. The influences of stakeholder groups—such as owners,

Figure P–1.  Link between business strategy, people, and rewards.

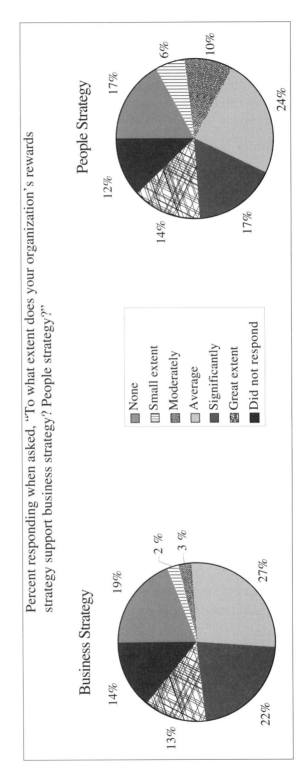

Percent responding when asked, "To what extent does your organization's rewards strategy support business strategy? People strategy?"

Business Strategy

People Strategy

Legend:
- None
- Small extent
- Moderately
- Average
- Significantly
- Great extent
- Did not respond

Business Strategy percentages: 27%, 22%, 13%, 14%, 19%, 2%, 3%

People Strategy percentages: 24%, 17%, 14%, 12%, 17%, 6%, 10%

Source:  *2001 Business, People, and Total Reward Strategy Alignment Questionnaire* (New York: Andersen, 2001)

customers, suppliers, government agencies, employees, and unions—were also studied.

- *Strategy Profile.* Three levels of business strategy were captured in the study:

1. General business strategy (GBS) reflects Michael Porter's classic three-strategy model of cost leadership, product or service differentiation, and focus.
2. Value chain strategy (VCS) characterizes the organization in terms of how and where it achieves competitive advantage, using Porter's value chain model as a framework.
3. Specific business strategy (SBS) captures specific choices made around growth and customer relationship strategies.

- *Organization Capabilities.* Information was collected about core competencies required for success. These competencies were then grouped into categories such as customer, products and services, management, people, and technology. The study not only addressed how an organization historically has competed, but also how it planned for critical changes to compete effectively in the future.

- *People Strategy.* This section covered three main points:

1. Organizational structure—the number of levels, percentage of line and staff, and the general design of the reporting relationships
2. Organizational processes—how an organization executes its business, and measures and communicates success
3. Organizational culture—the general norms and attributes of the organization

- *Reward Strategy.* This section identified how the participants created reward programs based on the various influences identified, and how critical changes in each area were reflected in the program through modifications.

The response form had nearly 1,000 questions and was used to collect information from more than 125 companies. Figure P-2 gives a profile of the questionnaire respondents by size of company (in terms of revenues and number of employees). The respondents reflect a cross section of American companies.

## Figure P-2. Respondents' profile.

Breakdown by revenues (in millions):

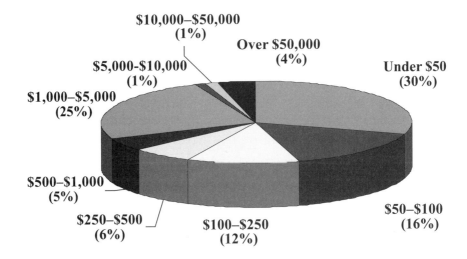

Breakdown by number of employees:

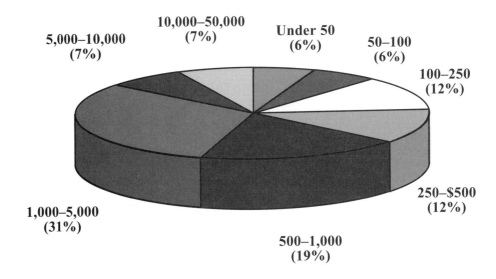

## What the Data Tell Us

The most powerful finding is that in the next three years companies seek to achieve more, in more varied ways. The preponderance of organizations indicated increases in the numbers of business strategy initiatives, means for adding value to their products and services, requirements for capabilities, and attributes for success. To achieve this, they will need more variety in their reward programs. Surgical reward programs—that is, individualized programs that afford greater differentiation among individuals, jobs, functions, and/or units—will drive success. This trend clashes with tradition, because historically corporations attempt to keep programs across the organization as consistent as possible. In the future, companies will achieve surgical rewards by defining reward strategies where tactics can be deployed differently to meet the needs of each situation. Accordingly, the strategy will be consistent even if its application is not. This will be done in two ways:

- Providing more reward tools in the management toolbox, which will allow management to customize the reward to the situation
- Increasing differentiation across the organization of rewards themselves

In addition, based on the findings from the questionnaire, two consistent themes are evident: First, individual performance will diminish in importance in the future while team and organization performance will gain in influence. Second, reward policies will focus more on long-term rather than short-term goals. While the data demonstrate that the diversity and complexity of the key messages being delivered are increasing significantly, the one clear and consistent message that companies are sending to their employees is, "We are in this together for the long haul."

## Using the Data

The information gathered from this study is used throughout this book to demonstrate norms for developing strategies and linking rewards to them. Readers can also request the full database findings of the survey by completing the questionnaire that comes with the CD-ROM that accompanies this book and returning it to manas.tm@buck consultants.com.

## Why Buy This Book

The only true best practice is the practice that works "here"—in your company! Even the myriad of texts that reveal "best practices" through case studies of world leaders in compensation fall short of a universal model. Indeed, they demonstrate that those practices work in those organizations because they fit: They belong with the organization's structure, core business processes, and culture that support the business strategy.

Rather than offering a one-size-fits-all prescription for design or lofty "be like me" generalizations, this book provides a step-by-step road map for the development of the appropriate Total Rewards Strategy to suit any company's broader corporate or business strategy. This book is not about a pay plan *design*—it is about defining the underlying design *process* to guide you through the pay design journey and find the unique solution. The user will find in this book a way to break down the business strategy into an operational set of principles to develop a Total Rewards Strategy in direct support of desired outcomes.

## How to Use This Book

Reward plan design is a fact-based art. Accordingly, this book is a guide for collecting, organizing, and interpreting the facts and perceptions required to make plan design choices in your organization. It illustrates the key decisions that need to be made and provides a foundation for making those decisions. Each user's journey through its pages should be personalized, and each outcome is unique. We encourage you to first read the book in its entirety to gain an understanding of its contents and methodology. Identify the tools and techniques that will make the most sense for your situation. Consider both the size and scope of the undertaking and the resources that you have to dedicate to the effort.

The accompanying CD-ROM includes additional design tools, exercises, facilitation guides, diagnostics, and process techniques for use hand-in-hand with this book. Use it to compile the materials that are most appropriate to your undertaking. The Buck Consultants Web site (www.buckconsultants.com) provides further materials and updates, as well as the underlying research findings that form the basis for many of the ideas presented.

Once you have read the book you will need to go back to use the specific topics, exercises, and process tools that make sense for your project. The more you have marked the book's pages, altered the tools to meet your organization's requirements, and made notations about where and how you may use the various methods described, the easier this second effort will be.

Finally, put this book in your professional "toolkit"—whether on a bookshelf or in a briefcase—and continue to refer to it. Bear in mind that reward plans have a limited shelf life—historically three years, and that is getting shorter as the pace of business change increases. Establishing sound compensation plans requires more than a one-time effort. Like any business process, it demands continual improvement. You will want to use the tools and resources presented here on occasion, just to verify plan designs and recommend changes—testing, measuring, and modeling along the way. Do not merely read this book. Refer to it over and over again as you design, refine, and/or redesign or enhance.

## How This Book Is Organized

We start by introducing the Total Rewards concept and definitions and the context for a design effort. The planning effort is described next. You will see that the design itself will be influenced by specific aspects of business, and you'll learn how to evaluate these influences within the Total Rewards Strategy context. The details of the design process, which are at the core of the book, are followed by a discussion of implementation and the process for measuring the ongoing effectiveness of the plans. Finally, the subject of planning comes full circle in the last chapter in the book, which provides alternative processes that may be used to augment the design effort. The complete breakdown of the chapters, and what you'll find in each one, follows.

*Chapter 1: Defining Total Rewards and a Rewards Strategy* will give you an understanding of a new, all-encompassing view of rewards that defines rewards broadly. You should begin to identify the rewards your organization offers—both formally and informally (sometimes invisibly). What rewards get broadcast? Which ones go unstated?

*Chapter 2: Planning the Total Rewards Development Process* scopes the effort you are about to undertake and provides a framework for creating and directing the design team. The tools and techniques provided can be applied whether you want to engage in an entire rebuilding, from start to finish, or merely measure, calibrate, or diagnose. Here you will find the project management insights for defining the appropriate size, structure, and membership of the design team and setting its mission and direction—again, whether you are forming such a team or simply need to identify the best sources of input. This is the beginning of Phase I of the Total Rewards Strategy Development Process: building know-how.

*Chapter 3: Developing an Understanding of the Organization* looks at the dimensions of a business that most directly influence reward designs, thereby allowing designers to create a company-specific framework for the development of reward plans. This is the foundation of the process, identifying how various data is to be used and analyzed and the thought process for determining what the data means to this effort.

*Chapter 4: Creating Linkage—Translating the Dimensions of Business into a Total Rewards Strategy* provides the taxonomy for interpreting the dimensions of business (as defined in Chapter 3) in order to build an understanding of the business and then to break it down into measurable criteria to use in the direct design of reward plans. This is the beginning of Phases II and III of the process: transferring know-how and linking employees to the business.

*Chapter 5: Leveraging People—Creating the Total Rewards Architecture* details the process for collecting, organizing, and analyzing the information collected. It contains what you need to know for taking the information about the business and turning it into a Reward Architecture and philosophy. Process tools and facilitation techniques are the foundation of this chapter. Reward Architecture and philosophy are the first half of the effort to align employees and their motivations to the business strategy. The second half of the effort is designing motivational reward programs, as described in the next chapter.

*Chapter 6: Turning Architecture into Program Design* provides technical details for analyzing design principles and creating reward plans in support of the architecture. You will develop the organization's Total Rewards Strategy at this point, through the application of a set of design principles; this chapter also marks the conclusion of the design and development process, setting the stage for implementation.

*Chapter 7: Delivering the Desired Key Messages* demonstrates how technical design represents a fraction of the battle. After building plans, the designers turn their expertise to delivering those plans to employees. Effective communications and implementation are key to gaining employee commitment. This is transferring and, as significantly, leveraging know-how (Phase IV) within the Total Rewards Strategy Development Process.

*Chapter 8: Sustaining Plan Effectiveness* starts Phase V of the Total Rewards Strategy Development Process. This chapter contains the insights and measurement process tools and techniques for analyzing plan effectiveness. It outlines steps and methodologies for ongoing refinement and adjustments and demonstrates the continuing need for follow-up and measurement. That's how the effectiveness of these plans are sustained for superior performance.

Chapter 9: *Approaches to Help Condense the Process* explores how not every situation commands the depth and commitment to resource deployment that the employee engagement development process requires. What is more, this book encourages you to customize its tools and approach to the specific requirements of the company you work for. Chapter 9 provides several condensed frameworks for doing just that. The reader will find several alternatives that may help to consolidate all or parts of the process.

If this process is about giving employees the knowledge they need to drive the organizational success, this book is about giving the reader the power to make it happen. It is intended to be a tool to help you manage the process of plan design and ongoing measurement and improvement. Its basis is the professional experiences of some of the best consultants in the field, built on the foundation of research, and it includes all the tools you will need. The CD-ROM provides two additional components that bring the book's pages to life: First, a series of Microsoft PowerPoint slides allow you, the user, to customize the approach for the situation at hand. This deck is itself a powerful toolbox for facilitating the process. Second, the diagnostic questionnaire will allow you to assess the key influences on rewards and compare your company's situation to norms.

# Acknowledgments

Both of us wish to acknowledge the clients that we have worked with over the years. If it were not for their needs, patience, and willingness to work in a partnership manner, none of this would have been possible and our lives and their organizations would be much different then they are today. The following come to mind:

Accor International
Albany International Corporation
Alleghany Corporation
Alpha Investments
Amerada Hess
American Management Association
Analog Devices
Ann Taylor
Apple Computer
AT&T
Atomic Energy Commission of Canada
Australia Mutual Providant
Automatic Data Processing
Ball Corporation
Banknorth Group
BASF
Bausch & Lomb
Baxter International
Becton, Dickinson and Co.
Bell Atlantic (now Verizon)
BellSouth
Ben and Jerry's Homemade
Bestfoods
BF Goodrich
Binary Tree

Cablevision Systems
Cap Gemini
Caxton
Cendant
Chanel
Chase Manhattan Bank
CIBA
Coca-Cola
Comcast
Computer Sciences Corporation
Coty Inc.
D. E. Shaw
Danbury Hospital
DoubleClick
Dynamics Research Corporation
Electronic Data Systems
Energy East
Englehard
E*TRADE
Exxon Mobil
FAMM
First Quality
FleetBoston Financial
Florida Power and Light
Georgia-Pacific

The Girl Scouts of the USA
Goldman Sachs Group
Guardian Life of America
Hannaford Brothers
Harvard University
Hasbro
Hatchette Filipacchi Magazines
Hershey Foods
The Home Depot
HSBC
International Business Machines
Irving Oil
J.C. Penney
K2 Digital
Kepner Tregoe
Ketchum
KeyCorp
Kmart
Laerdal Medical Corporation
Limited
L'Oréal USA
LVMH Moët Hennessy Louis Vuitton
M&T Bank Corp.
Martha Stewart Living Omnimedia
The May Company
McGraw-Hill
MCI (now part of WorldCom, Inc.)
McKinsey & Co.
Merrill Lynch
Metropolitan Life Insurance
Mikimoto
Morgan Stanley Dean Witter & Co.
National Fuel Gas
New Power
Northeast Utilities
Nortel Networks
New York City Board of Education
New York Life Insurance Company
Oceanconnect.com
Office Depot
Ogden Entertainment
Ohio Casualty
Omnicom
Oxford University Press

Pacific Telesis
Payless ShoeSource
PDVSA
Pegasus Investments
PerkinElmer
Perot Systems
Philip Morris Companies, Inc.
Phillips-Van Heusen
Praxair
Prudential
Qantas Airways
Quest Diagnostics
Register.com
Revlon
Roche Vitamins
Royal Caribbean Cruises
Saint Raphael's Healthcare System
Saks Incorporated
SBC Communications
SCA
Sears, Roebuck and Co.
Shell Oil
Securities Industry Automation
    Corporation (SIAC)
Smith College
Sony
Stamford Financial Group, The
Stanley Works
State Farm Insurance
State Street Corp.
Sun Chemical
Swissotel
Textron
T-FAL
Travelers
University of Massachusetts Medical
    School
USAA
Vermont Public Service Corporation
Wal-Mart Stores
Wilson Greatbatch Technologies
WorldCom
Ziff Brothers Investments

But of course, there are others. First, it took administrative muscle to get the job done. Specifically, Keith Marshak, who spent many an overtime hour on our behalf, and Joanne Larsen, who cracked the whip, deserve all the praise that is due them. Second, there is the editorial team at AMACOM that gave this book a life (at the expense of us having one), most notably, our development editor, Christina McLaughlin, whose significant contribution dramatically enhanced the quality of the work product. We cannot express our gratitude to her. Also, there are the efforts of our associate editor, Erika Spelman, and copy editor, Karen Brogno, and finally, Adrienne Hickey, the executive editor who saw its promise.

Third, the contributions of the following consultants and clients of Buck Consultants, whose stories are included where noted, are also acknowledged: David Browne, Kristen Busang, David Bushley, Howard Fine, Martha Glantz, Mary Horowitz, Toni Jackson, David Leach, Jeffrey Miller, Antoinette Petrucci, James Scannella, Gary Starzmann, and Scott White.

Last, there are the colleagues with whom we've worked in a combined six wonderful professional services firms (Andersen, Buck, Clark Bardes, HayGroup, Towers Perrin, Watson Wyatt). Too many to name, the challenge and insight that we have gained through sharing ideas with these coworkers serves as the foundation for our thinking. Besides, you know who you are . . .

## Chapter 1

# DEFINING TOTAL REWARDS AND A REWARDS STRATEGY

DESIGNING A REWARDS STRATEGY BEGINS with the broadest view and understanding of the concept of "total rewards." This term includes all types of rewards—indirect as well as direct, and intrinsic as well as extrinsic (see Figure 1-1). From an employee's perspective, it is everything the employee takes away from his or her relationship with an employer. The operative word here is *everything!* Yet this definition is inconsistent with how reward plan design is generally practiced; very few companies take such a holistic view.[1] In this book, however, the term *Total Rewards* represents the requirement for "31 flavors." People have different tastes; variety responds to those differences. The more broadly rewards are defined, the more likely you are to touch upon what motivates the broad constituencies represented by your employees. But if rewards are not defined as broadly as possible, the range of alternative reward strategies and satisfied organizations will be very limited. Besides, our data suggest that a more limited view of rewards is also a more costly view, as organizations may tend to respond to every situation with cash.

## Total Rewards

Total Rewards begins with Total Remuneration, a subset of Total Rewards. Total Remuneration (TR) comprises all the elements of rewards that can be valued in dollar terms. TR begins with base cash—the fixed and recur-

1

Figure 1–1. Total rewards.

| Definition | Reward Elements | Common Examples |
|---|---|---|
| TOTAL REWARDS | Other Noncash Rewards | • Quality of Work & Life<br>• Affiliation<br>• Development |
| TOTAL REMUNERATION | Perquisites | • Cars<br>• Clubs<br>• Counseling<br>• Contracts |
| | Benefits | • Retirement<br>• Health & Welfare<br>• Time Off w/Pay<br>• Statutory Programs |
| TOTAL | Long-Term Variable | • Stock/Equity<br>• Cash<br>• Incentive (Long-Term) |
| TOTAL DIRECT CASH | Short-Term Variable | • Incentive (Short-Term)<br>• Bonus/Spot Awards<br>• Contract |
| TOTAL CASH | Base Cash | • Base Salary<br>• Hourly Wage |

Intrinsic

Extrinsic:

All things onto which we can assign a dollar value

Source:  Adapted from Todd Manas, "Combining Reward Elements to Create the Right Team Chemistry," Workspan (November/December 2000), p. 47.

ring wage. Building on base cash is any short-term variable pay. Short-term variable pay is compensation that is paid for the result of work measured in increments of a year or less; it typically varies from one period to the next. Annual base cash plus annual variable cash makes up Total Cash Compensation (TCC). TCC plus the present value of all long-term incentives (LTI) is Total Direct Cash (TDC). (Long-term incentives are the variable compensation provided for measurement periods in excess of one year.) Add the value of benefits and cash-bearing perquisites, and you derive Total Remuneration—the total of all that can be valued in dollar terms (see the sidebar, "Are Benefits a Reward?").

> **Are Benefits a Reward?**
>
> According to the definition used in this book, they certainly are. What's more, employees are not entitled to benefits, and while there are statutory requirements, they are minimal. Moreover, even though they are legislated, the company still pays for them.
>
> Generally, though, most employees, and even some managers, do not consider benefits a reward. Ask your employees and managers what they believe, and you will begin to gain insight into how rewards are defined at your organization.

## Noncash Rewards

In addition to the elements of Total Remuneration, organizations offer employees rewards in various forms that, while measurable, may or may not have a dollar value. As the dynamics of the labor market shift, these other noncash rewards take on greater significance for several reasons.

Noncash rewards are the components of the employment compact, or employer/employee relationship, that matter most to today's workforce. People do not leave jobs for money—they leave jobs for opportunity. When considering data from research institutes such as the Gallup Organization across what represents hundreds of thousands of employee responses

> **The Employment Compact**
>
> A compact is an agreement or covenant. The term is used here to reflect the unwritten contract that exists between an employer and an employee for the exchange of value. Accordingly, the employer offers rewards as payment for the employee's service; it is the reason a company has a position and why a person works for that company. The employment compact provides a means for an employer to define its job offerings and differentiate itself in the labor market. Establishing this unique identity requires knowing the characteristics of the compact that are most meaningful to the employees being recruited and retained and articulating those characteristics as rewards.

to anonymous attitude studies, the results are consistent. The top three reasons people leave jobs all involve opportunities—the opportunity to grow and develop, to learn new skills, and to be in an environment where they are appreciated. On a list of the top eight reasons why people leave jobs, pay ranks at number eight. People seek the opportunity to contribute, and they want to feel their contribution is appreciated. At the same time, chief executive officers rank customer satisfaction and employee retention as the top two measurements of value creation.[2] Customer service is a proven by-product of employee satisfaction, which in turn is directly linked to rewards and recognition.[3]

In addition, noncash rewards are the only real way to differentiate your employment offerings. Cash is a commodity, so it cannot differentiate one company's employment compact from another; it is the intangibles that distinguish. Besides, when it comes to money, someone will always pay more. It is by broadly defining Total Rewards to include other noncash rewards that employers truly distinguish themselves in the labor market from the competition and earn employee commitment. It is a matter of focusing the employment compact on the rewards that matter to the workforce you are trying to create, not on the cash elements traditionally measured by companies. Organizations spend a lot of time measuring Total Remuneration. But what matters to employees is the total package—the Total Rewards.

Often, responding to employee requirements is circumstantial. The effects can be immediate or longer term. Consider two current events:

1. At the time of the authoring of this book we are experiencing a dramatic shift in the world's economies. This has had a profound impact on the labor market, shifting the U.S. labor market from an all-out war for people (the boom years saw more of a fight for bodies than a true war for talent) to a very focused series of battles for key talents. This reflects a long-term impact requiring adjustments to Total Rewards Strategy.

2. The events of September 11 posed an immediate circumstance that caused a rewards response. Consider that, according to a survey by Buck Consultants, "When faced with the harsh reality that terrorism can occur even in this country, employers have responded with increasing security, providing employee assistance programs, and granting additional time off, especially in the areas located in the vicinity of the attacks."[4] Unarguably, these employers gained significant good will capital with their people.

These illustrations point up the need to stay attuned to one's environment and be able to be flexible in your responses.

Finally, other noncash rewards yield a greater return on the monies invested. Our recent research demonstrates that smaller organizations understand how noncash rewards can have a greater return on each reward dollar invested, enhancing the economical impact of the Total Rewards package.[5] They typically compete for the same caliber of talent but often offer fewer benefits and lower salaries. They make up for this through a work environment and experience that rebalances the Total Rewards equation. And while it may be true that cash gets you in the game, it doesn't win it for you; smaller organizations have been successful at winning the talent game for a lower total cost through other noncash rewards that are categorized into three areas—affiliation, quality of work and life, and training and development.

- *Affiliation.* Affiliation captures the benefits of belonging to a company over a period of time. Those benefits range from the quiet satisfaction of job stability to the excitement of working for a winner. Over time, affiliation builds value much in the way time spent in a home builds value for its owner. The homeowner enjoys the home—living in a specific neighborhood, being part of that community, and participating in local events. All the while, the home accrues value to the homeowner for these reasons (in addition to any market appreciation that may occur at the same time). The same principle applies to the employee who affiliates with coworkers and works in an industry, company, and geographic area. Such an employee builds a kind of personal equity—socially, professionally, and financially. In a home, that equity is realized both while you live there and when you sell; for affiliation it is realized while the employee works for the organization and when he or she leaves (for example, retires, transfers, terminations).

- *Quality of Work and Life.* This area refers to the challenge that the employee receives at work and the personal satisfaction derived through that challenge. The exposure to projects, people, and specific opportunities to share in the value that the company creates for the community is all part of this reward element. It represents the personal and professional fulfillment of the employee.

- *Training and Development.* This area represents the investment that an organization makes in its employees' human capital. It comes in many forms, including training for a current job, building competency for a future job, or learning a life skill.

In conclusion, if other noncash rewards matter to the workforce that you are building, then they need to matter to you as an employer. They are fundamental in any company's ability to attract and retain the talent required to meet its business needs.

There are myriad potential rewards, and the combinations and permutations for organizing and delivering them to employees are infinite. The critical difference comes in the development of a Total Rewards Strategy.

## Total Rewards Strategy and Its Context

Total Rewards Strategy is a plan for allocating reward resources in a manner that directs the business to the successful execution of its objectives. There are three main factors involved in developing and managing this plan: a thorough understanding of the total value of all of an organization's reward elements vis-à-vis its stated market competitive objectives (money), the strategic allocation and distribution of money to each element (mix), and the articulation and delivery of specific and deliberate expressions to employees about what a company values and expects (messages). These three defining dimensions of Total Rewards Strategy are displayed in Figure 1-2 and explained as follows:

1. *Money.* This is the "what" dimension, or the elements that are considered to be rewards in the marketplaces where you compete for talent and the competitive levels that you establish for yourself in those marketplaces. This is the content and level of rewards, and it is where Total Rewards in the employment compact are defined.

2. *Mix.* This is the "how, who, when, and where" dimension. It determines how program eligibility is established, who participates in the plans, and how rewards are delivered. It organizes rewards into the most efficient means of delivery. Money and mix together are the architecture of rewards, and they are used to create the blueprint for developing reward plans.

3. *Messages.* Messages are the "why" dimension—conveying the values and expectations that need to be delivered through rewards. Purposefully articulating specific messages allows a company to focus employees on desired business outcomes and the competencies to be successful. Messages forge alignment of both plans and people's efforts. This is the philosophy of the rewards (or compensation philosophy), the overarching premise of reward programs. It

Figure 1-2. Reward strategy and objectives.

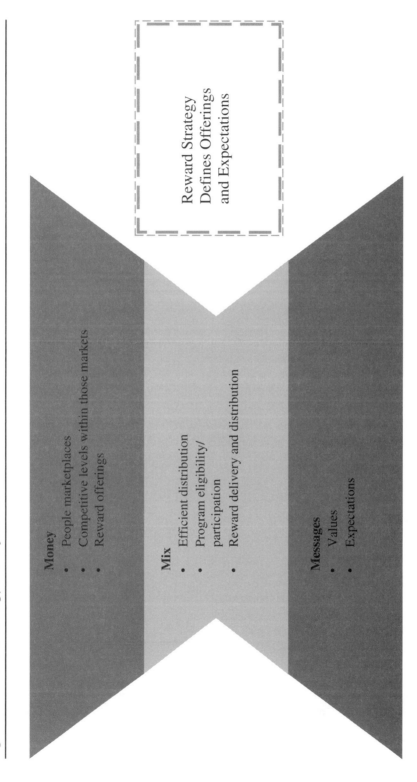

Reward Strategy
Defines Offerings
and Expectations

**Money**
- People marketplaces
- Competitive levels within those markets
- Reward offerings

**Mix**
- Efficient distribution
- Program eligibility/participation
- Reward delivery and distribution

**Messages**
- Values
- Expectations

defines at the highest level how you want your plans to be viewed. It is the statement of the plan's imperative—what it is designed to accomplish (see the sidebar on how "Attracting, Retaining, and Motivating Are Noble Pursuits").

---

### Attracting, Retaining, and Motivating Are Noble Pursuits

There are pundits who would have us believe that the mantra "attract, retain, and motivate" is passé as a reward philosophy. This is not so. If anything, traditional plans are passé. "Attract, retain, and motivate" remains a viable imperative for reward plans.

Ask your line management, "Why do we have reward programs?" Invariably, you will hear that reward programs exist to capture your fair share of the labor market, keep the best of the talent you have acquired, and direct employees' efforts toward certain outcomes—in other words, to attract, retain, and motivate.

Now ask your line managers, "Which of our plans are focused on attraction? What about retention? Motivation?" These are different goals, requiring different tools and techniques. Consider the CEO of a company who, having been told that his company was at the fortieth percentile for pay and benefits and the bottom quartile for performance, said, "Our turnover is low because of our culture; people like to work here. The market is inconsequential." One may reply to such a statement by saying, "That's a good retention strategy. But with your corporation underperforming its peers, this doesn't seem to be an effective motivation or attraction strategy." You may learn that these ends remain as important as ever—it is the plan design's ability to achieve them that has fallen behind.

---

## The Total Rewards Strategy Development Process

The recommended process is the Employee Engagement Process, as outlined in Figure 1-3. It is a thorough and tested process that provides a complete set of steps through which you can design and evaluate your plans. In today's business world, change happens so fast that frequently time is not a luxury. This book advocates this detailed, five-phase process to help you adapt your company's rewards strategy to fit the needs and objectives of your organization. If after reading this book you find you do not have the resources, time, or requirements (business need) to go through the whole process with your organization, consider the three methods for condensing the program, as outlined in Chapter 9, or select the tools and processes to fit your needs. Or, if you are not sure, the condensed approaches allow the reader to develop the company's requirements.

*Phase I (Building Know-How)* sets the scope of the employee engagement effort and defines the most appropriate means for gath-

Figure 1-3.  Five phases of reward strategy development.

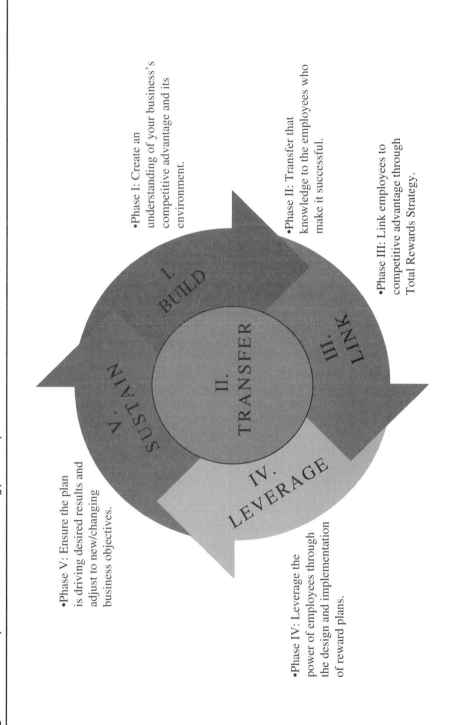

•Phase I: Create an understanding of your business's competitive advantage and its environment.

•Phase II: Transfer that knowledge to the employees who make it successful.

•Phase III: Link employees to competitive advantage through Total Rewards Strategy.

•Phase IV: Leverage the power of employees through the design and implementation of reward plans.

•Phase V: Ensure the plan is driving desired results and adjust to new/changing business objectives.

ering and organizing key input. Here, tools and processes are used to build an understanding about the aspects of the business and its environment that drive reward designs. This phase is developed in Chapters 2 and 3.

*Phase II (Transferring Know-How)* runs throughout the life of the design effort and supports every phase of development and renewal. It is about communicating the key aspects of the design process, reward designs, and the business to employees and plan designers.

*Phase III (Linking Employees to Know-How)* develops the organization's philosophy, architecture, and Total Rewards Strategy. This is the point at which the information is translated into design. Clearly this phase is the heart of the process, and it is developed, in detail, in Chapters 4 through 6.

*Phase IV (Leveraging Know-How for Success)* requires communications and implementation; they are the foundation for success and have their own phase in deference to their importance. Implementation is about creating buy-in among your employee base, focusing employees on key aspects of business success. While technical design is important, delivering the key messages is critical. This phase is covered in more depth in Chapter 7.

*Phase V (Sustaining Plan Effectiveness)* provides for ongoing follow-up and measurement. It illustrates the importance of continuous improvement and renewal of ideal and communications. This phase is covered in Chapter 8.

A word about involvement and engagement. Creating quantum leaps forward in business performance requires engaging employees in the business; allocating reward resources through an effective Total Reward Strategy is the most effective means for aligning people with business outcomes and engaging them in strategic results. Accordingly, the process described is the Employee Engagement Process. The approach *involves* employees.

The condensed approaches are designed to engage employees in business outcomes; they sacrifice employee involvement for the sake of speed and/or efficiency. Accordingly, there are benefits and challenges to their application. The user needs to be cognizant of those and choose wisely.

## Turnover and Employee Motivation Issues

There are eight causes of turnover that are consistently identified in one form or another by confidential employee surveys conducted by myriad human resources (HR) consultancies that do research in this area. They are listed here in order from the most to the least significant:

1. Opportunity to learn new skills (e.g., on-the-job training)
2. Coaching and feedback from manager
3. Nature of work
4. Ability of top management to lead the company successfully in the future
5. Recognition for a job well done
6. Respectful treatment by supervisors
7. Training and development opportunities (e.g., formal training)
8. Pay—both direct and indirect

The facts demonstrate that people do not leave organizations for money. Therefore, although money is certainly a motivator, it is not the most effective motivator.

Ask yourself or your line managers, "Why do people work here?" Begin a list of the reasons why the people who come to your organization stay in it and, most important, give their best efforts to it. Build from your earlier discussion of benefits as a reward. Be as thorough as possible, and list all of the things that people get out of their relationship with your organization. Use Figure 1-1 as a framework for building your own company's definition of Total Rewards.

Now you have taken the first step toward the creation of your organization's Total Rewards Strategy. In a very fundamental way, you have begun to define the elements of the money dimension by broadening your organization's view of rewards. Keep going—you are about to see how to use this broader view to plan the Total Rewards Development Process. Step by step, you will work toward your goal—engaging your employees more fully in achieving the strategy of your organization.

## Chapter 2

# PLANNING THE TOTAL REWARDS DEVELOPMENT PROCESS

THIS CHAPTER IS DEDICATED TO beginning Phase I of the Total Rewards Development Process—building know-how. This approach will engage employees in truly transformational growth. Rewards are the most powerful tool in the line manager's toolkit to help the employee make the connection between her success and company success. Accordingly, the first step to linking business strategy and rewards strategy is to determine what will make your business successful and then communicating that knowledge to employees. The Employee Engagement Process creates the message; rewards are used to deliver the message. To begin the process, you must determine the objectives you hope to achieve. Those objectives should include:

- Educating employees about your business and its path to success
- Communicating to employees how they affect that success
- Explaining how rewards are related to success and encouraging that success
- Building a customized design process around your objectives

This first phase of the Employee Engagement Process has a set of predefined steps and deliverables that are illustrated in Figure 2-1. You'll find tools and techniques available on the CD-ROM that also closely follow

Figure 2–1. The building know-how phase.

| Phase I: Build Know-How | 1. Initiate Project Planning | Conduct Environmental Analysis | | 4. Build a Common Understanding | 5. Analyze Organizational Readiness | 6. Initiate Business Case |
| --- | --- | --- | --- | --- | --- | --- |
| | | 2. Internal | 3. External | | | |
| Timeline | $t_1$   $t_2$ | $t_3$   $t_4$   $t_5$ | | $t_6$   $t_7$ | $t_8$   $t_9$   $t_{10}$ | $t_{11}$   $t_{12}$   $t_n$ |
| Events | • Select executive leadership<br>• Define team membership and roles<br>• Determine scope<br>• Notify stakeholders<br>• Facilitate project planning | • Identify reward strategy imperative<br>• Define internal influences on design<br>• Determine degree of business strategy penetration<br>• Define critical success factors<br>• Articulate vision | • Facilitate employee focus groups<br>• Conduct document review<br>• Interview key executives<br>• Assess culture<br>• Assess competitive positioning<br>• Complete competitive analysis | • Organize inputs<br>• Complete fact/perception matrix<br>• Complete SWOT analysis<br>• Complete gap analysis | • Define scope and readiness for change<br>• Determine the requirements for change | • Develop cost/benefit analysis |
| Deliverables | • Workable project plan<br>• Project involvement strategy<br>• Prereading | • Executive input<br>• Employee focus group input<br>• Business strategy materials<br>• Input on the influences of reward design | | • Organized influences on rewards and team's interpretation | • Evolution versus revolution design platform | • Business case for change |
| Responsible Parties | | | | | | |

these steps. Here is a description of how to use the design team approach to plan the project (step 1). Collecting the requisite data (steps 2 and 3) and building a common understanding of the insights gathered to establish a path forward (steps 4 through 6) are the subjects of Chapters 3 and 4.

Figure 2-1, which corresponds to page 9 of 99 on the CD-ROM, provides the initial project plan for Phase I. Use it to identify who will be accountable for the various events and deliverables, and to identify and record unique requirements for your project.

## Total Rewards Strategy Process Owners

Strategy is not a document; it is a plan for allocating resources that is continually evaluated, adjusted, and manipulated to meet the needs of the business. As an example, many organizations have an executive responsible for business strategy. Total Rewards Strategy, too, is a living process within an organization that requires input and direction from stakeholders at every level and vantage point. It requires an ongoing means for continuous review and improvement. Sophisticated users of Total Rewards Strategy processes identify line and staff leads who have ongoing accountability for maintaining the freshness of the reward programs. Many organizations rely on just a few of the employee and adviser groups available to them.[1] The inclusion of a greater number of valuable sources will guarantee a more successful and comprehensive reward strategy, not to mention greater buy-in and therefore greater ease with which the organization will be able to implement the final reward strategy and resulting programs. Figure 2-2 demonstrates that companies generally don't include employees enough.[2] In the design/evaluation process, employees fill three pivotal roles as process champions, process owners, and process facilitators.

The process champion is a senior executive with the authority to make changes to reward plans. She will see this project through to fruition as the head of the project's executive committee and be primarily responsible for setting the overall direction of the effort. The process owner should be a senior line manager who will ultimately serve on, or lead, the steering committee. The process facilitator is generally a seasoned member of the human resources (HR) or compensation and benefits function. This is not a HR-owned process; rather it is a HR-facilitated process. Human resources will organize the design team by assessing the criteria for membership, articulating roles and responsibilities, and determining how employee involvement and communication will be accomplished.

Figure 2-2. Employee involvement in Total Rewards Strategy design.

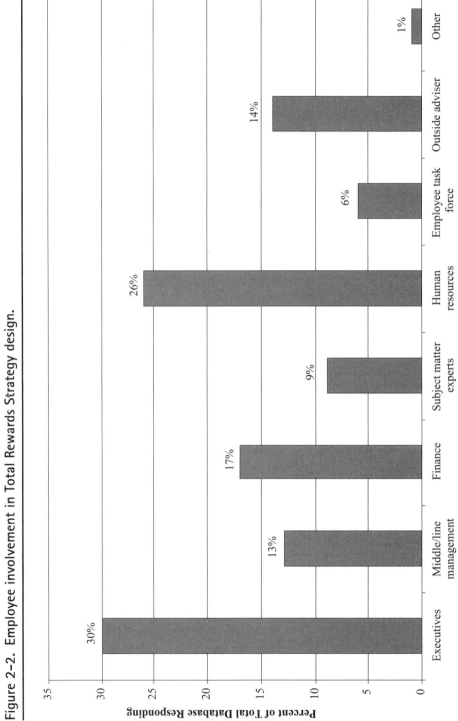

The three participants should first define or "scope out" the project. Establishing scope can be achieved by defining the business case for change.

---

## CASE STUDY: EFFECTIVE DESIGN TEAMS

Building an effective design team at the onset is critical to the long-term success and viability of the plan. When done correctly, the team processes and technical, corporate, business, operational, and people knowledge that can be structured for effective design. An excellent example is the team structure deployed for the design process at a chemical plant of a multinational chemical company.

The task was seemingly simple: The plant had reengineered its manufacturing processes to be more team oriented and to leverage its investment in property plant and equipment (PP&E). It had undertaken, in the truest sense of the term, a "radical redesign" and now it needed to create the management processes—including performance and rewards—to support its new team-based operating model. Beneath the surface, however, the complexity of the situation stood to doom the effort from the onset. For one thing, the European-based concern brought with it the culture of both its parent and its industry—not to mention its hundred-year-old tradition. Additionally, the new operating model did not come with instructions; there was no history on which to base future operating costs, metrics, and efficiencies for the plant—only projections.

In considering the business case, several points were obvious. First, buy-in at every level would be critical to future success and that buy-in would not come easily. The company's history and traditions naturally rejected change; it would be necessary to work within the culture to create a solid case for rewarding differently. Second, the expertise required to make this effort a success was deemed to be broad. Many of the new operational processes were still being developed as the Total Rewards Strategy project was being initiated. The lack of understanding and the need for building competency across the organization played heavily into how the team needed to structure itself. Finally, the centralized nature of the company's decision-making and operating model required a very high approval line for the process. Before any change could be effected it needed to be reviewed by very senior leadership.

Since this effort required senior executive sponsorship for success, the head of U.S. manufacturing was asked to be the project champion. He could give the effort direction and directly affect future adjustments. He also was a key player in the approval process. The process owner was the head of the plant. He could provide both expertise about the plant and knowledge of the people who worked there. The facilitator was the director of compensation and benefits, a deep technical expert.

The team consisted of various line and staff functionaries from within the company, mostly at the plant level. Besides the plant HR and accounting managers, employees from every walk of plant life were included. Each shift, expertise area, and level was represented. This served the team well not only in having expert representation but in facilitating communications. The reason was simple: It combined the best knowledge of the operation with expert facilitation and design. What's more, because these people "represented" their peers and colleagues, the entire process was destined to be a success. The value of the team effort cannot be overstated.

## Reward Plan Development Business Case

The next step in the process requires the design team to make the "business case for change." Team members should organize information required to articulate why the reward program should be reviewed and changed, and why it should be done within some specified time period. They also need to determine who should be involved; the expected impact on the organization; and the anticipated return on this investment in money, time, and energy. Remember that people usually find change difficult, and they tend to resist it. While the existing program may have shortfalls in its ability to achieve desired outcomes, it may not be appropriate to change every aspect of the reward program at the present time. Accordingly, this step sets priorities and defines what should change, how it should change, and when it should change.

An effective business case allows plan designers to assess the current programs vis-à-vis the future desired people strategy. This is assessed by determining the plan's fit with the organization's future structure, process, and culture using *gap analysis,* which is an examination of the difference (or gap) between the present and the desired future. The business case process facilitates the dialogue on subjects such as the degree of change, the breadth of change, and the speed of change (e.g., evolutionary versus revolutionary change).

The business case also develops priorities, timing, and appropriateness for the changes required. It allows for an analysis of the impact of changes in the reward programs. There may be financial savings or costs, efficiencies, and increases in employee satisfaction that may be accrued to the organization based on the changes in the different types of programs. The business case provides a review point for determining what kinds of redesign will make some sense. It provides the road map for change with the objective of closing gaps. Figure 2-3 outlines the framework for a reward plan development business case. It can be customized as page 5 of 99 on the CD-ROM.

The business case is referred to throughout the development of reward plans and their assessment. Accordingly, the business case itself is not completed in this stage but rather is developed as a starting point; it gets refined, evaluated, and updated throughout the process. At this stage develop just enough detail to determine if and how the process should move forward and establish the scope of the effort. Use the definitions in Figure 2-3 (the "why-what-where-when-who-how-how much" tool) to make design decisions and apply them to the initiation of the business case.

---

### THE CASE FOR THE BUSINESS CASE

Even when viewing the internal and external influences during the building know-how phase, the depth and type of analysis that you undertake, and the extent to which a business case needs to be developed, is unique to every situation.

Consider the case of overcoming the boundaries created by the different cultures of two countries. A $1 billion U.S. division of a French company was designing its Total Rewards Architecture. Generally, Europeans tend to view U.S.-style compensation programs with a certain skepticism. The French stakeholders had specific expectations for data gathering, in terms of sources of input, level of analysis, and the depth of the details. They were looking for a fact-based analysis of the U.S. market to support any recommendations; any analysis of employee expectations would be meaningless to the parent company and not worth the investment. By giving consideration to the parent company's culture and business requirements, the team was able to work more efficiently. Simply outlining the various programs offered by U.S. companies (i.e., the plan designs, features, prevalence, and data to provide a sense of how widespread various programs were) was all that was necessary; the parent company understood what programs it did not have and why change was required.

Figure 2–3. Defining why–what–where–when–who–how–how much.

In commissioning and scoping the project, start by defining:

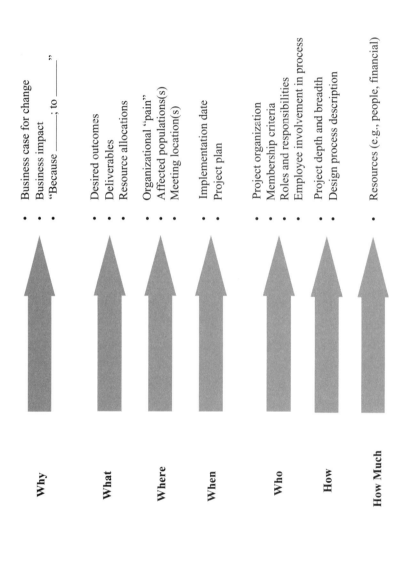

Why
- Business case for change
- Business impact
- "Because _____; to _____,"

What
- Desired outcomes
- Deliverables
- Resource allocations

Where
- Organizational "pain"
- Affected populations(s)
- Meeting location(s)

When
- Implementation date
- Project plan

Who
- Project organization
- Membership criteria
- Roles and responsibilities
- Employee involvement in process

How
- Project depth and breadth
- Design process description

How Much
- Resources (e.g., people, financial)

## Issue Resolution (Why)

In a concise sentence or two, state the reason this effort is being considered and the objective to be achieved. This statement typically is made up of two parts. The first is generally a "because" statement: "XYZ company is initiating this study because it does not achieve the required return on its investment from its reward plans." Or maybe a company is doing it simply "because its plans have not been studied in five years." The idea is to provide the various constituencies with a concise expression of why it's necessary to undertake this project now. It provides everyone involved with a broad sense of why they are committing resources to resolve an issue.

The second half of the statement is an active objective that is framed as a "to" sentence. "We seek to enhance employee understanding of our business" and "We want to update the programs and ensure that their design is reflective of current practice, business, and our people" are examples.

## Objective (What)

In undertaking this initiative, ask yourself: What are the desired outcomes that you are attempting to achieve? By identifying three to five objectives about what this project will do, and what you will get out of it, you set the course of the effort.

For example, in conducting this study XYZ will:

- Assess the competitive nature of its reward program designs and, as appropriate, redesign plans to be consistent with its strategic objectives.
- Create the positive connection between what it is attempting to achieve as a business—its strategic plan—and the messages that it delivers through rewards.
- Engage employees in a thoughtful process about the business and demonstrate to them how they impact its outcomes.
- Develop an understanding about competitive reward designs in order to make decisions about how to deliver rewards to employees.

The above outcomes are most often gained through specific deliverables. This dimension of the business case outlines those deliverables, illustrating what the company will get for its investment.

## Diagnosis (Where)

For the primary issue (the why) and underlying objectives (the what), identify the specific reward elements or business operations where you are experiencing the most pain. This is to be the focus of your effort, and it may be described in a specific program, employee population, business unit, function, geography, or in general. For example, "XYZ delivers cash rewards to employees in two primary forms: through merit increases and an annual discretionary bonus. Over the years the differentiation between employees in the application of merit has diminished to the point where there is practically none. The bonus is now paid regardless of performance." The "pain" of employees coming to understand that they are not automatically entitled to a bonus would be consistent with the objective "to reenergize our pay-for-performance philosophy."

## Timing (When)

Based on the importance of the objective, or the size of the issue and the pain it is causing, managers should determine how quickly the effort must be completed. Consider that this effort can have significant impact, but only if you pursue it to the appropriate level of detail. Accordingly, given limited resources, the need for thoughtfulness must be balanced against the requirement for speed. Consider here the cyclicity of workload among the participants and the timing of the compensation cycle. Often it is effective to start with a required deliverable date, new fiscal year, or board meeting and work the project plan back from then.

## Involvement (Who)

Identify the key contributors to solving the issue. Later in this chapter there is insight into creating various design teams (see the section on "Composition of the Project Team"). Based on this discussion, name names, putting people in roles on the teams. Here the business case developer should assess generally the categories of people who should be involved in the process. Figure 2-4 illustrates the basic structure for the project team.

Based on the depth of the initiative, the following groups will need to be involved:

- *Executives.* Executives can assist in defining strategy, clarifying objectives, and approving the new plan designs. They may serve on the executive committee or steering committee.

Figure 2-4. The project team structure.

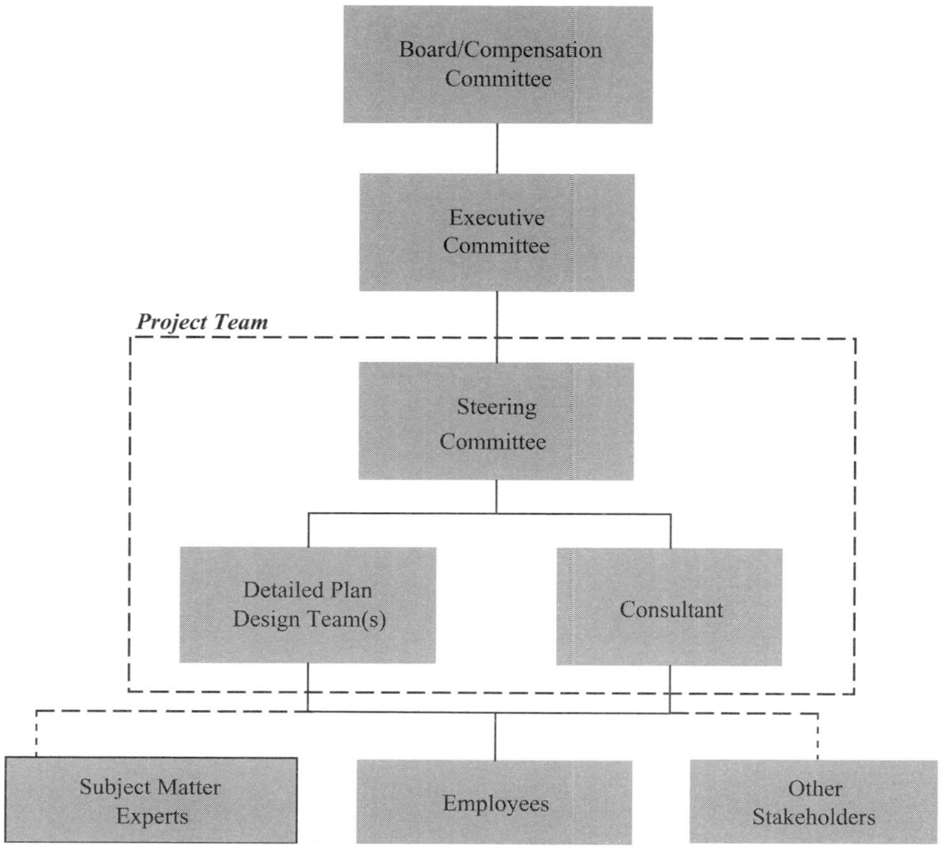

- *Line Managers.* As middle managers, they can provide subject matter expertise to the design process, serve as members of the steering committee, or be involved on the design team itself.
- *Employees.* Those who represent the company as members of the design team and provide direct input should be involved.
- *Consultants.* They can be helpful in providing an external perspective on reward plan competitiveness and design, expert facilitation, or oversight.
- *Suppliers, Customers, or Other Stakeholders.* Their role is also to provide an external perspective.

## Project Scope (How)

It is time to assess the depth of the effort required and the most appropriate design approach based on the points developed in the business case. If you determine in the business case that a complete overhaul is required, use the Employee Engagement Process espoused in this text. If you will be merely adjusting a rewards program that works fairly well, you may use the process to customize an approach for your situation. The approach in this book usually takes six weeks to six months and requires a team of approximately eight to twelve members. If you need results faster than the recommended approach, or you merely want to assess the effectiveness of existing plans before commissioning a team, there are three alternatives—the conclave, the expert panel, and the reward strategy audit—each of which is discussed in Chapter 9. The conclave and expert panel methods condense the suggested approach; the audit tests plan effectiveness. You will likely need to mix and match these approaches with tools and techniques from the CD-ROM to meet your unique requirements.

## Cost/Benefit Modeling (How Much)

To determine the resources to be applied to this effort, there are two primary considerations: the potential costs associated with meeting the previous six dimensions of the business case versus the savings inherent with this project. As the business case is yet to be fully developed, consider the extent to which you are over- or undercompensating and the costs relative to your desired competitive positioning in hard and soft dollars (e.g., payroll in excess of what is required, turnover, and the resources required to commit to this effort). You should also consider the inefficiencies inherent in delivering rewards and how improvements may drive successful completion of business plans. Balance these two considerations against the desired impact (why) and objectives (what) to ensure the team is addressing the most important requirements.

## Gap Analysis

Gap analysis is a systematic process for reviewing the difference, or the gap, between what your plans currently deliver and what they need to deliver in the future. Here, you will assess gaps at a strategic level; there will be discussion later about using gap analysis to assess individual plans.

Begin by taking inventory. Throughout the process and on into sustaining plan effectiveness, you will take inventory of plans and processes. You will want to make a list of all the reward programs you are currently managing by identifying the following:

- *Name.* What is the plan's designation or name? This will be covered in greater detail in the design phase in Chapter 6, but every plan should have a proper name.

- *Type.* Identify the type of plan (e.g., base pay, short-term incentives, long-term incentives).

- *Eligibility.* List all the populations of employees who are eligible to receive a benefit from the plan.

- *Historical Payout.* Over the period of this plan's existence, how has it delivered rewards? If the plan has been operating for an extended period, go back three to five years, or one business cycle in a cyclical industry. The most efficient means for evaluating payout is as a percent of target; to determine plan effectiveness, payout as a percent of target can be compared to overall corporate performance, for example, relative to peer companies.

- *Plan Cost.* What does this plan cost the organization? Consider payroll and administrative costs. Design and reevaluation costs should also be captured.

- *Objective.* What is the plan designed to achieve? Why does it exist? What key messages should this plan deliver?

- *Effectiveness.* On a scale of one to five, give this plan a subjective evaluation of its ability to achieve its objective. How well does this plan achieve what it is designed to do? Does this plan deliver the messages it is designed to deliver?

- *Return on Plan Investment (ROPI).* Brainstorm and list all the benefits derived from this plan. Calculate the financial impact of those

benefits that yield a dollar return; for those benefits that do not provide a dollar impact, identify the benefit in some other terms. In
addition to improved financial performance, plans frequently yield
benefits that include:

- Increasing awareness of business objectives
- Improving employee morale and/or customer satisfaction
- Reducing turnover

While each of these may be quantified, they are at least one step
removed from a financial impact. To determine ROPI, compare the
costs associated with each plan to the financial benefits derived.
Where the financial benefits exceed the costs, the ROPI is positive—
the nonfinancial benefits represent extras. Where the financial benefits are less than the costs, the ROPI is negative; designers need to
assess whether the nonfinancial benefits exceed the costs.

- *Last Review.* Make note of the date the program was last reviewed.

Analyzing gaps is a matter of determining the degree to which each
plan identified in the inventory has "face validity" in the future organization. A reference point here is to consider the current program vis-à-vis the
why and what statements developed previously. These define the objectives
of the redesign effort, and desired outcomes. Use them to determine the
extent to which each plan is part of the problem or the solution.

## Composition of the Project Team

With the gap analysis complete, the project team can begin to take shape.
Figure 2-5 shows how the team structure will function together. To develop
the team, start with the executive committee, which is headed by the
reward process champion. This committee must provide both high-level
guidance and final approval authority. Having two to three executives in
place to assume these roles and responsibilities will help to gain participation across the remainder of the roles.

The steering committee provides recommendations to the executive
committee. It oversees the development of the reward plan's philosophy
and architecture and gives the detailed plan design team(s) specific guidelines as to the amount of latitude it has. The steering committee should
contain three to five executives.

Now turn your attention to the design team. Executives frequently
ask, "Why involve employees in the design of the corporation's reward

**Figure 2-5. Project team roles and responsibilities.**

A typical project team organization includes many roles and participants:

| Group | Role/Responsibility | Deliverables | Criteria for Membership |
|---|---|---|---|
| **Executive Committee** | • Design guidelines<br>• Approve final plan<br>• Act as project champion | • A working reward plan<br>• Update periodicity | • Approval authority<br>• Leadership position |
| **Steering Committee** | • Provide direction to design teams<br>• Define architecture | • Further refinement of executive guidelines<br>• Project plan | • Interim approval authority |
| **Detailed Design Team(s)** | • Oversee and support design team activities<br>• Refine architecture<br>• Develop plan deails<br>• Outline involvement requirements<br>• Conduct research | • A project that meets executive guidelines | • Representative of the employee population<br>• Subject matter expertise<br>• Respected by peers |
| **Employees** | • Share information | | |

---

**The One Percent Assumption**

It is frequently necessary to demonstrate the value-add of a new design or program. One fun way to conduct this analysis is to begin with "the one percent assumption." The idea is to take some unarguably low number to begin the analysis—let's say one percent. Generally, you start by asking the question, "Will doing X yield an improvement of one percent?" If it doesn't, don't bother! That's a good place to start. So, if you consider raising the bar on the level of person who works for you from the fiftieth to the seventy-fifth percentile (a calculable cost), determine the net benefit of a corresponding one percent increase to, for example, volume. If the cost is outstripped by the benefit, it's hard to argue against the project.

---

plans?" The answer is simple. If you want to know what motivates your employees, ask them. From one perspective they are "the corporation's reward plans." Reward programs define the employee compact—the relationship that the company establishes with its employees. In that way, they represent the very basis of how the organization values its employees and focuses their activities toward specific outcomes. Rewards create the foundation of communications to employees about the company's expectations, values, and commitments. True, there are other processes that are used to gain employee input (those will be reviewed in Chapter 9), and you must consider the implications of varying degrees of involvement. However, effective Total Rewards Strategy development is the result of a facilitated, three-dimensional design team process.

Also, gaining employee input is the first step toward empowering employees to develop a core HR process that engages their commitment to company objectives. By involving employees in the input and design process you are facilitating buy-in and engagement on the back end. Consider that knowing what is on your employees' minds allows you to say, "You told us X and we are responding with Y." Or, "You told us X and here is the business reason we cannot do that."

Executives most often do not want to involve employees out of fear that it will in some way set an expectation that something will happen—for example, pay will increase. To the contrary, involving employees in the process and managing the message about this effort allows you to better control the expectations of your employees. After all, their peers are on the team, providing them with the straight scoop.

Employees are stakeholders in this venture, too. By identifying the employee groups that will be directly and indirectly affected by the project and its impact, you can select employees who represent varying populations. Assessing the impact on various groups of employees can help to establish project involvement strategy and communication requirements.

Accordingly, the design team should be constructed to consider every possible corporate dimension including:

- Employees representing each organizational level (vertical) and function (horizontal), as well as each business unit, demographic group (age, race, gender), and location
- External stakeholders, including customers, suppliers, owners, regulators, and advisers
- Subject matter experts (SMEs), including human resources, finance and accounting, operations, legal, and sales/marketing

If the workforce is unionized, the company must consider how to involve the union's representatives. There are legal requirements to consider, so be sure to discuss this issue thoroughly with your legal counsel.

A detailed design team develops the Total Rewards Strategy under the guidance of the steering committee. Each major program element typically has its own design team because the volume of work in a full design effort can be significant; accordingly, you will most likely require one or more of these teams. In addition to the previously stated value of a three-dimensional representation of your organization, the key benefit of a design team is to marry the technical expertise that resides within the various SMEs with the business knowledge of your employees. Your employees know the company's operating processes more thoroughly than anyone else. Take advantage of both the technical knowledge of your subject matter experts and the operational knowledge that resides within your employee base; the combination is the most powerful tool for developing plan designs. What's more, the best way to ensure employee buy-in at implementation is to involve employees from the start.

Although employees are not experts in reward plan design, they do get paid, and they understand how it feels to work at your company. You can educate the team on the design process and provide the technical background team members need to ask the right questions in the design process by assembling a package of reading material culled from the popular press or business journals. This book is designed to provide the employees on the design team with the background knowledge they will need with regard to the process and how to make design decisions (key influences on design). Readings should include current articles on topics being considered and should be distributed throughout the process. The

CD-ROM contains additional materials for determining team member-ships and identifying employees to fill roles (other than the criteria listed in Figure 2-5) based on the requirements of the effort.

Finally, there are fundamentally four roles that a consultant can play in this journey that are not mutually exclusive (in other words, in the design process, a consultant may play one or more of these roles). Assess where and how the consultant can add the most value, allocating con-sultant dollars to those initiatives. These roles are:

- *The Expert Witness.* Many times clients will say, "Gee, if I put this idea forward to my board or my boss, it won't have nearly the impact as you, 'the expert,' putting the same idea forward." And candidly, this is quite true. The outside consultant, who does not have a vested interest in the design of your programs, is often more effective than an inside employee in the role of expert witness.

- *The Subject Matter Expert.* A second potential role for a consultant is to serve as a subject matter expert. Consultants, by the nature of their jobs, are exposed to more varied program designs and corporate cultures than most practitioners. Accordingly, consultants can add value if they can bring subject matter expertise from their various engagements to the specific design requirements of your company.

- *The Expert Facilitator.* A good consultant can facilitate a group through the design process, keeping it both on track and on subject.

- *The Pair of Hands.* After a decade of downsizing and reengineering, many organizations are simply short of human resources talent. This is not necessarily a bad thing. The design process is one you may undertake once every five years or so; accordingly, the need for a design expert and/or an extra pair of hands may be something you would rather rent than buy.

## Project Planning

You can now apply the "why-what-where-when-who-how-how much" tool to initial project planning. This tool is used in project planning much as it was when developing the business case; only now you have peeled back the onion several layers and are working at a deeper level of detail.

- *Team Objective (Why).* To ensure that the people involved and affected understand the scope of their involvement, define this project in terms of why this particular team is being commissioned. What is its pur-pose and fit within the engagement?

- *Deliverables (What).* Defining desired outcomes in terms of deliverables in the beginning will ensure that the deliverables and expectations are clearly understood by all parties. It also allows you to focus the data collection effort as executives may have specific requirements for analysis, background discovery, and written documentation.

Establishing what these deliverables will look like saves time along the way. It also helps to assess the resource requirements to get to final implementation in terms of time, technology, money, and expertise. Be respectful of your employees' time. While it is easy to talk about design teams and their breadth and depth as requirements, don't forget that there is a considerable amount of time and effort that goes into the design process. At the start, contact employees regarding time commitments, and identify the expectations of each member with respect to his or her commitment.

- *Geographic Considerations (Where).* Where the design team meets and how its members work together is as important as the locations of the affected employees. The design takes on considerably different attributes based on the geography of your organization. Your team should be constructed to adequately represent all the employees affected. Accordingly, the logistics of how the team will meet, work together, and achieve its commitments must be considered at the beginning.

- *Timing (When).* The planned implementation date is typically a given; it is up to the project team to establish a project plan to meet that date. The team should develop the timeline and agree to it.

- *Affected Parties (Who).* It is important to identify the groups that will be impacted by the effort. Certainly employees at potentially every level in the organization will be affected. Other stakeholders should also be considered.

The mere fact that the plan design team is meeting—that is, that you have assembled employees, had several meetings as a team, and collected a plethora of information—means that employees know that this design effort is under way. As a consequence, they'll have some expectation about what that design effort may yield. The team should begin to communicate with employees about the status of the effort. Remember customers and suppliers are stakeholders, too. Their input with regard to measures and perceptions, in particular, will prove valuable. Decide whether and how to get input from these groups.

- *Design Process (How).* This book provides a means to involve employees in the development of a management process to engage employees in business outcomes. The process is, however, highly cus-tomizable through the insights and tools provided. Defining the design process—how to accomplish this effort—occurs here. You've collected enough input now to determine the requirements for redesign; use the project planning tools to determine how those requirements will be addressed.

■ *Design Process (How Much).* With the design process defined (How), allocate resources to the effort. Consider the people, time, monetary, and physical space resource requirements to bring the effort through to fruition.

## The Transfer of Know-How

It is essential at this point to communicate the message developed in Phase I to the employees who make the success of the company a reality. This communication phase—or the process of transferring know-how—is the continuous thread that supports design, implemen-tation, and assessment by communicating the project's progress, designs, and, ultimately, the strategy and the programs. It is about cre-ating awareness of how this company operates, energizing employees to provide input and effort, and leveraging the power that is within your workforce. It is important to begin this process early and to define how team members will communicate with one another and deliver a con-sistent message about the project outside the team.

---

Spinoza's Law: "Nature abhors a vacuum."

or

Manas's Law: "Absent fact, rumors fill the void."

---

Communication begins when the process begins, and it runs contin-uously throughout. To facilitate this communication process, break it down into steps.

While implementation of the communication process is described in Chapter 7, the process should start here in the planning stage. Getting it right, and getting it right early, is critical. The communication of business strategy broadly through the organization is pivotal to its successful implementation and execution. At the same time, compensation is the most powerful tool that management has for communicating that strategy and linking employees to it.[3] This holds true for reward strategy as well. How people get paid is far more important than how much. And yet organizations, by their own admission, are dreadfully poor at implementation.[4] Figure 2-6 nearly condemns the HR professional for failing to grasp the importance of communication when it comes to reward strategy. As is evidenced by the data, human resources has neither taken the time itself to fully grasp strategy nor provided the resources required to foster complete understanding among the line managers. Communication creates the necessary connection between performance and rewards. Understandably, it is time- and resource-consuming. However, the lesson from the field is clear: Invest the energy necessary to get communications correct.

> *"A good plan violently executed now is better than a great plan executed next week."*
>
> GENERAL GEORGE S. PATTON

To initiate this communication effort, the team needs to come to several agreements. First, you must ensure that affected executives and decision makers have the information they need as you go along. Ask your executive sponsors how they want to be updated and how much detail they need. Develop a feedback loop to ensure that information is communicated throughout the team. One team might assign each member a specific executive with whom they have to meet periodically and update.

Communication with other employees and stakeholder groups is a bit trickier. Learning from political "spin doctors" is valuable here. The first and most important element is to agree to and articulate the team's key message(s) about the effort. Fall back to your business case and build consensus among the members about what they want to say about this effort; then develop this information into coherent statement(s) and agree to maintain those key messages.

Determining the key message, what to communicate, and how much to communicate is driven by the level of detail that the team wants to present to the organization. Obviously, the decision of what to communicate, how much to communicate, and when to communicate needs to be made over and over again as the process develops. In this way, the depth of the communication effort can continue to be increased as the programs take shape.

Finally, the members should agree on how they communicate with one another. Besides being candid, frank, and confidential when meeting, team members should set boundaries for communicating between sessions, too. Consider:

Figure 2-6. The breadth of communications.

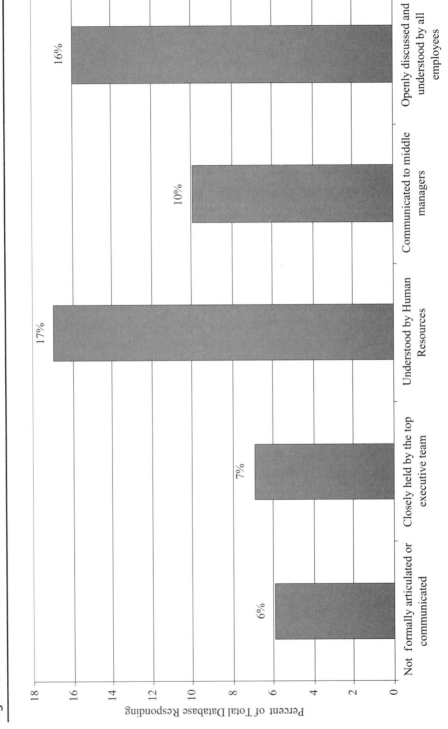

▪ *Establishing a Team Web Site or Notes Database.* It will be important, as the amount of information that drives this effort grows, to have a central repository. Team members need to know not only where they are in the process, but how to frame the various pieces of information for decision making and design. Members will need to access information as it is collected, too, in order to prepare for design team meetings. This is critically important for two reasons: First, each team member is working on an assignment for the team both between meetings and in conjunction with a day-to-day workload. The team member's ability to access information quickly to see how other work streams impact his or her efforts is critical. Second, to make design team meetings efficient, the members need to be informed before coming in.

▪ *Utilizing Standard Subject Lines on E-Mails.* Most of us are inundated with voice and electronic mail messages. One approach to ensure that the team reads project-related e-mails is to agree to a standard subject line. This way recipients can immediately see that the e-mail relates to the project.

▪ *Establishing a Consensus on Scheduling Contact.* To ensure that the process is flowing, the work is getting done, and key decisions are being made, some kind of regular contact among team members must be scheduled. If the team is spread across various locations, it is best to set a standard day and time for a weekly dial-in conference call. Typically you may have the core of the team—the majority of people in one single place—meet and dial into a virtual conference center. There can easily be a standing agenda that covers:

- Progress on the last meeting's "go do" list
- Progress relative to the project plan
- Identification of critical work streams for the coming week
- Decisions on process, scope, and design
- Evaluation of what to communicate outside the team
- Definition of next steps
- Management of work streams between meetings
- Discussion of open items

A phase-by-phase communications approach allows the design team to manage the amount of information out in front of the organization, the timing of the delivery of various key messages, the approval process, and

Figure 2–7. Phased communication planning.

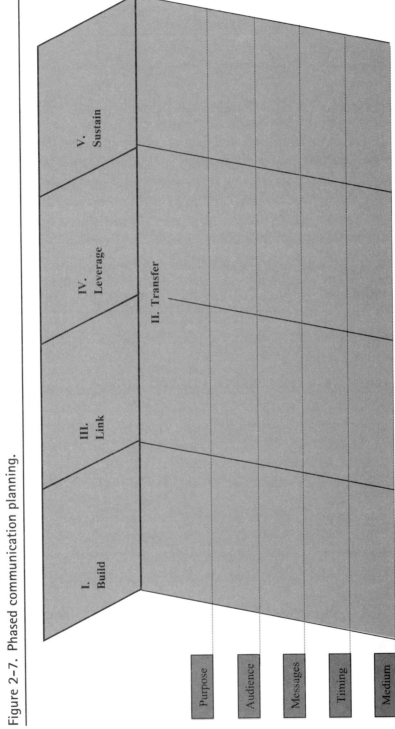

the intrateam communications. It is a recognition that communications as a phase in plan development and implementation are core to the process and run throughout the life of the Total Rewards Strategy. Figure 2-7 provides the tool to manage this effort (see also page 48 of 99 of the CD-ROM). This tool gets the team to define the critical communications strategy decisions early in the process. It should include:

- *Purpose.* What is the purpose of this particular communication? Is it, for example, to simply inform (a reasonable purpose at this stage of the process), or are you trying to move people to act (more likely in the final phases)?
- *Audience.* Who are the audiences for my communications? The audience dictates the level of detail required as well as the key message.
- *Messages.* Key messages describe the spin you want on these issues.
- *Timing.* When do you want your messages out? And with what frequency?
- *Medium.* What is the medium for your message(s)? Define how you will get your messages across, but consider at least two mediums to ensure that the meaning is delivered.

By building the team and initiating the business case, you've gone a long way toward creating the momentum to redesign. You are now about to study the key influences in the design process and how to use them to inform the designs themselves. From there you will see how to energize the team toward effective outputs. As a result, you will emerge more knowledgeable about the company and have the tools to leverage that knowledge to drive success.

Now you're ready to go!

## Chapter 3

# DEVELOPING AN UNDERSTANDING OF THE ORGANIZATION

BY THIS POINT, THE SCOPE of the effort has been established and the appropriate expertise has been brought together in the design team. That team needs to turn its attention to building up the repository of information that it will need to link their employees' day-to-day activities to the achievement of strategy and, ultimately, the transformation of the business. This information is the foundation of the Total Rewards Strategy and reward plan design. The development of a reward strategy requires a thorough understanding of the unique context within and around which your organization conducts business. Certainly there are an infinite number of details that you can consider; the process that is described throughout this book is dedicated to defining, collecting, organizing, analyzing, and transferring the information necessary to propel your business forward by leveraging employees' capabilities through reward design. This chapter defines what you need to know to accomplish this by outlining the key business influences on rewards.

## Defining What's Critical

Figure 3-1 provides the framework to describe the factors that most directly influence Total Rewards Strategy (TRS) development. Here in Chapter 3 the concepts and the relevant requirements for information are defined; Chapter 4 describes how and why these factors influence reward

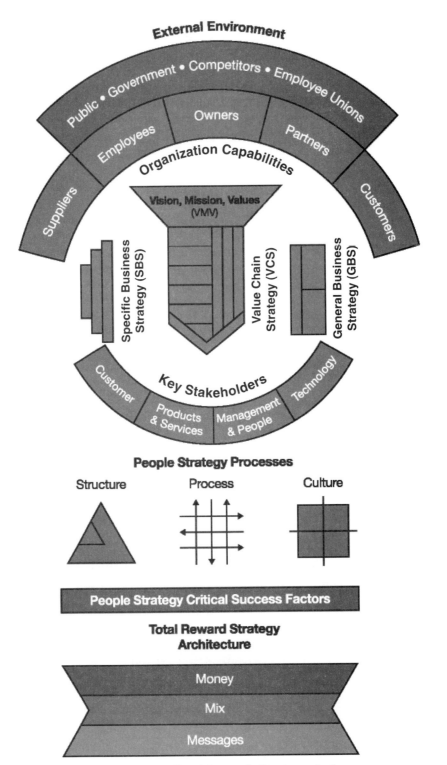

Figure 3-1. Factors influencing Total Rewards Strategy design.

architecture and their role in the design process. The primary influences on TRS are:

- *External Environment.* This comprises the powerful forces (e.g., governments, competitors, employee unions, and the public) that are external to the organization but exert significant force on organizations throughout the entire process, including the actual detailed plan design stage.

- *Key Stakeholders.* These influences are made up of individuals or groups normally associated with a desire for the organization to succeed. Those forces include owners, employees, partners, suppliers, and customers. All can be influential in reward architecture and design.

- *Vision, Mission, and Values.* These influences are the overarching reasons for the existence of organizations. They provide the most fundamental answers to the universal questions of who, what, when, where, and how.

- *Business Strategy.* Business strategy includes the detailed plans that determine how resources will be acquired and deployed in fulfillment of the organization's vision, mission, and values. Their influence is categorized into general, value chain, and specific business strategies.

- *Organization Capabilities.* This category includes those capabilities that the organization needs to possess in order to execute its business strategies. These capabilities can be numerous, but generally fall into the categories of customers, products and services, management and people, and technology.

- *People Strategy.* This refers to the internal people-related environment (i.e., the environment within which the employees will work). It consists of the organization's structure, processes, and culture.

- *People Strategy Critical Success Factors.* This area includes the people-specific goals and imperatives that need to be successfully attained if the organization is to fulfill those goals and objectives determined to be necessary for its business strategy and organizational capabilities.

The rest of this chapter is dedicated to defining the aspects of each of these conceptual frameworks that will be important to your organization as it develops an appropriate reward strategy to complement and reinforce its overall voyage to success.

The depth and degree of common understanding the design team creates at this stage of the process will serve it well as it makes choices from among the various "downstream" alternatives in the reward strategy and as it details program design phases of the process. The following sections further explain each of the aforementioned factors.

## External Environment

In the external environment there are a myriad of factors that impact a business such as the public, competitors, government, and employee unions.

These influence your designs in two dramatic ways: First, your ability to attract and retain—and to a lesser extent motivate—employees is directly influenced by the external view of your organization. A thorough review of materials such as analysts' reports on your company/industry will help the design team understand the perception of your industry and its future potential. If you understand the demographics of the workforce you are creating, use that to determine the most desirable attributes of organizational life and assess your company's ability to deliver on those requirements. Clearly, broadening the organization's definition of rewards and focusing its communications extends the value of this approach. Some industries (e.g., tobacco, firearms, or alcohol), when competing for the same talent (e.g., a marketing person), may need to establish different competitive rates for total rewards, as well as a different mix, than other industries. Also, identification of desirable industry attributes allows a company to fundamentally alter the reward programs themselves and/or management's ability to use those programs, yielding a competitive advantage in the labor market.

Consider a recent college graduate from a top school, able to pick from any number of job offers. Your company's products, its positioning of those products in its competitive markets, the perception of the product and your industry, and your ability to reward the individual employee, all these things are on the prospective employee's mind. These attributes need to be on your mind as you design your reward program because you need to fundamentally articulate what your company will be providing back to prospective employees in return for their investment of time in your company. It goes deeper than money; it gets to all of the intrinsic and extrinsic rewards that the prospective employee will take away from the relationship, as discussed in Chapter 1.

In addition to affecting the ability of your organization to recruit, the government may have a substantial influence on the way that your organization employs people. Some industries (e.g., financial services and medicine) have employment regulations that heavily affect hiring minimum qualifications. Other industries require specific qualifications such as a CPA license, Series 7 exams, and medical degrees. Still other fields (e.g., airlines) have designated work hours for key machine operators such as pilots. In addition, governments have, to some extent, determined the level of social engineering employee/employer rights balance by providing legislation that covers the entire scope of employment from compensation and benefits (FLSA, ERISA, ADEA) to safety (OSHA) to employee/employer rights (ADA, FMLA).

Competitors will always have a significant influence on the design of the reward strategy. In addition to vying with rivals for financial, technological, physical, and other resources, the competition for human talent will be an overriding obstacle to overcome in the future if your organization is to be successful.

## EXTENDING RETENTION IN BAD TIMES: NEGOTIATING THROUGH A CHAPTER 11 BANKRUPTCY FILING, BY JAMES SCANNELLA

Companies facing severe financial difficulties are forced to make tough decisions to remain viable. Downsizing, reductions in force, and/or forced sales of whole divisions are steps that may need to be taken. Each involves the termination of significant numbers of employees. Yet should these steps not restore financial health and a bankruptcy filing be required, the HR picture changes quite drastically. Flight of key employees becomes a key concern, as many components of the company's Total Rewards lose their luster. The company's best hope for emergence typically lies with current key employees, who may be scattered at all levels throughout the organization. Adding complexity, the compensation programs proposed by companies in Chapter 11 risk challenge by disgruntled creditors and rejection by the court.

In one particularly troubling case, a U.S.-headquartered manufacturer, wholesaler, and licensor of footwear (annual revenues of approximately $250 million; 2,300 employees) suffered a steady decline in revenues in the late 1990s. Financial difficulties peaked in 2000, and employee turnover reached unacceptable levels. Unwilling to wait for a seemingly unavoidable Chapter 11, the CEO implemented an employee stay bonus. The plan provided that cash bonuses would be payable to select key employees in March and May of 2001, but only if those employees had not resigned prior to that date. In January 2001, the company filed for bankruptcy under Chapter 11. Shortly thereafter, the creditors objected to the stay bonus program on the basis that it offered excessive bonus opportunities. This action undermined the credibility of the CEO in the eyes of the employees and threatened a resumption of key employee flight. A review of market practices confirmed that the bonus opportunities were excessive, but only in light of the required stay periods. The solution was to develop an employee retention program that consisted of several components delivered in two phases; the extended timeframe incorporated by the two-phased approach more accurately reflected the projected period of time required for the turnaround. While phase 1 was in excess of marketplace norms, phase 2 was structured at or below market, acting as an offset. This approach allowed the company to deliver what the CEO had promised, extend the retention period with additional incentives, and not exceed overall market norms. With court approval of the two-phased plan, turnover of key employees remained negligible. Ultimately, the estate was able to deliver a fully functional operating company to the strategic buyers bidding for the assets.

*James Scannella is a compensation consultant with Buck Consultants.*

Employee unions are a force that influences the design of reward strategies for both the members and nonmembers of bargaining units. The resulting reward program designs are often a tortured result of the collective bargaining process. In addition, most organizations design their reward strategies (and specifically the reward program) for nonunion employment groups with at least one eye on any employee union reward programs that result from collective bargaining.

The information that the design team chooses to collect and analyze will depend to a great degree on the significance these environmental external factors have on the ultimate success of the organization. If these factors (individually or collectively) exert significant influence on the organization, then that influence will need to be understood and subsequent plan designs will need to reflect its importance.

## Key Stakeholders

Key stakeholders influence a company's ability to reward as well. Stakeholders can be divided into five categories: owners, partners, employees, suppliers, and customers.

  1. *Owners.* Owner stakeholders ultimately influence the entire range of company issues, from business strategy through people strategy to reward strategy. For this exercise, the most important way to view this category is to determine whether the organization is tightly controlled by a few owners or whether owners have little or no control over business operations. To the extent the organization is owned by the public at large without any large shareholder, the freedom to design reward strategies is great. If, on the other hand, the organization is tightly held by one or only a few shareholders, the influence of those shareholders will be significant on the overall reward architecture and even possibly on plan design itself. Accordingly, it is important to know the breadth of the ownership structure and the influences that those owners have on the business and plan designs.

  2. *Partners.* Partner stakeholders are the individuals or organizations that assist your organization in bringing products and services to your customers. They can provide value anywhere along the value chain. They can help the organization in raw material acquisition (such as purchasing cooperatives), or they can assist in value chain processes (such as independent radiologists do in healthcare organizations). Logistics and distribution partners can assist in the transportation of products (such as in trucking and the railroad industry). When these partners are concentrated and critical to the ultimate value received by your organization's customers, then they will often influence reward architecture.

  3. *Employees.* Employee stakeholders exert their influence to the degree there is an abundance or dearth of talent to be acquired at a low- or high-wage rate. Obviously, if there are a few highly specialized individuals (i.e., actors with marquee value), then the influence on the reward strategy will be great. If the business's requirement is for a large number of unskilled laborers, then the employee stakeholder influence on reward architecture will be minimal.

  4. *Suppliers.* Supplier stakeholders have a similar pattern. If there are only a few (e.g., the Arab oil cartel in the 1970s) where critical supplies

are provided, dramatic impacts may be felt along the entire value chain that cause the reward architecture to be of a certain type.

5. *Customers.* Customer stakeholders are important to consider when designing a reward strategy. If there are only a few customers that purchase products or services, then the impact on reward strategy will be great. If the customer base is broad and very few customers account for any substantial amount of purchases, then the influence on reward strategy architecture and plan design will be insignificant.

---

### BIGGER THAN BOB

A few years ago, "Bob," the owner of a well-known hedge fund with $4 billion in assets under management, needed help in developing an exit strategy. He personally was worth an estimated $800 million and wanted to sell the business and retire. The dilemma was that, since he was the key to the success of the business, no one wanted to buy the business from him without him! The solution was to make the business "bigger than Bob." An equity-based Total Rewards Strategy seemed to be the means to that end.

In the hedge fund management arena, top fund managers are highly compensated; the mix of pay is highly leveraged toward short-term cash incentives. What Bob needed to do was create a nontraditional economic model that made both short- and long-term sense for the principals of the company. Then he needed to recruit several key candidates to become part owners through their efforts (in lieu of short-term cash) over a period of several years. The difficulty this created was that this required Bob to sell the value of this economic model to a highly compensated group who were used to instant gratification. What these new stakeholders gave up in short-term cash "bought" their shares of the business from Bob, provided them with superior long-term returns, and served to transfer ownership from Bob. The new model allowed the organization to more than double the money in its funds under management in five years and created an organization that is the result of the efforts of Bob and several other people. It has also allowed Bob to position his majority stake for sale as the company is now perceived to be "bigger than Bob."

## Vision, Mission, and Values

There are books written on the creation and refinement of organization vision, mission, and values (VMV) statements; this book will not recreate those efforts. Core, however, to the design process is the need to understand how these three important influences impact the reward architecture and detailed program elements.

Vision is how the organization sees itself in the future—say, three to five years from now. It is a compelling statement that moves the organization to some future desired state. It defines for the organization and its employees what success will look like, what they aspire to become, and/or how they want the outside world to see them. Examples of various vision statements are provided in Figure 3-2. The design team needs to determine whether a vision statement exists; the extent to which it is operative, communicated, and understood; and the degree to which employees perceive it to be compelling.

Mission defines, at a high level, how the organization plans to achieve its vision. What will it do, and what actions and outcomes will it strive to achieve to accomplish its vision? Sample mission statements are provided in Figure 3-3. Determine if a mission statement exists; the extent

Figure 3-2. Vision: the compelling statement of how we see ourselves.

Vision is a compelling statement, designed to rally the organization to a specified cause. It will answer the questions:

- What do we see ourselves as?
- How do we want others to see us?
- What does success look like?

Examples include:

"To be the best consumer-products company in the world, with all of our products either number one or number two in their category."—Phillip Morris

"To have a Coca-Cola within arm's reach of every consumer in the world."—The Coca-Cola Company

"To be known as the the leading authority on girls...." The Girl Scouts of the USA

Figure 3-3. The "how we are going to get there" mission.

---

**Mission defines, at a high level, how the organization plans to get there. Examples of effective mission statements are:**

"To Teach"
Martha Stewart Living Omnimedia's first mission is to provide homekeepers everywhere with the "how to" information, ideas, and confidence they need to raise the quality of lifestyle in their homes.

"To Do"
MSLO's second mission is to turn our large media audiences into real "doers" by providing them with products, tools, materials, and other resources they need, under powerful brand labels, for do-it-yourself ingenuity "the Martha Stewart Living" way.

---

to which it is associated with the company's vision; and the degree to which employees understand the company's mission.

Core values define what the organization will value as it sets upon the journey of its mission to accomplish its vision. Values describe the specific behaviors, attributes, and competencies that are important to achieve overall success. The design team needs to clarify the degree to which the organization is values based and, if it is, define what those values are.

## Business Strategy

Business strategy is a detailed plan for the allocation of resources in order to win in the marketplace. It is founded on business objectives, knowledge of the competitive environment, and an appraisal of the organization's resources and capabilities. It is assessed against values and goals, industry environment, resources, capabilities, and management. Overall business strategy is often supported by various functional substrategies, including human resources, marketing, sales, R&D, and finance strategies. Each functional substrategy is executed through its supporting pillars; human resources strategy includes recruitment, succession planning, training and development, employee relations, and reward strategies. It is through this linkage that Total Rewards Strategy must support business outcomes. Business strategy can be viewed at three levels, each of which has a significant influence on TRS design.

The first level is general business strategy (GBS), which describes why a customer chooses one company's products or services over another. Examining GBS defines the overall objectives of any business by answering the question, "Why choose me?" This represents the foundation of your strategy. Figure 3-4 illustrates Michael Porter's[1] three forms of GBS— product/service differentiation and the cost advantage of a low-cost provider. A product/service differentiatior offers something that sets itself apart from the others—it could be quality, choice, or service. Alternatively, a low-cost provider competes on price. In its simplest form, ask the question, "Why do customers use our company's products/services?" Remember that Porter tells us that a successful company is one or the other, but not both. A derivation of these two strategies is what Porter calls a *focus strategy*, which reflects either a low-cost provider or a product/service differentiator in a specific market. A niche product/service or geographic area may define that market. Figure 3-5 indicates the distribution of GBS types, based on our research. The design team must know the answers to the questions asked in this paragraph and thus know the company's GBS. Understanding any planned changes to GBS, for example, shifting from differentiation to cost leadership, is equally as important.

Value chain strategy (VCS) defines how an organization adds value to the products or services it sells. Figure 3-6 provides this framework and illustrates that organizations add value to the goods/services they produce along a critical path. Each link in the value chain represents some process that has an additive effect on the product or service the organization plans to acquire, build, and deliver to its customers. Every link in the chain must increase the value and/or do so at a cost that is preferably lower than that of competitors. Taken together, the value added is greater than the cost, so the difference between cost and value is margin. It is critical to understand the key pathways along which goods and services pass and where your organization adds value and/or reduces costs, as can be seen in Figure 3-7. Organizations are significantly increasing the number of stages where they intend to have or create a competitive advantage. What is more, the most dramatic influence comes in those stages of the value chain most influenced by people and technology.

Specific business strategy (SBS) articulates what your business plan is designed to accomplish and how it will meet its goals. There are any number

*(text continues on page 54)*

**Figure 3–4. Forms of general business strategy (GBS).**

A business strategy requires adding value to customers to build competitive advantage.* It comes in three forms:

**Cost Advantage**

Maximizing every opportunity to increase efficiency.

Sources Include:†

- Economies of scale
- Economies of learning
- Production efficiencies
- Design
- Material costs
- Capacity utilization

**Differentiation Advantage**

Matching the customers' demand for differentiation with the firm's capacity to supply it requires:‡

- An understanding of customer needs/preferences
- Commitment to the customer
- Knowledge of organization capabilities
- Product/service differentiation

**Focus** (i.e., delivering a cost or differentiation advantage to a specific buyer)

*Michael Porter; *Competitive Advantage* (New York: Free Press, 1985).
†Robert Grant; *Contemporary Strategy Analysis* (Cambridge, Mass.: Blackwell Publishers, 1991), p. 153.
‡Ibid., p.176.

Figure 3–5. General business strategy (GBS).

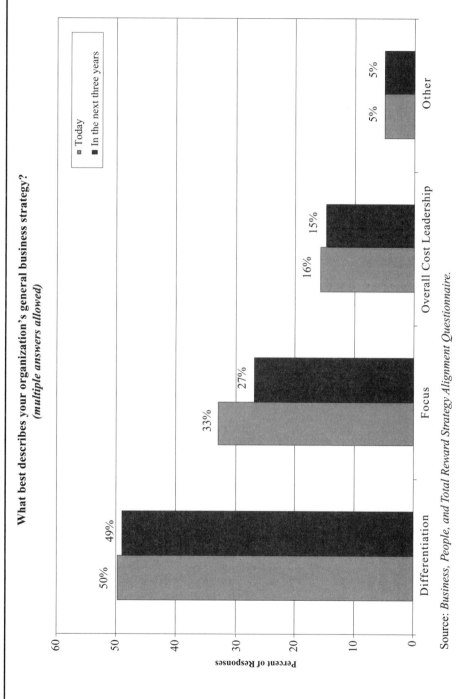

**What best describes your organization's general business strategy?**
*(multiple answers allowed)*

Source: *Business, People, and Total Reward Strategy Alignment Questionnaire.*

**Figure 3-6. Porter's value chain.**

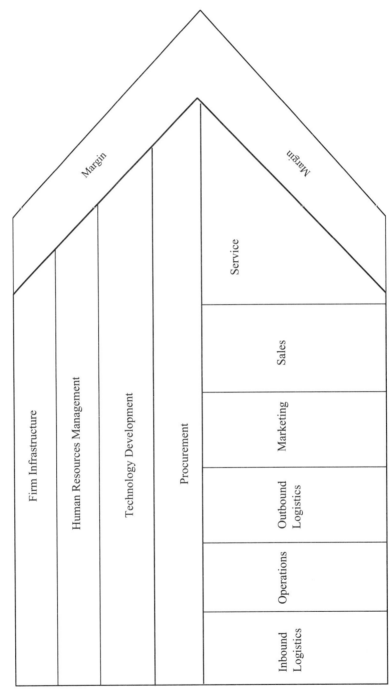

Source: Adapted with the permission of The Free Press, an imprint of Simon & Schuster Adult Publishing Group, from *COMPETITIVE ADVANTAGE: Creating and Sustaining Superior Performance* by Michael E. Porter. New York, 1985, p. 37. Copyright © 1985, 1998 by Michael Porter.

Figure 3-7. Value chain strategy (VCS).

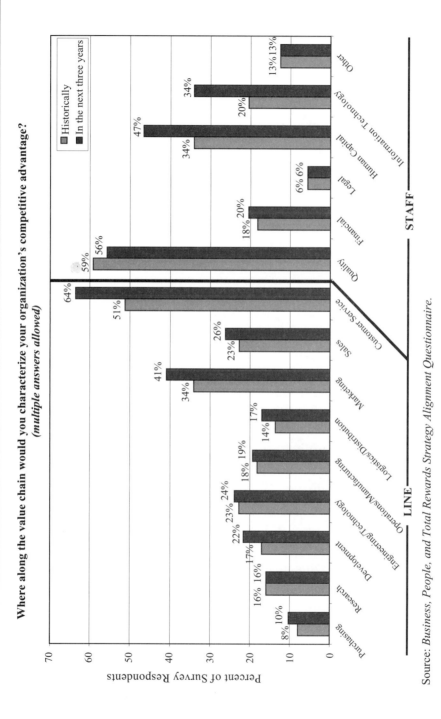

**Where along the value chain would you characterize your organization's competitive advantage?**
*(multiple answers allowed)*

Source: *Business, People, and Total Rewards Strategy Alignment Questionnaire.*

of SBSs that can be pursued in any number of forms. Likewise, success can be defined in a variety of forms. It is not possible to identify them all. The authors' research and experience lead to three broad categories of specific business strategy, each with its own influence on reward design. These are:

- *Growth.* Growth—either organic or inorganic—may be accomplished through expansion into new markets, geographically or vertically, or through acquisition of competitors, suppliers, customers, etc.
- *Process Optimization.* These are strategies that improve any core processes in order to magnify their impact on adding value/reducing cost.
- *Maintenance/Reduction.* These activities address an organization's existing offerings (e.g., being known for that "one thing"). An organization may increase its profits, for example, by getting out of less desirable businesses.

Figure 3-8 indicates a dramatic increase in the number of specific business strategies that organizations will pursue in the next three years. It should be easy to see how these various strategies both look different to your customers and require different people strategy critical success factors. Consider, for example, that the underlying processes required for success vary dramatically between a company that constantly pursues operational excellence(e.g., through Six Sigma) and one on a strong acquisition binge. Likewise, what the people need to know and to do well are different, too. (People strategy will be clarified later in this chapter.) Accordingly, the underlying metrics will need to support the articulated SBS; it is imperative that design team members understand how the organization goes to market.

## Organization Capabilities

Organization capabilities are the people-related aspects of an organization through which the business strategy is transformed or translated into the executable code of a people strategy. It is the transmission between the business strategy engine and the people strategy wheels. It defines what the organization collectively must do well to succeed.

### The Balanced Scorecard as a Framework for Valuing Organization Capabilities

This book is intended to be descriptive and not prescriptive. Accordingly, it uses commonly accepted frameworks to demonstrate that rewards can

Figure 3–8. Specific business strategy (SBS).

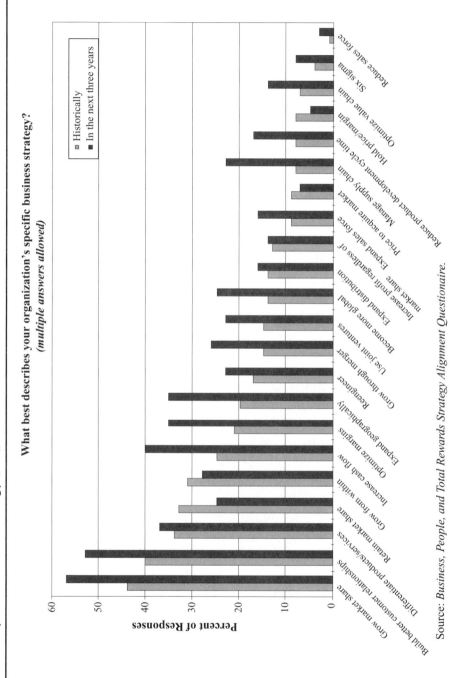

What best describes your organization's specific business strategy?
*(multiple answers allowed)*

Source: *Business, People, and Total Rewards Strategy Alignment Questionaire.*

be developed to fit whatever model your organization embraces. One popular framework that has been particularly influential is the balanced scorecard. Robert Kaplan and David Norton have authored two books on the subject that demonstrate the concept's capability of linking people to strategy. In the first, they suggest that the balanced scorecard (BSC) translates an organization's mission and strategy into a comprehensive set of performance measures that provides the framework for a strategic measurement and management system.[2] Figure 3-9 is adapted from their text; it illustrates how the framework is used to take the reward influences discussed up to this point (from strategy to capabilities) and wraps it around a useful model. There will be further discussion about the balanced scorecard in subsequent chapters; here it is important to point out how it makes the connection from strategy and organization capabilities to people.

The foundation of the balanced scorecard is that leading-edge organizations view their business through four "perspectives." As depicted in the center of Figure 3-9, these perspectives are financial, operational, customer, and employee in nature. What Kaplan and Norton had discovered, and subsequently built their thinking around, was that successful companies defined metrics for each of those views of their business and used those metrics to translate how they impact the successful execution of strategy to people. The steps in this cyclical process are: clarifying strategy, communicating the linkages, planning and metric setting, and feedback to readjust.

Executing strategy requires that you be good at certain things; it stands to reason that those things are what should be defined, communicated, measured, and ultimately compensated for once they are achieved. These things that people need to do well are the organization's capabilities. They can be articulated through the four-perspective framework of the balanced scorecard. As it relates to people and pay, two points are critical. First, adopting the varied perspectives allows a company to move beyond the traditional financial measurement models by incorporating metrics that are generally more easily understood by employees and that imminently reduce the line of sight for the vast majority of people. This is not to imply that the ultimate goal of a for-profit enterprise is anything less than increasing the wealth of the owners. It is merely to say that adopting a balanced perspective facilitates the creation of subordinate metrics that people can understand and affect, with the knowledge that those measures ultimately drive the company's end objective.

Figure 3-9. The balanced scorecard as a strategic framework for action.

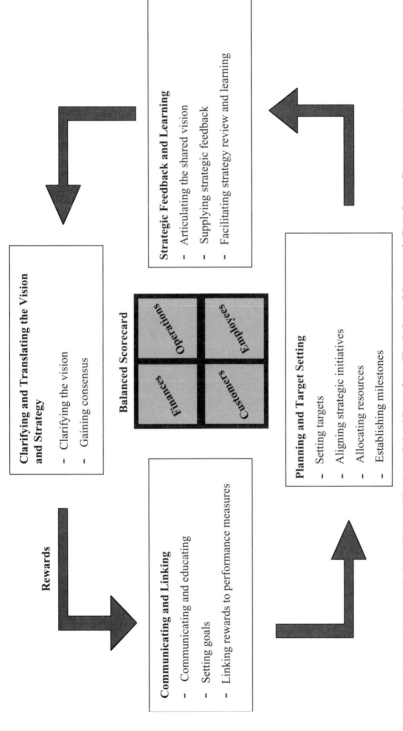

**Clarifying and Translating the Vision and Strategy**

- Clarifying the vision
- Gaining consensus

**Rewards**

**Communicating and Linking**

- Communicating and educating
- Setting goals
- Linking rewards to performance measures

**Balanced Scorecard**

Finances | Operations
Customers | Employees

**Strategic Feedback and Learning**

- Articulating the shared vision
- Supplying strategic feedback
- Facilitating strategy review and learning

**Planning and Target Setting**

- Setting targets
- Aligning strategic initiatives
- Allocating resources
- Establishing milestones

Second, linking balanced scorecard plans to compensation creates more robust change.[3] Previous research has demonstrated that the most sophisticated users of the balanced scorecard link their measurement plans to compensation, most specifically through annual incentive plans. However, as is frequently the case with compensation, "how" is more important than "how much." In fact, very clear key messages can be delivered with very little pay. Accordingly, the balanced scorecard framework is more about educating employees than compensating them. Most often companies link it to compensation to get people to pay attention.

One example is that of a biomedical testing laboratory where the balanced scorecard was used to deliver annual incentive compensation to employees throughout the organization. The design flowed from the organization's vision to the descriptions of the responsibilities of each job. Each employee could articulate the vision and concisely state how her role did something that delivered a result, which, in turn, impacted a customer to drive value and achieve the corporate vision. It was systemic, and the payoff for this effort was less than 4 percent of payroll—an incredible return on investment.

As defined previously and shown in Figure 3-1, organization capabilities fall into four categories. The first is customer capabilities, such as acquiring new customers, building better customer relationships, and matching services to customers needs. The second category encompasses product- and service-related capabilities (e.g., providing excellent customer services, creating innovative products/services, continuously improving products/services, bringing new products and services to market, and creating and building brand identity). Third are management and people capabilities. Management capabilities are required for achieving growth and profit; executing mergers, acquisitions, or strategic alliances; entering new markets; deploying resources effectively; and organizing around customer requirements. People capabilities include attracting and retaining the best employees, creating employee commitment, creating an organization without boundaries, developing a truly global organization, achieving a capacity for change and training, and developing the workforce. Fourth are organization capabilities relating to technology and information—for example, managing intellectual capital, applying state-of-the-art technology to key processes, and even creating a new economy technology strategy.

Most organizations realize how critical it is today, and how much more critical it will be in the future, to build an extensive list of organization capabilities across customers, products/scrvices, management and people, and technology. Such organization capabilities are needed to support all of the different levels of business strategy, from the general to the value chain and to specific strategies. Figures 3-10 through 3-14, which are derived from the *Business, People, and Total Reward Strategy Alignment Questionnaire*, provide some interesting insights into how businesses respond to questions about current organization capabilities and where they expect to significantly increase capabilities in the near term.

The findings in each of these areas point up another key aspect of the balanced scorecard and its application in the design of performance measurement and reward programs. Fundamentally, the four areas of organization capabilities provide metrics and insight into three of the four perspectives of the balanced scorecard—operational, customer, and employee. Kaplan and Norton indicated that, in addition to viewing organization performance through the four perspectives, one should strive to use measures that are both historical and forward-looking, or predictive, in their inclination. In Figure 3-10, which depicts the findings of organization capabilities relative to interactions with customers, it is interesting to note that the ability to acquire new customers is virtually flat (i.e., expectations slightly decline for the near future). A common measure of customer acquisition activity may be, for example, market share, which is clearly historical in its view. Meanwhile, organizations expect a somewhat dramatic increase in efforts related to building relationships with existing customers, meeting their needs, and solving their problems. This illustrates the link between strategy and capabilities through the use of balanced scorecard–based leading metrics. The respondents who indicated the requirement for building customer relationships are ripe for moving off traditional financial measurements toward a more balanced—and forward-looking—approach. This requires defining the requisite capabilities necessary to achieve strategy and the metrics that support their execution.

Consider a high-tech company that's more interested in understanding its customers' businesses, and in building the future requirements of customer products, than in market share. The solution may be a balanced scorecard plan where the measures are based on customer partnering. By getting into the development labs of its customers, and understanding the requirements for the next generation of products, the high-tech company has a clear predictor of its future business.

The correlation between value chain strategy and organization capabilities is also worth noting. Figure 3-7 illustrated that the most significant impacts to the value chain will be derived through people and technology.

*(text continues on page 65)*

Figure 3-10. Organization capabilities: customers.

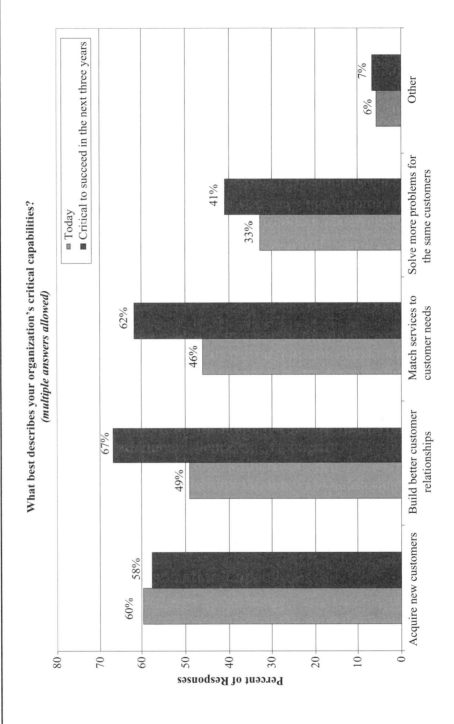

What best describes your organization's critical capabilities?
*(multiple answers allowed)*

Legend: ■ Today  ■ Critical to succeed in the next three years

Acquire new customers: Today 60%, Critical 58%
Build better customer relationships: Today 49%, Critical 67%
Match services to customer needs: Today 46%, Critical 62%
Solve more problems for the same customers: Today 33%, Critical 41%
Other: Today 6%, Critical 7%

Percent of Responses

Figure 3–11. Organization capabilities: products and services.

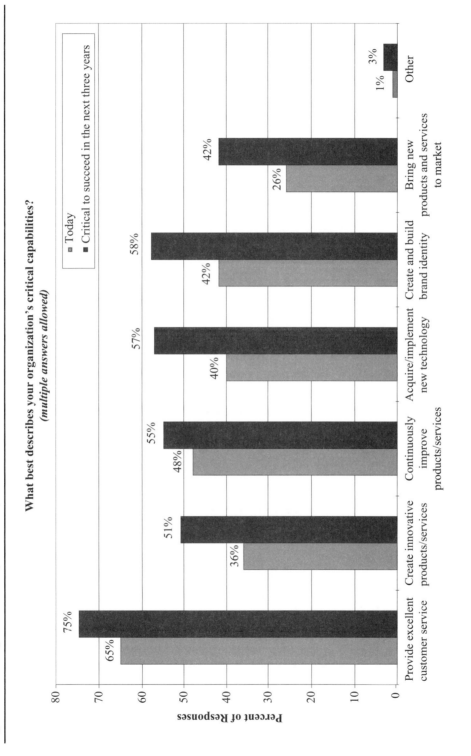

**What best describes your organization's critical capabilities?**
*(multiple answers allowed)*

Figure 3–12. Organization capabilities: management.

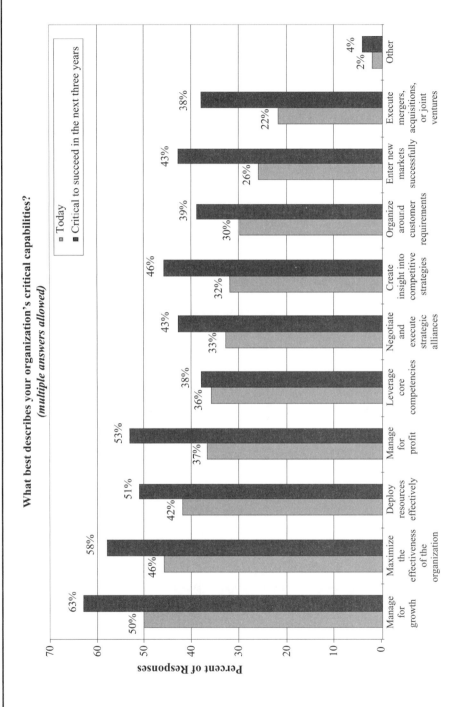

**What best describes your organization's critical capabilities?**
*(multiple answers allowed)*

Figure 3–13. Organization capabilities: people.

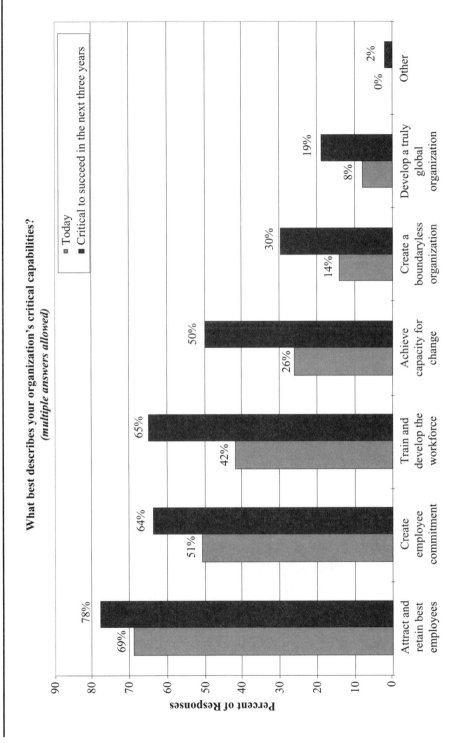

What best describes your organization's critical capabilities?
*(multiple answers allowed)*

■ Today
■ Critical to succeed in the next three years

Percent of Responses

Figure 3–14. Organization capabilities: technology.

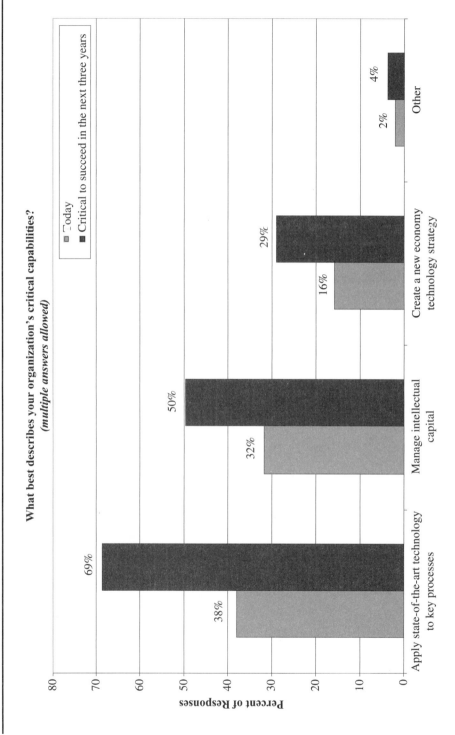

**What best describes your organization's critical capabilities?**
*(multiple answers allowed)*

□ Today
■ Critical to succeed in the next three years

That parallels the results of the data driving Figures 3-11 and 3-14. Getting and keeping the right people, training and developing them, building their commitment, and achieving the capacity for change are reported as those organization capabilities that will most drive future success. Likewise, managing intellectual capital and using technology are gaining in their importance, too. Applying a balanced scorecard framework allows an organization to better measure and manage the requirement for these capabilities. What's more, it facilitates the differentiation between historical and prospective metrics. Consider that investing in the training and development of people is as much an investment in the future as investing in infrastructure; unfortunately, however, most organizations do not view it that way and cut training costs at the first sign of economic uncertainty. But also think about the difference between measuring employee commitment and measuring turnover. The latter is simply a quantification of the number of people who departed in some period of time past; the former is a good predictor of the likelihood of people leaving in the future. As pointed out previously, organizations have used this measure to predict customer satisfaction and profitability.

However your organization wishes to define organization capabilities, remember, they must be defined so as to provide the critical input for development and definition of the final conceptual framework of people strategy.

## People Strategy

People strategy is a general term used to describe the foundational concepts applying to the people component of business strategy. All businesses have financial, technical, marketing, operational, and customer service strategies. Most organizations also have people strategies (written or unwritten) that provide a road map for employees and other stakeholders to understand the way in which people will contribute to the accomplishment of the overall and component business strategies. The people strategy can be broken into three parts: (1) organizational structure, (2) management processes, and (3) culture. These components are discussed in the next sections.

### Organizational Structure

The most useful analytical concepts to understanding organizational structure consist of three sets of information that represent a simplification of many of the various conceptual frameworks.

First, organizational structure is understood by the number of organizational levels that exist in the company. Simply, this reflects the management layers separating employees from the CEO. The CEO's direct reports are typically classified as "level one," "level two," and so on.

Second, the organizational structure can be understood by the balance, or percentage, of positions and incumbents allocated to line versus staff roles. This is also represented by the percent of total employees who are staff and how those staff members are distributed within the organization. Typically, staff functions are either centralized or decentralized.

Third, organizational structure can be understood by determining the "key organizing themes" of the various management levels. These themes are functional, geographic, or product- or process-oriented. A simple structure defines each employee group along one theme; complex structures use two or more themes. In Figure 3-15, the critical information elements to collect and analyze with regard to organization structure are defined pictorially.

In Figures 3-16 through 3-18 can be seen the distribution of responses to the three analytical concepts that allow us to understand organizational structure. As the reader can see, organizations are very different. For example, while some organizations (21 percent) have fewer than three organizational levels, 3 percent of the respondents have between nine and eleven levels. With respect to the issue of line versus staff roles, it can be noted that while 8 percent of the respondents had less than 5 percent of their employees in staff positions, a full 13 percent of respondents had more than 50 percent of their employees in staff positions.

Organizational themes are important to understand because they are reflected in the way an organization budgets and allocates resources. If the organization keeps track of critical performance measures by product, then installing an incentive scheme that rewards based on geography is an uphill battle. This is true especially if the executive management organizing theme is governed by product. In today's complex organizations, it is not unusual to have different themes by layer as well as multiple themes within the same organizational layer.

## Management Processes

If structure defines how you organize to get the business of the business done, management processes define how you measure and communicate success. It is the managerial accounting of the human resources world. You need to understand its various components in order to make

*(text continues on page 71)*

Figure 3–15. Three components of organization structure concepts.

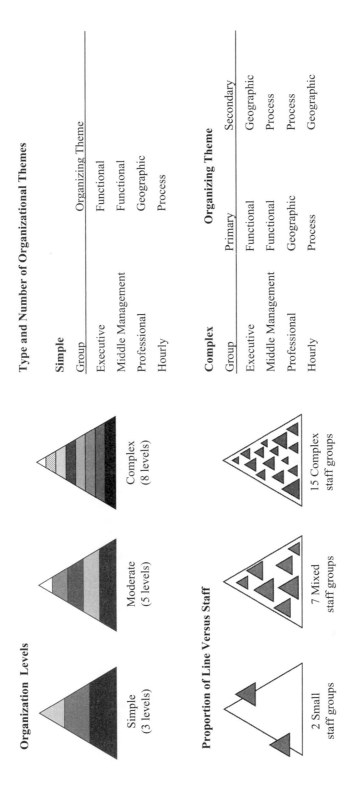

Figure 3-16.  Organization structure: number of layers.

**How would you characterize your organizational structure?**

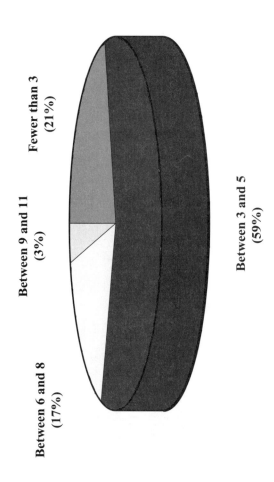

Fewer than 3
(21%)

Between 9 and 11
(3%)

Between 3 and 5
(59%)

Between 6 and 8
(17%)

Figure 3–17. Organization structure: line/staff ratios.

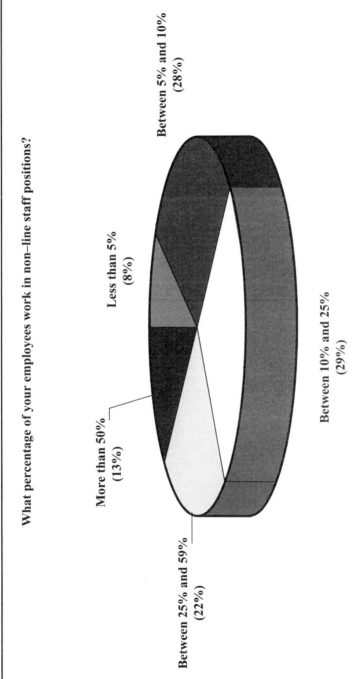

**What percentage of your employees work in non–line staff positions?**

Between 5% and 10%
(28%)

Less than 5%
(8%)

More than 50%
(13%)

Between 10% and 25%
(29%)

Between 25% and 59%
(22%)

Figure 3–18. Organization structure: organizing themes.

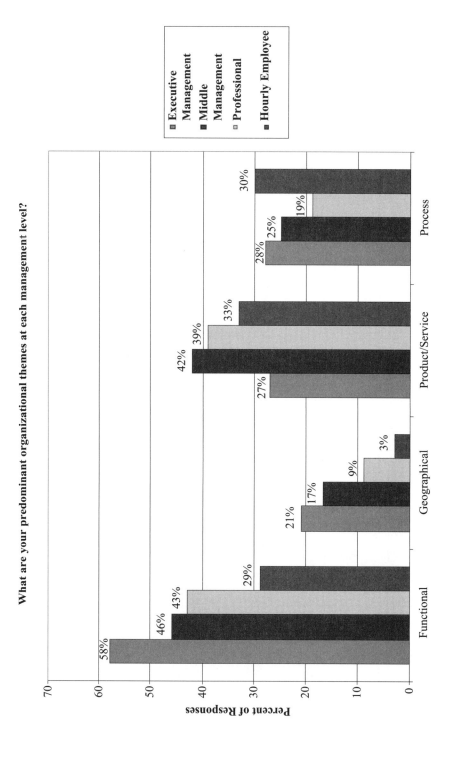

What are your predominant organizational themes at each management level?

informed rewards decisions. As before, different conceptual approaches can be used to build an understanding of organizational processes for the purpose of developing appropriate rewards strategies. Henry Mintzberg utilizes a series of processes ("design parameters") that he refers to as planning and control systems, liaison devices, and degree of centralization and decentralization.[4] Some combinations of these processes, as shown in Figure 3-19, can be simple and useful. This framework allows an assessment of each of the following management processes.

- *Knowledge and Innovation Management.* This area represents the depth and breadth of knowledge required to produce the organization's products and services and the overall need for effectiveness of innovation.

- *Decision Making.* This area includes what decisions are made by whom and where within the organization those decisions have an effect. Assess the information required by and provided to the decision makers, the degree of guidance in various forms, the impact of an inappropriate decision, and the time frame within which the decision must be made. Summarize the knowledge you gain in simple terms, such as the degree of centralization/decentralization of the organization's decision-making process, along each of the major functional/organizational vertical segments.

- *Resource Planning, Allocation, and Monitoring.* When it comes to resource deployment, many organizations are extremely "planful" and have long time horizons for the planning processes. Other organizations are more reactive and their planning processes are short-term in nature.

- *Supervision.* With this organizational process you can analyze the type and degree of supervision exercised within various organizational units. Some organizations have employees under very close supervision while others have some or all employees substantially free to execute their job responsibilities without direct supervision.

- *Communications and Contacts.* This organizational process explains the various aspects affecting the flow of information within the organization and how the organization communicates with individuals and companies outside its own organizational envelope. A key to reward strategy design is to determine the extent and the speed of communications exchange. For example, when the flow is quick and open from top to bottom and between departments, the organization becomes more creative and requires less planning.

Figure 3-19. Management process framework.

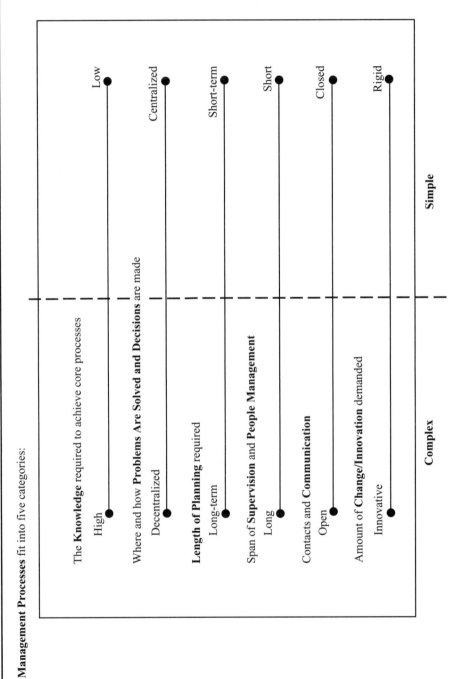

**Management Processes** fit into five categories:

- *Change Management.* This organizational process is increasingly important because few aspects of organizational life remain the same for long periods of time. It is important to understand the degree to which the company identifies the need for change-oriented intelligence gathering and interpretation and how well it understands the opportunities and threats that are posed by the various internal and external changes. Only a very small percentage of organizations participating in the *Business, People, and Total Reward Strategy Alignment Questionnaire* have completely met their objectives in each of the organizational process groupings. Figures 3-20 through 3-24 indicate the degree that respondents felt they had met their objectives in each of the various organizational processes tested. Clearly there is great need and opportunity to improve on present organizational processes. For the reward strategy design team, these needs, successes, and failures must be reflected in Total Rewards Strategy and plan design.

## Organizational Culture

Culture defines the norms of a company. What is it like to work there? How do employees communicate with one another and share work? What do employees think and perceive about their relationship with their employer?

Organizational culture has been defined as the glue that binds an organization together. It is, as Sherriton and Stern[5] define it, "the environment or personality of the organization." They organize culture into three aspects:

- Ritualized shared patterns of beliefs, values, and behaviors
- Management environment—style, philosophy (what is said/done/rewarded), systems and procedures in place
- Written and unwritten norms/procedures

To appreciate just how important culture is, consider this quote by Lawrence A. Bossidy, former chairman and chief executive officer of Allied Signal, Inc. and now chairman of Honeywell International: "My primary challenge during these years has been the same as the one that no doubt faces many companies . . . that is to say, creating a culture in which people focus on where they are going, instead of where they have been."[6]

As with the other aspects of this approach to information gathering and knowledge development, there are many alternative ways of thinking about culture. Collective assessment of organizational culture

*(text continues on page 79)*

Figure 3-20. Organizational processes: managing knowledge.

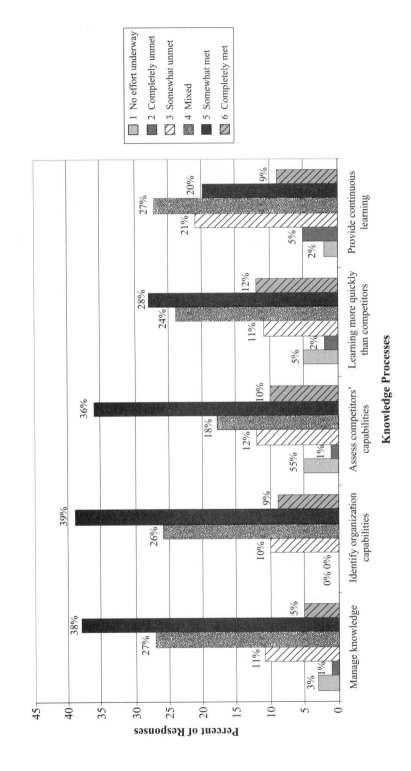

How would you rate your organization's success in each of the following key areas?

Figure 3–21. Organizational processes: decision making.

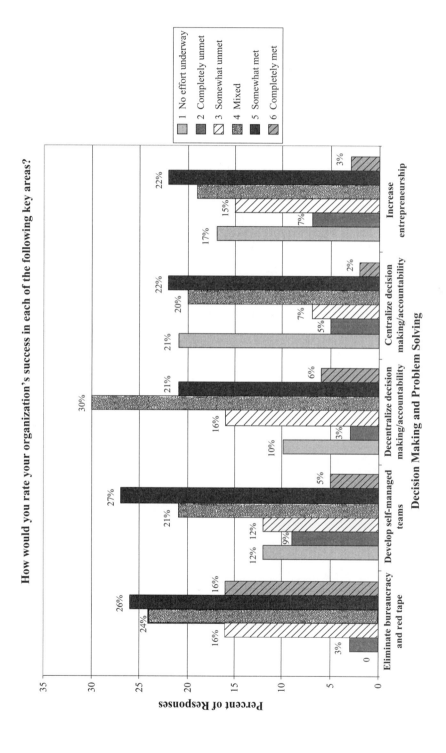

How would you rate your organization's success in each of the following key areas?

Legend:
1 No effort underway
2 Completely unmet
3 Somewhat unmet
4 Mixed
5 Somewhat met
6 Completely met

Decision Making and Problem Solving

Percent of Responses

Figure 3–22.  Organizational processes: contacts and communications.

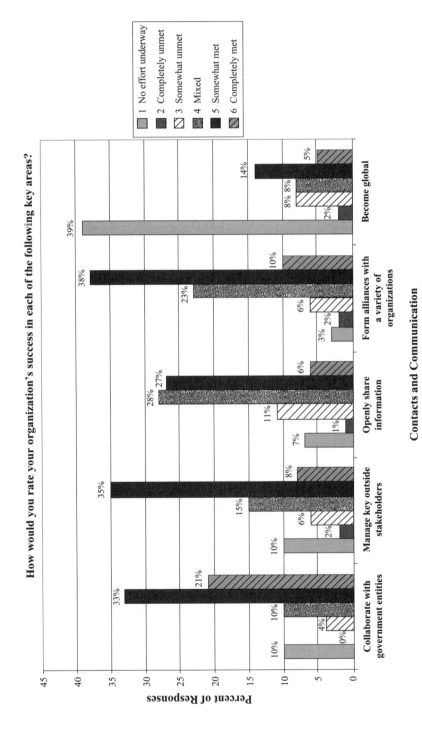

Figure 3-23. Organizational processes: supervision and people management.

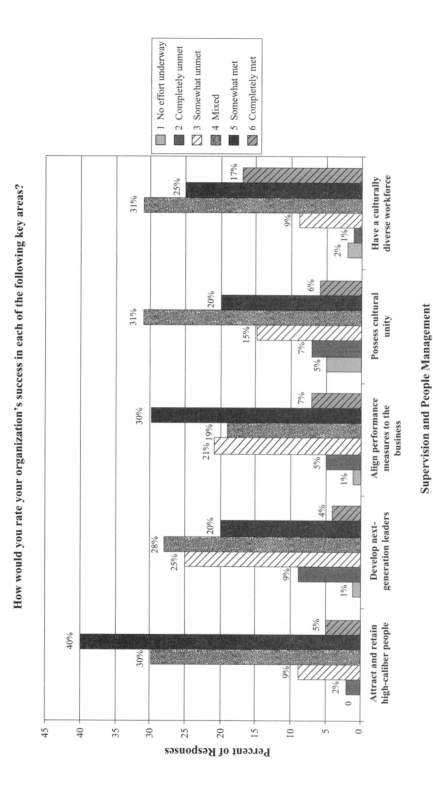

How would you rate your organization's success in each of the following key areas?

**Supervision and People Management**

Figure 3-24. Organizational processes: change management.

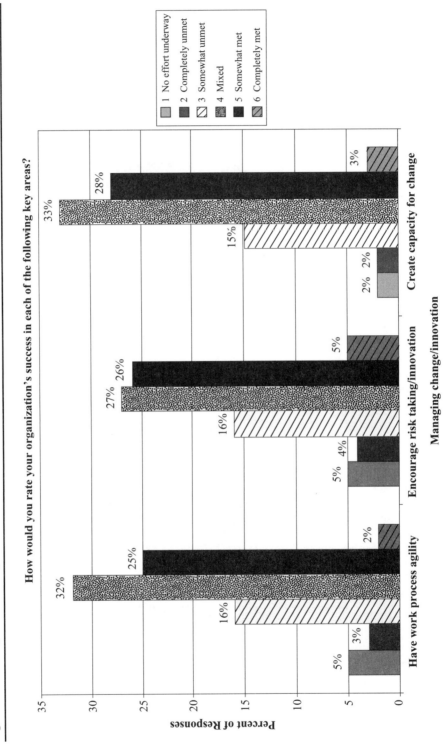

literature provides eight general dimensions within which ideas can be framed.[7] They are:

1. Truth and rationality—ideas about what is real and not real, and how those truths are discovered
2. Time and time horizons—its importance and how it is measured
3. Motivation—underlying reasons for achievement and supporting systems, e.g., rewards, punishment
4. Stability versus change—the propensity toward security or risk taking
5. Orientation toward work—task versus social focus
6. Collaboration/cooperation—how work is most effectively or efficiently accomplished
7. Control/coordination—the degree of concentration or shared decision making
8. Focus—the extent to which it controls, or is controlled by, its internal and external environment

*Corporate Culture and Organization Effectiveness* by Daniel R. Denison lists another fairly complete set of cultural items.[8] Denison measured culture in terms of eighteen indexes organized into four areas—organization climate, job design, supervisory leadership, and peer leadership. His study of these indexes led him to create the culture and effectiveness model. It illustrates the interrelationships of four elements that impact effectiveness:

- Adaptability—internal flexibility and external focus
- Mission—meaning and direction
- Consistency—normative integration and predictability
- Involvement—informal processes and formal structure

Another effective outline on organizational culture is described in the book *Organizational Culture and Leadership* by Edgar H. Schein.[9] He defines the culture of a group as "a pattern of shared basic assumptions that the group learned as it solved its problem of external adaptation and internal integration, that has worked well enough to be considered valid and, therefore, to be taught to new members as the correct way to perceive, think, and feel in relation to those problems." According to Schein, the key characteristics of culture are:

- The organization's environment
- The nature of human activity
- The nature of reality and truth
- The nature of human nature
- The nature of human relationships
- The nature of time
- Information and communications
- Subcultural uniformity versus diversity
- Task versus relationship orientation
- Linear versus systemic field logic

Schein organized these cultural attributes to define the difference between a functional organization and a learning culture. This framework is summarized in Figure 3-25.

A core principle applied throughout this book is that it matters less how the various influences on TRS are described, but rather that they are done. Accordingly, any of these different frameworks may be appropriate. However, the cultural concept that has been particularly helpful for us is the one defined in *People, Performance, and Pay* by Flannery, Hofrichter, and Platten.[10] They outlined the existence of four general cultural types: process, functional, network, and time-based. They are defined as follows:

1. *Functional Culture.* In a functional culture, stability, reliability, and consistency are the watchwords of the organization; customers are passive, cycle times lengthy, competition limited. Work in the functional culture is designed around the specialization of individuals. It is identified by management hierarchies in which decision making is clearly set apart from execution: Bosses boss, and workers work. Performance is measured in terms of size, return or equity, and industrial reputation.[11] Some good examples of a functional culture include a hospital operating room or the flight of a commercial aircraft. With commercial aircraft, mechanics, pilots, flight attendants, and air traffic controllers are all involved, but you want the pilot to fly the plane and the flight attendant to attend to the passengers, and not the other way around. Likewise, in brain surgery the surgeon should perform the operation, not the nurse.

2. *Process Culture.* Process work cultures are designed around processes for consistently meeting obligations to customers while contin-

Figure 3–25. Characteristics of culture.

| | **Functional Organization** | | **Learning Culture** |
|---|---|---|---|
| Organization–Environment Relationship | Environment Dominant | Symbiotic | Organization Dominant |
| Nature of Human Activity | Reactive/Fatalistic | Harmonizing | Proactive |
| Nature of Reality and Truth | Moralistic Authoritative | | Pragmatic |
| Nature of Human Nature | Humans Basically Evil | | Humans Basically Good |
| Nature of Human Relationships | Groupism Authoritative/Paternalistic | | Individualism Collegial/Participative |
| Nature of Time | Past Oriented Short Time Units | Present Oriented Medium Time Units | Near Future Oriented Long Time Units |
| Information and Communication | Low Level of Connectivity | | Fully Connected |
| Subculture Uniformity Versus Diversity | Highly Uniform | | Highly Diverse |
| Task Versus Relationship Orientation | Primarily Task Oriented | Task and Relationship Oriented | Primarily Relationship Oriented |
| Linear Versus Systemic Field Logic | Linear Thinking | | Systemic Thinking |

Source: Edgar Schein, *Organizational Culture and Leadership.*

ually improving quality.[12] A team approach to work dominates the culture. Planning, execution, and control are integrated as close to the customers as possible. A team-based chemical or pharmaceutical manufacturing plant, where each participant is equally skilled at each job, fits this definition. The results required—a consistent product or service (e.g., a consistent dosage or chemical formula)—are the most important thing.

3. *Time-Based Culture.* Focused on maximizing the return on fixed assets, flexibility, and technical agility, time-based cultures limit the levels of management hierarchy while increasing the use of program and project work groups that cross functional boundaries. Individuals in time-based organizations are encouraged to develop multifunctional expertise and competencies. Rather than using traditional accounting measures such as return on assets, organization performance is assessed through a more dynamic measure such as economic value added (EVA) and by the competitive position that new products or services achieve in the marketplace.[13]

Examples of time-based culture abound in today's high-tech world where organizations strive for speed to market. They accept a certain level of impression or error to gain first-mover advantage. The cellular telephone industry is an excellent example. Cellular service providers need to get into a region first in order to be successful.

4. *Network Culture.* Work in the network culture is designed around alliances that bring together the necessary proficiencies and competencies to successfully complete a specific venture (e.g., the development of a new product or the production of a new movie). The traditional management hierarchy is replaced with "producers" who coordinate and direct the efforts of the network through the specific venture's life cycle.[14]

However an organization chooses to think about culture, it is certain that the understanding must be a strong consideration in the development of the reward strategy.

## People Strategy Critical Success Factors

Once the previous conceptual models are developed and information is collected and rationalized, the all-important question becomes: "What do the people within the organization need to do to ensure the organization wins?" These are the people-related critical success factors.

Understanding the development and interpretation of these critical success factors will determine the ultimate value that will be created by the complementing reward strategy. It is generally a lack of real understanding of these factors that has resulted in the most serious misadventures in reward strategy and created the fertile ground for sayings such as: "Be careful of what you pay for, you'll usually get it." This is otherwise known as "You get what you pay for!"

People strategy critical success factors (PSCSFs) outline how the organization and, most important, its people need to behave, work together, and achieve results in order to be successful.

These PSCSFs are defined by different organizations in a myriad of ways. For example, they may be defined as a core of collective competencies that drive employees toward the specific behaviors and knowledge/skills/abilities that define success. Alternatively, PSCSFs can be defined through a series of internally focused measures. They identify what the organization must achieve to be successful in working together across the company. Either way, the PSCSFs are internally oriented.

> **Breaking Down the Entitlement Culture**
>
> Here is a story about Charles Deming. At an initial meeting, a potential client said to Dr. Deming, "Our problem here is that we have too much deadwood." Deming replied, "Did you hire those people dead or did you somehow kill them along the way?" Whenever a company wants help breaking down its culture of entitlement it should be asked the parallel question: "Did you hire entitled people or did you, through your actions, entitle them?" When considering reward designs in the vein of breaking down entitlement mentality, start from this negotiating point and move on from there: Everything the company offers its employees is a reward, and they are entitled to nothing.
>
> Some specific strategies for breaking down this mentality include:
>
> - Shifting compensation from fixed to variable pay systems
> - Shifting from short- to long-term compensation
> - Breaking old paradigms—just doing something different or breaking some old "rules"
> - Creating new tools for compensation delivery that pay for value or strategic impact, not tenure

## Conclusion

This chapter has defined (using various conceptual models and categories of information) what should be gathered and understood by those

## A BABY BELL PEOPLE STRATEGY OF THE FUTURE

In 1990, the head of human resources for one of the large Baby Bells was under severe pressure to increase the hiring rates for radio frequency (RF) communications engineers because the line organization was experiencing difficulty completing its business strategy of "dominating the wireless world of the future." The HR executive wasn't completely sure how many engineers he needed, but he guessed over 300 new ones within a few months. Well, when you employ more than 30,000 employees, hiring 300 more doesn't seem like many.

However, back in 1990 the average person didn't have a cell phone, the wireless revolution hadn't really begun, and the universities were not really producing RF communications engineers in volume, at least not yet.

Not only were there relatively few graduates being produced, but few existed in the general population (the wireless industry was relatively new in terms of providing jobs for graduates of technical schools). Without the demand there wasn't much supply. To make matters worse, this Baby Bell's competitors were also seeking out RF engineers, and one of the potential sources for this talent pool—other telecommunications organizations—was most likely going to be hiring in similar numbers.

The problem facing the Baby Bell was that it needed to put "people before strategy." In other words, there was no executing the strategy if the people weren't there. The answer to this problem had to come from a nontraditional hiring source. Although the company deployed scholarship, work-study, and intern opportunities, the numbers and the time horizon were still not sufficient to fill the immediate hiring requirements. The solution was to hire the professors in addition to the students, creating for the elders the opportunity to be part of the initiation of a new industry. The recruitment equation was to offer more than just money; the professors got to continue to "teach" in a real industrial laboratory.

People strategy critical success factors don't always develop over time; sometimes a technology jump can disrupt the market and create unexpected needs.

individuals undertaking the development of a reward strategy. Many alternative concepts exist in the literature, and all have at one time or another provided design teams with insights that later proved to be valuable.

Figure 3-26 summarizes the material presented in this chapter and

## Figure 3-26. Key influences on reward designs.

| Influence | Definition | Need to Know |
|---|---|---|
| **Environment**<br><br>■ **Government**<br>■ **Competition**<br>■ **Union Influence** | The business environment and markets within which a company operates. The regulatory and legal climate, the competitive landscape and the company's fit within that landscape, and the influence of organized labor. | • *Degree of design freedom*<br>• *Industry norms*<br>• *Union preferences* |
| **Stakeholders**<br><br>■ **Suppliers**<br>■ **Employees**<br>■ **Owners**<br>■ **Partners**<br>■ **Customers** | All of the parties that have an interest in a company's success. The number, breadth, and diversity of these parties and their direct influence on both operations and decisions. | • *Owners' preferences and requirements*<br>• *Degree of design freedom*<br>• *Strategic allegiances* |
| **Organization Capabilities** | The capacities that the organization needs to possess to execute its business strategy. | • *Requirements for success; metrics* |
| **Business Strategy**<br><br>■ **General Business Strategy (GBS)**<br><br>■ **Value Chain Strategy (VBS)**<br><br>■ **Specific Business Strategy (SBS)** | The company's plans to win in the market.<br>Low cost provider; product service differentiator; focus; operationally excellent/customer intimate.<br><br>Stages and functions where strategy is achieved.<br><br>Go-to-market orientation. | • *Articulated GBS, VCS, SBS*<br>• *Planned changes*<br>• *Degree of penetration*<br>• *Metrics as a link to capabilities* |
| **People Strategy**<br><br>■ **Structure**<br>■ **Processes**<br>■ **Culture**<br>■ **Critical Success Factors** | How the company is organized, the business is measured and managed, and core attributes that drive success are defined.<br><br>The capabilities that must reside in our people to meet the demands of the marketplace. | • *Organizing themes*<br>• *Measurements and performance processes*<br>• *Required behaviors and attributes* |
| **Reward Strategy**<br><br>■ **Money**<br>■ **Mix**<br>■ **Messages** | Plan to allocate reward resources to support business. Elements; competitive markets; positioning.<br><br>Efficient distribution.<br><br>Purposeful words and phrases about offerings and expectations. | • *Reward elements for success; markets and positioning*<br>• *Efficient distribution*<br>• *Desired messages* |

provides you with an outline of the key learning points. Chapter 5 will provide the team framework for building a common understanding of these points among the design team members.

Remember this, however: While there is always an impatience to begin the design/redesign phase by the organization and design team (since they already understand the organization), redesigning the programs without a common understanding of the various aspects of the preceding conceptual frameworks would be like Columbus attempting to sail without his fearless crew.

Chapter 4 will outline how each of the conceptual frameworks impacts the key considerations affecting decisions. It will address questions such as: How competitive should overall rewards be? How should fixed and variable pay be balanced? What should the key messages of the reward program be?

# Creating Linkage— Translating the Dimensions of Business into a Total Rewards Strategy

THIS CHAPTER PROVIDES THE DESIGN team (commissioned in Chapter 2) with the means for linking people to the business by illustrating how each of the influences (defined in Chapter 3) should be interpreted into the design. Linking employees to business outcomes is about taking the influences of the business and designing the dimensions of the Total Rewards Strategy (TRS)—money, mix, and messages—in a way that shares knowledge and fulfills the requirements of the plan. This knowledge about what makes a company successful, and how its employees affect that success within the context of the business influences on design, has to be built, transferred, and leveraged. Motivation is about answering that age-old question, "What's in it for me?" This requires knowledge of the business, a means for interpreting that knowledge, and use of that knowledge to motivate employees through rewards. You want to align the successes of your company with those of the employees, both intrinsically and extrinsically, who contribute to it always while demonstrating how that connection is made. Total Rewards Strategy is the foundation of what links employees to the organization. Reward plans will provide the leverage!

Unfortunately, there is no silver bullet. For much of our professional lives we have searched for the secret decoder ring that allows one to align all the variables and find the path to the Holy Grail. What the search has demonstrated instead is that there's no one right path; the possible iterations and permutations do not allow it to be so. Instead, this book can only show you the map and let you find your own way.

Having said that, here is some guidance that demonstrates how each business influence—within the framework of the model we've chosen to use—impacts Total Rewards Strategy design. For each influence we will give specific insight to money, mix, and messages—the three dimensions of reward strategy identified in Chapter 1. As a refresher:

- *Money* refers to the determined people markets, competitive level, and reward elements.

- *Mix* is the design to distribute those elements most efficiently.

- *Messages* are the deliberate statements about the company's values and expectations that it delivers through rewards (see Figure 1-2).

There is good news and bad news. The good news is that you are given a reference guide against which you can assess your own plan design choices. This guide is proven, since it is based on empirical evidence and the experiences of the consultants who provided materials and insight for this text.

The bad news is that it leaves you to resolve conflicts. Each influence on reward design is treated individually; to do otherwise would be, in a one-dimensional text, impossible. Naturally, contradictions will exist. It is up to you, the reader, to reconcile these contradictions.

This chapter illustrates how each business dimension influences Total Rewards Strategy. Use Figure 4-1 (see also page 66 of 99 on the CD-ROM) to establish priorities, assess fit, and resolve the conflicts. As the sum of all the factors' collective influence is equal to 100 percent, each one's importance can be assessed and prioritized. As you do this, consider the frequency with which a specified response comes up, and also consider the impact of the collective influences on your organization, by defining the messages that are most critical to reinforce in your company. Much of what's covered in this chapter has its most significant influence on the degree of freedom that the designers enjoy. Accordingly, the design team needs to assess its limits in terms of both design freedom and timing. In that way the decision may be either what to do or when to do it.

Figure 4–1. Identifying Total Rewards Strategy alternatives.

| | Business Strategy | | | Organization Capabilities | People Strategy | | | People Strategy Critical Success Factors |
|---|---|---|---|---|---|---|---|---|
| External Environment Key Stakeholders | General (GBS) | Value Chain (VCS) | Specific (SBS) | | Structure | Process | Culture | |
| Briefly Describe Linkage | | | | | | | | |
| Money | | | | | | | | |
| Mix | | | | | | | | |
| Messages | | | | | | | | |
| Relative Influence | | | | | | | | = 100 % |

## Key Stakeholder Considerations in the External Environment

The external business environment and an organization's key stakeholders dramatically influence reward plan designs. Of particular influence are a company's ownership structure, the regulatory environment, and competitive posture.

---

### CHANGING OWNERSHIP, BY DAVID BUSHLEY

A leading medical malpractice insurance company, organized as an exchange, was converting to a public company. As an exchange, the focus was internal and did not foster a performance orientation. The change required that the culture shift toward one that established solid external benchmarks, set challenging goals, and focused people on their accomplishments.

The approach was to establish a competitive peer grouping in conjunction with the investment bankers to measure corporate performance and the achievement of strategic objectives. A performance-based executive Total Rewards philosophy was designed—including short- and long-term benefit plans—to measure and reward success relative to that peer group, in terms of the strategic initiatives. The design put more pay at risk, increasing the leverage of each executive's total cash compensation.

The ultimate success of the organization, and ultimately the program, was the development and implementation of tiered, line-of-sight objectives. Executives realized that in the new world as they were faced with it, the company's success rested with employees at all levels. Real culture change, toward a broader performance orientation, required that higher performance expectations be instilled at every level. Accordingly, a single budget created the funding for all incentive plans. The combination of pooled dollars and cascading metrics force cooperation and teamwork to drive success.

*David Bushley is National Director, Financial Services Industry Rewards Consulting, for Buck Consultants.*

Whether a company is publicly or privately held influences its orientation toward rewards. Private companies' programs need to reflect the tenor of the owners, defining for employees what it means to work there (almost saying, "Work here for me"). Family businesses, more than any other category, have a unique opportunity to define how the family wants the company to be viewed in its relationship with its people. Figure 4-2 illustrates these relationships. There is a stratification of reward offerings that is more pronounced in privately held companies, generally reflecting the critical nature of specific people or roles.

In determining the money axis of the TRS architecture, private companies forfeit some flexibility in terms of what they can offer. How the owners define their employee/employer relationship significantly influences both competitive level and mix.

Public companies, of course, have more flexibility in terms of offerings but less in ability to personalize their messages.

A company's competitive positioning and product offerings are pivotal, too. In other words, what the company does and its posture in that market should be reflected in its rewards plans since both factors significantly influence a company's ability to attract, retain, and motivate people. Consider the following issues:

- *General Profile of the Industry.* How a company's products and services are viewed by consumers influences employees' feelings about working in that environment. Consider that people generally feel better about working for helping, healing businesses than other businesses; this is intuitive because many companies with positive images pay less for the same jobs as other businesses. Any company can leverage this issue, however. Look back to Chapter 1 and the number-one reason employees give for leaving a company. Conversely, creating a learning and nurturing environment—one where everyone is pulling for the same outcomes—establishes a place people want to be. Make your workplace that place.

- *Company's Competitive Posture in Its Industry.* The profile of your company in the market influences your employees' and potential employees' perceptions of the company—everyone wants to work for a winner.

- *Leading Hallmarks.* Define what your company is known for and reflect that in your Total Rewards Strategy.

Figure 4-2. Ownership structure and its impact on TRS.

| Reward Strategy Dimension | Linkage | Ownership-Based TRS | |
|---|---|---|---|
| | | Closely Held | Widely Held |
| Money | • Owners have powerful influence on the use and allocation of the reward resource | • Above market for top management<br>• At or below market of nonmanagement | • Approaches market median overall |
| Mix | • Few owners tend toward high variable | • High variable (if employee controlled)<br>• Low variable (if process limited) | • Moderate variable<br>• Moderate base/fixed compensation |
| Messages | • Few owners focus on financial returns<br>• Many owners tend to serve multiple stakeholders | • High risk/high reward<br>• Individual contribution rewards | • Traditional or market-average risk and reward<br>• Organization-based rewards |

In addition to ownership structure and competitive positioning, a company's customers, suppliers, and the government regulatory impact on its operations all influence the designs.

When considering customers, assess the following linkages:

- *The Significance of Products/Services to the Customers' Business.* Is your product/service of critical importance or low impact? This factor influences the money and key messages dimensions.

- *The Degree of Partnership Between a Company and Its Customers.* Any relationship between a company and its customers informs the mix and key messages dimensions.

- *Distribution of Products/Services.* The distribution of a company's products/services to either a few (and therefore powerful) customers or many (and therefore less influential) customers most influences the messages.

Key messages should inform employees of the company's relationships, ensuring they understand who you are, what you do, and how it influences your customers' businesses. At the other end of the value chain from customers are suppliers. When considering suppliers, the most powerful influences are:

- *Number of Suppliers.* Consider the number of suppliers—from few to many—and therefore the degree of influence those suppliers yield on the company.

- *Integration of Suppliers.* Consider the extent to which your suppliers are integrated in the product development and manufacturing process. Look at the number of links along the value chain where they provide a product/service.

- *Flexibility.* Consider the flexibility you have to choose suppliers.

- *Length of Supplier Relationships.* Are your supplier relationships short- or long-term?

Figure 4-3 illustrates how your company's relationships with its customers and suppliers will impact your Total Rewards Strategy. Here, too, this particular influence may first be considered in terms of degrees of freedom to design. For example, when a company is dealing with very few, powerful customers, its ability to control price is limited. This lack of flexibility clearly influences the company's ability to increase wages. At

Figure 4-3. Suppliers/customers and their impact on TRS.

| Reward Strategy Dimension | Linkage<br>High to low degree of: | Supplier/Customer-Based TRS | |
|---|---|---|---|
| | | Few/Powerful Influence | Many/Diluted Influence |
| Money | • Suppliers integrated into products/services<br>• Impact products/services have on customers | • High: Surgical differences to rewards; highly competitive for key positions<br>• Low: Median position with limited differentiation | • High: Very differentiated reward plans<br>• Low: No influence on design |
| Mix | • Flexibility of choice<br>• Strategic partnerships<br>• Established relationships (e.g., length of time, long product development cycle) | • More fixed than variable | • More leverage |
| Messages | • Impact on value chain<br>• Product risk profile | • Importance of strategic alliances<br>• Supplier/customer management | • Distribution of product/service in market |

the same time, the key messages in this powerful customer relationship need to clearly reinforce customer focus.

Finally, the degree that the regulatory environment influences your business must be considered. Figure 4-4 outlines these relationships. In heavily regulated businesses, where the freedom of markets and/or control over products/services is limited, the degree of freedom the company has to design is, as a rule, also reduced.

If you were to rate the regulatory environment of companies on a scale of one to five, with one being "heavily regulated" and five being "regulation free," it would be intuitive to suggest that the higher degree of regulation, the lesser the degree of freedom one has to design. However, in practice, what sometimes happens is that regulations spur the need for increased thoughtfulness and creativity. In today's business environment all types of companies are competing for the same limited resource— talented people. Highly regulated industries face this challenge from a more limiting perspective. Accordingly, they need to be better at brainstorming alternatives and use a broader brush when painting. This is typically accomplished most effectively by building the messages and then supporting them with money and mix.

## TRS Considerations and Vision, Mission, and Values

This is a threshold condition; you either have a statement of your vision, mission, and values and you use it as a communications tool or you don't. It's not the purpose of this chapter to espouse the virtues of corporate vision, mission, and values. Many companies have them, however, and they do make good communications tools. If you are vision, mission, and values–oriented you know it, and you should leverage it to every advantage. Accordingly, the extent that they are operative within your organization dictates the extent to which they should be linked to compensation. Figure 4-5 illustrates the linkage. At a minimum, appreciate that if something is valued, then it should be paid for, and if there is an aspiration—and a plan for achieving that aspiration—then rewards should be linked to its accomplishment.

Consider, too, that if vision, mission, and values reflect what the organization wants to be, how it plans to get there, and what it will value along the journey, rewards give directions to get there. At this point design team members need to ask these questions:

- *How deeply embedded in the organization are vision, mission, and*

Figure 4-4. Government regulatory environment and its impact on TRS.

| Reward Strategy Dimension | Linkage | Government Regulatory–Based TRS | |
| --- | --- | --- | --- |
| | | Heavily Regulated | Regulation Free |
| Money | • The degree of government regulation impacts the free market for organizations and employees | • The lack of effective competitors tends to produce a lack of restraint on employee reward levels; therefore reward levels tend to be higher and focus only on limited definition of competitors | • Industries and organizations tend to have broad-based market reward levels |
| Mix | • The degree of government regulation impacts whether the product is system controlled versus employee controlled | • Heavily regulated industries tend to have high levels of noncash rewards and low levels of variable compensation | • Organizations in regulation-free industries tend to have lower noncash rewards and higher variable pay |
| Messages | • The degree of government regulation increases and decreases the risk orientation and time frame | • Organizationwide incentives<br>• Lower risk and reward<br>• Long-term rewards | • Complete set of organization, business unit, team, and employee incentives<br>• High risk and reward<br>• Short- and long-term rewards |

Figure 4-5. Vision, mission, and values and their impact on TRS.

| Reward Strategy Dimension | Linkage | Vision, Mission, Values–Based TRS Considerations | |
| --- | --- | --- | --- |
| | | Focus: Internal Organization | Focus: External Product/Market |
| Money | • Acquisition and retention of talent | • Low turnover encouraged to maintain investment in people | • Target industry-average turnover<br>• Targeted for greatest attraction |
| Mix | • Shared outcomes and degree of control over results; motivation of target | • High base salary<br>• Low short-term variable<br>• High long-term variable<br>• High market benefit | • Low base salary<br>• High variable pay<br>• Short-term pay<br>• Market benefits |
| Messages | • Direction of focus on key objectives and outcomes | • Focus on organization performance of critical success factors<br>• Long-term development<br>• Organization, business unit–based metrics | • Focus on customer and core capability–based metrics<br>• Short-term development<br>• Team- and individual-based rewards |

*values?* In some organizations these are a fundamental part of their identity; in others they represent a waste of time.

▪ *Do vision, mission, and values provide plan designers a focal point around which to create linkage and leverage?* The focus of your effort will be to leverage the value that is within your workforce. Determine if your company's stated vision, mission, and values provide a point of leverage—or if potentially they can.

▪ *Should vision, mission, and values, or their potential linkages to the business, be further developed?* If the opportunity exists to link employees to a compelling future state and leverage their power along the path—and more often than not, it does—then use this as a development point. If not, linkages among vision, mission, and values need to be further accentuated with business strategy.

---

## AFFILIATION WITH A WINNER, BY GARY STARZMANN

The Colonial Pipeline Company is based in Atlanta, Georgia. As an energy supply company, we faced the new realities of being a highly scrutinized business coupled with tougher competition and increased price pressure. We recognized that continuing to operate the world's largest liquid pipeline pursuant to our imperatives surrounding operational excellence mandated that we acquire the best talent from the oil and gas industry, as well as a cross section of other industries.

This presented two significant challenged for us. First, from a recruiting perspective our location forced us to compete against name brand success stories, including Home Depot, Delta Air Lines, UPS, and Georgia Pacific. What is more, being outside of the epicenter of the United States' oil and gas industry (Houston, Texas), where we would enjoy name recognition, challenged our ability to attract the top talent. "What would motivate talent from the oil and gas industry to move to Atlanta, or any of our field locations, given that we are neither a dominant player geographically, nor one of the big names in the industry?" asked Rhonda Brandon, Vice President of Human Resources for Colonial.

The second key challenge was dealing with the vestiges of our industry's compensation and benefits practices, which tended toward stable, employment-for-life employer/employee compacts. In fact, historically, Colonial's own compensation and benefit arrangements were more traditional than progressive, reminiscent of our oil and gas roots. The prevailing mentality in our organization was one of entitlement, not high performance.

The answer, although simple on the surface, came in the form of a Total Rewards Strategy that had at its core Colonial's vision, and put into the hands of management the tools they required to execute our business strategy. A core tenet of our vision is "to have the passion to drive unparalleled change and foster an environment that inspires individual growth and stimulates achievement." Today, there are constant internal pressures upon performance, accountability, and achievement, driven by the strong external demands of zero tolerance around spills and environmental impact and heightened government scrutiny. The business strategy that we have chosen to achieve our vision is built on operational excellence. We needed to align our people systems and processes with this new view of the world. To do so, we specifically addressed the requirements of attraction and motivation—assuming, correctly it turns out, that retention would take care of itself.

For compensation and benefits systems we redesigned around messages that fostered excellence by designing several interrelated programs. First, we introduced a companywide goal-sharing program, based on Colonial Pipeline's performance. This focused all employees on the requirement for flawless execution by the company as a whole. Annual base pay increases were linked to a clearly defined team- and individual-based performance management system, and placed completely in the hands of first-line supervisors and team leaders. Here our emphasis was on driving improvements through change and team and individual achievement. The communications of our health and welfare and retirement benefits were directed toward letting our people know that these benefits are not a "given contract" between the company and the employee. Rather, they are designed to protect the employees' ability to continue to contribute and earn, and provide for their long-term financial success while they do so. A progressive set of work life benefits, built on a high commitment to training and development, round off our Total Rewards package. Here the design was suggesting to employees and recruits that this is a great place to learn and grow, and that we take care of you while you do. The result is a motivation-driven reward system to focus employees on success at various organizational levels.

The results of the new designs are twofold. First, we increased the level of awareness and motivation toward the achievement of our business strategies and plans. People became connected to the business, and felt better about its success. Second, it allowed us to gain the share of mind of those highly qualified candidates whom we had not previously attracted. This was true both inside and outside our industry. By building our human resource philosophy under a Total Rewards umbrella, including performance-based compensation and competitive benefits and work life practices, we have created a buzz that gets people not only to know about us—they want to be a part of us!

*Gary Starzmann is Director of Compensation and Benefits, Colonial Pipeline Company.*

The design team should decide what its effort in this regard will be, based on its commission, structure, and resources. If vision, mission, and values are well developed and ingrained in the company's culture, then the team needs to collect those materials and be ready to process them in design. If they do not exist, then the team can:

- Develop straw model vision, mission, and values as a component of this process and report those back to the executive committee.
- Agree to design without them, using the fact that they do not exist as a design consideration.

The CD-ROM provides more examples and techniques pertaining to the articulation of vision and the linking of metrics.

## Key Messages

Build reward messages that inspire the organization to become the company it's capable of, drive behaviors to get you there, and pay for the things you value on your journey. In developing key messages, use vision, mission, and values as the filter to determine the appropriateness of any particular reward element. Every design alternative and resource allocation decision can be assessed against this threshold.

## Money

Ensure that your offerings are commensurate with the type of organization you espouse to be. In short, if you value something you should pay for it. If you have told employees certain things about what it means to work for you, deliver on those promises through reward programs. Conversely, be sure your reward offerings aren't in conflict with the messages of your vision.

## Mix

If you are striving toward a vision statement that is three to five years away—or even aspirational—organize rewards for the long term. This means not only a broader use of long-term compensation, but also benefits, perquisites, and noncash rewards that reflect the employment compact (e.g., training and development).

---

### VALUES-BASED COMPENSATION

One of the world's leading not-for-profit organizations was looking to move away from its traditional salary structure. Because of its highly diverse business operations, global reach, and very decentralized operating model, there did not seem to be a central theme around which to organize rewards. There was, however, one core facet to this organization that was foundational—its core values.

To capitalize on this theme, the organization designed a job evaluation system that used its core values as the premise for defining compensable factors. As these factors were rather broad, a corresponding broad-band system was built. While the structure is not unusual, the creation of a job evaluation scheme that is based on core values is. Here's how it works:

- Organization values are well defined, communicated, and developed. They are ingrained into each employee's workday.
- Parameters for how each job impacts on those values are documented on a job description. The purpose of job documentation (i.e., how the questionnaires are organized and structured) is solely to define and illustrate how a particular job impacts the organization and lives its values.

- A job-worth hierarchy is built.
- Bands are defined around like degrees of influence, being considerate of the values-based hierarchy.
- Market anchors are defined within each band by market anchor, based on the hierarchy.
- Jobs are managed to the appropriate market anchor, based on the hierarchy.

## TRS Considerations and General Business Strategy

There are considerations to be made in your business strategy as you develop your Total Rewards Strategy. Here are some of them that impact on general business strategy (GBS).

### Key Messages

The first and most critical key message is to clarify any confusion about your company's GBS. This alone will yield significant advances in linking employees to the business. It is key that you define GBS and articulate it so that everyone knows how you compete. In the case of a low-cost provider strategy, you want to continually tell your employees that you compete on price and it is everyone's job to drive costs out of the business. Total Rewards Strategy must drive efficiencies by demonstrating how efficiencies are derived and then rewarding for those efficiencies.

A product/service differentiation strategy requires that employees understand your point of differentiation, and you need to do everything you can to continue to strengthen that offering. Defining the critical points of differentiation to the customer, and paying for anything that strengthens them, is the key message. Figure 4-6 illustrates the relationship between GBS and TRS.

### Money

Money will vary significantly between the two GBSs. (Because the focus strategy is a differentiation or low-cost-provider strategy in a specific market or geography, it isn't discussed as a separate GBS here.) Product differentiation strategy calls for pay that can be focused on the point of differentiation, through vehicles such as person- or team-based pay. At these points of differentiation you may tend to compete at a higher percentile in

Figure 4-6. General business strategy and its impact on TRS.

| Reward Strategy Dimension | Linkage | GBS-Based TRS Consideration | |
|---|---|---|---|
| | | Low-Cost Provider | Product/Service Differentiator |
| Money | • Across the full spectrum of Total Rewards | • Functionally based<br>• Below or at median, with limited to no above median | • Person-based<br>• At median to above median surgically<br>• High use of noncash rewards |
| Mix | • Rewards focused on GBS outcomes | • Increased leverage; lower fixed, higher variable<br>• Longer term | • Balanced short- and long-term |
| Messages | • Fair, equitable<br>• Mediocrity<br>• Tenure<br>• "Our market focus"<br>• "What we are to our customers" | • Increased efficiency/reduced cost<br>• Focus on key points in the process where costs can be impacted, processes reengineered | • Focus on key points of differentiation |

the market and deliver offerings that are commensurate with the desired tenure. A low-cost provider strategy requires that reward costs be managed with greater efficiency. This demands increased offerings in the area of intrinsic rewards with lower overall total remuneration costs. To achieve this requires that employment costs be managed—for example, by having fewer people making relatively more money or a typical-sized workforce making at/below the median.

### Mix

Mix, too, varies significantly by GBS. In a cost-based strategy you want to have as much money as possible in variable, not fixed, pay. There is great effectiveness in linking variable pay plans to any form of cost reduction through vehicles such as profit sharing and gain sharing. Look for the areas where there is the greatest opportunity for reduced cost, and focus specific team- or function-based programs in those areas. Use pay to drive cost out of the business. For product/service differentiation strategies, use leverage to deliver on the increased total remuneration at the point of differentiation. Increased opportunities for long-term variable pay exist in an effort to reward and retain the talent that delivers the differentiation.

## TRS Considerations and Organization Capabilities

As these considerations articulate what needs to be done well to achieve success, how they are incorporated into a plan's design is meaningful. Key messages, which are defined as the articulations of what the company values and its expectations, are used here to inform employees about the behaviors, results, and performance expectations. Use the leverage of reward plans to link employees to core capabilities through metrics.

The money dimension should be heavily influenced by organizational capabilities. Review the value chain analysis, and the degrees of specialization versus differentiation of the workforce, to assess the degrees of freedom and differentiation. Focus rewards—cash and non-cash—where leverage from capabilities is most significant.

Mix, too, follows capabilities. The point of efficient distribution is to get a "bang for your buck." Use mix to effectively organize rewards, putting emphasis on the right behaviors and results as well as the populations from whom they can be derived.

W. Edwards Deming believed that individual success is 80 percent influenced by the process to which that individual is assigned. In reward plan design, the key is to distinguish how organization success is process limited and people impacted. As a rule you might think that the airline industry is heavily process limited with little opportunity to be people impacted. It is, after all, highly regulated, capital-intensive, predominantly unionized, and has few suppliers (since airports control price, time, and frequency). But Southwest Airlines has been able to break that model by finding the points of greatest people impact and capitalizing on them to influence the process. The surprise is not that Southwest found them, but that it took so long for someone to identify and capitalize on them.

For example, no one would be surprised to learn that flight attendants have more influence on customer satisfaction than any other single factor. Accordingly, they most significantly influence passengers' level of enjoyment of a flight and therefore their likelihood to use that airline again. In that regard, the industry is people impacted and should focus on enhancing those impacts.

The number of things that employees will need to be good at is increasing. This trend will have a dramatic impact on recruitment and retention-oriented programs. It requires organizations to be better overall at more things, stretching the fundamental tenet of differentiation.

## Value Chain Strategy–Based TRS Considerations

Like GBS, the first most important aspect of value chain strategy (VCS) is that you have articulated it and that you can use it to deliver to your employees the messages about how and where you add value to your products and services. Of course, compensation is the primary means for delivering those messages. Use them to identify the specific points along the value chain where your GBS is affected most significantly. Figure 4-7 illustrates these linkages.

In defining money and mix, focus on the critical links in the value chain and reward the appropriate people and behaviors. Ensure that rewards are focused on how and where each link in the value chain adds value, varying mix to reflect emphasis. Seize this opportunity to magnify the links that have the biggest impact by putting noncash compensation, in the form of training and development, into these critical aspects of the business.

Ensure that the employees working in the most critical value chain links get the message. Use rewards to both differentiate and to illustrate what is important along each value chain link.

Figure 4-7. Value chain strategy and its impact on TRS.

| Reward Strategy Dimension | Linkage | VCS-Based TRS Consideration | |
|---|---|---|---|
| | | Even Value Chain Strategy | Surgical/Key Value Chain Strategy |
| Money | • To the extent value is added evenly throughout the process versus when the value is added only in key chain elements | • Competitive reward level reflects the profitability across all positions | • Key value chain positions paid substantially above market |
| Mix | • Mix reflects individual versus process control of product/service | • All positions reflect industry-standard mix | • Rewards reflect organization's key contributor positions, with high variable, low base, and others at industry mix |
| Messages | • Messages reflect contribution and product/service cycle time | • Organizationwide rewards for all positions<br>• Low-risk reward and longer-term variable compensation<br>• High benefits | • High/variable rewards for key positions<br>• Other positions are proportionally lower high risk/high reward for key positions<br>• Low overall benefits |

## Examples of VCS-Based Strategies

As an example, a value chain–based reward strategy would consider where value is created and differentiation is defined along the value chain to establish elements in direct support. It would likely facilitate different pay positions and elements horizontally. Accordingly, and as a matter of policy, you may pay more—and utilize more unique forms of rewards—at those points along the value chain where your products/services are differentiated in the market to enhance the talent pool. Likewise, a low-cost provider may seek to structure a variable pay plan that further drives cost out of the business.

Value chain core competency identification is a tool that facilitates determining the fundamental driver of differentiation at each stage in the value chain (see Figure 5-4 and CD-ROM page 20 of 99). Furthermore, core competencies can be further broken down to the specific behavioral requirements for achieving a point of differentiation. If they are directly linked to rewards, you would have a value chain–based strategy.

Let's take the example of two successful retailers: Wal-Mart and Nordstrom. For the most part, Wal-Mart competes on price while Nordstrom competes on service. The success of Wal-Mart is driven by its ability to manage buying, then get the product from the point of manufacture to the consumers' hands as cheaply as possible.

Nordstrom, of course, is known for its merchant capabilities. Its sales and customer service associates are unparalleled in any retail setting.

Applying value chain–based compensation, as illustrated in Figure 4-8, to the pay policy for Wal-Mart, one would want to pay the folks that design, manage, and improve the supply chain commensurate with the best logistics people from wherever they can be found. Because the supply chain function commands long-term investments, you don't want to encourage the employees in this function to take short-term risks.

At Nordstrom, one would want to recruit the best floor sales staff and customer service associates. The emphasis would be short-term with high leverage.

Many organizations plan to reduce cost or demonstrate product or service differentiation across more stages of their value chain over the next three years. In other words, they anticipate being better at more of the capabilities that drive success in their industry. This trend is having a significant influence on the design of TRS dimensions. It forces organizations to focus more key messages on more value chain links, calling for an increased use of more surgical or differentiated reward designs.

Figure 4–8.  The retail industry value chain.

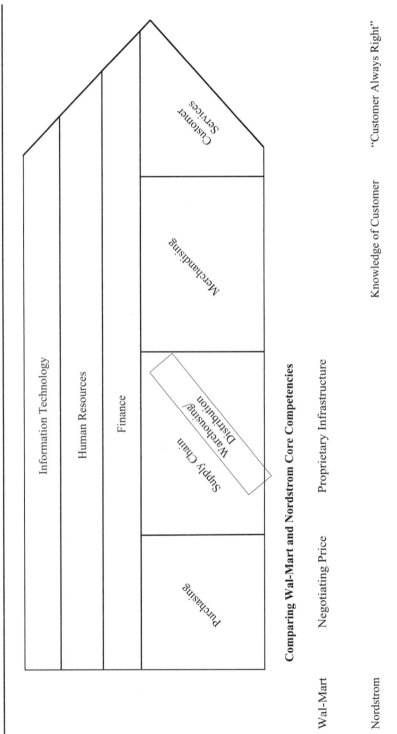

**Comparing Wal-Mart and Nordstrom Core Competencies**

Wal-Mart          Negotiating Price      Proprietary Infrastructure

Nordstrom                                                          Knowledge of Customer      "Customer Always Right"

It is also noteworthy that there is a general shift in how value will be added from the traditional tail-end value chain stages (e.g., sales, customer service) to the front end (e.g., purchasing) and back end of the value chain. Maintaining supplier and customer relations will take on increasing significance.

## TRS Considerations and Specific Business Strategy

Because of the number and diversity of specific business strategy (SBS) approaches, it isn't practical to articulate strategies for each. One basic rule applies: Ensure consistency. Rewards provide the most powerful management tool in delivering consistent messages about what the organization and its employees are working together to accomplish. It is the means for linking employees to corporate objectives and leveraging their capabilities. But only if they know the direction. It is like this: If I stand in the middle of a circle with no preference for direction, I can make one of 360 choices. Rewards narrow that decision field; strive to bring it in as tightly as possible.

Specific business strategies fall into three broad categories—growth, value chain optimization, and maintenance/reduction. To the extent possible, those should be defined and communicated to enhance the power of the influence of reward programs. Figure 4-9 illustrates the money, mix, and messages decisions for each category of SBS.

---

### USING COMPENSATION TO DRIVE BUSINESS INTEGRATION, BY DAVID LEACH

Industry consolidation caused three marketing services organizations to merge; these professional services firms competed head-to-head in certain business segments and markets, while each had business lines that were complementary. Management believed the new organization would lead to increased efficiencies in their operations and synergies for the group in serving existing clients and new markets. The three separately had found that their businesses had stagnated; the strategy was to foster growth by creating a significantly larger presence in the marketplace.

One condition of the merger was that each firm was to retain its existing compensation and benefits plans, at least through some integration period. When the economy declined, and the integration failed to yield the results predicted, none of the executives in any of the three entities received an incentive award after their first full year of operating together. The lack of incentive payments put pressure on employee morale; employees blamed the merger for failures to meet goals, further exacerbating the normal level of distrust that comes pursuant to most mergers.

The investors did not allow the situation to fester: They hired a new CEO, who was charged with taking the three independent business units and uniting them into one powerful firm. His approach was to first have each of the executives interviewed by a third party to gather input and identify issues. The comments from the executives were indicative of the problem overall. Invariably, each responded only in the "I," referring to his or her particular business unit. Although integration, cooperation, and teamwork were encouraged, there was no reward for actually doing so. In essence the new entity had gotten what it paid for—a group of people who were very collegial to one another but who made no real effort to share resources or integrate their practices.

The solution was to blow up each of the existing three compensation schemes, and replace them with a single "New Co. Total Rewards Strategy." Specific focus was put on an incentive plan designed to encourage and reward for the efficiencies and synergies derived from the overall organization.

The results were obvious from the top down. First, the division presidents began working more closely with one another, sharing resources across units and developing mutual trust and respect. As other employees witnessed this increased cooperation, they, too, started better working with their counterparts in other organizations. Within that second year the company realized much of the increased efficiencies and synergies from the business integration they had been seeking.

*David Leach is Regional Director, Compensation Consulting, for Buck Consultants.*

## Examples of SBS

Let's review two examples. Two categories of SBS are market share growth and value chain (or margin) optimization. Within the first, there are two fundamental approaches: organic growth (e.g., expansion into new markets by opening facilities) or inorganic growth (e.g., expansion through acquisition).

Figure 4-9.  Specific business strategy and its impact on TRS.

| Reward Strategy Dimension | Linkage | SBS-Based TRS | | |
|---|---|---|---|---|
| | | Growth | Optimize Value Chain | Maintain/Reduce |
| Money | • Portions of the organization that are expected to grow, optimize, or reduce will need rewards to be invested | • Competitive levels will be at or above market for executives and will probably trail market for rest of employees | • Staff positions assigned to regulate and improve value chain effectiveness will be high | • Below market |
| Mix | • The degree to which the process is people or machine limited | • Low base<br>• Emphasis on short- and long-term pay for results<br>• Average benefits | • Variable pay for optimizing staff<br>• High development rewards | • Low base<br>• High variable<br>• Low benefits<br>• Low perquisite |
| Message | • Messages best conveyed through variable pay for results | • Targeted incentives at key aspects of execution | • Continuous improvement | • Project-based<br>• Exit strategy incentives<br>• Turnaround incentives |

Growing market share generally requires an investment in people. There is a competency to opening new markets that is distinct from maintaining existing accounts. Reward systems need to be structured around the timing and markets that the organization is focused on supporting through recruitment and relocation strategies. There can be more influence on person- or team-based pay with time horizons that are within the window of the company's plan. Likewise, acquisitions place different demands on reward systems, the least of which include portability and flexibility. This speaks to plans that are more open in their architecture.

A value chain or margin optimization strategy, on the other hand, says that the company has a good piece of market share for its products or services, but now it needs to enhance the profitability of that space. Legitimately, this approach is irrespective of the VCS or GBS and can be accomplished by:

- Leveraging the product/service differentiation that the company has built, or reducing the extent to which it competes on price for the established customer base, by increasing price
- Reducing costs along the value chain

Here, too, reward approaches need to reflect the desired outcomes. In the first case, reward strategy supports sales and pricing strategy. In the latter case, reward approaches that examine the value chain and direct cost-containment efforts have greater impact.

The number of SBS initiatives that companies will pursue over the next three years is increasing from an average of four to six.[1] This indicates that organizations will likely also correspondingly increase their requirements for core capabilities. This has the potential to dilute the impact of reward plans if they are not focused. Key messages and a differentiated approach to plan design and use is fundamental to success.

## TRS Considerations and People Strategy

Chapter 3 defined people strategy in terms of structure, process, and culture and provided several models for understanding and gathering information about each. Now let's look at each element separately to demonstrate how it informs the design process.

## Structure

The predominant organizational themes influence the money dimension of TRS. Whether the primary focus is functional, geographic, product/ service, or process organized dic- tates the company's reward offer- ings, competitive markets, and positioning. Consider how people in the organization tend to move (e.g., within functions but across geographies, or vice versa) and align rewards with those normative models.

> **In Design, Capitalize on Your Size**
>
> Every company should capitalize on its size, whatever it is. Big companies need to be efficient and gain economies of scale; small ones need to be fast and nimble. Program designs and their hierarchy, structure, and levels of bureaucracy should reflect these conditions.
>
> The organization of work and jobs needs to reflect the management process of the company. Be swift where you can be—bureaucratic where you must be.

Most significantly, the number of management layers will drive mix. Flatter organizations—those with fewer organizational layers— need to strive for consistency in terms of eligibility and participation in short- and long-term plans.

All three influential characteristics of structure—number of layers, predominant themes, and percent of employees who are in staff positions—influence key messages. Take advantage of each and reinforce the flow and importance of communications.

---

### STRUCTURED FOR SUCCESS

Two major consulting organizations have very different organizational structures. Both are in the same subset of industry, both consult to some of the same clients in mostly the same service areas. They are essentially the same size in terms of revenue and have grown at almost the same pace over a ten-year history. One is organized geographically primarily and by practice secondarily. The other is organized primarily by practice. While both consulting firms provide excellent service and advice to their clients, the geographically based organization operates with one-third of the administrative overhead of the one organized by practice. Over the past twenty years, one of the consulting firms has evolved toward becoming an integrated provider of advice to predominantly middle-market organizations, while the other has dominated the large company market.

Why did two firms with similar backgrounds evolve to such dissimilar end-businesses? It has to do with organization structure and rewards.

Where geography ruled one organization, the result was great client relationship managers and good, but not great, consultants. Long-term relationships developed as consultants stayed at home in their geographic area. The geographic-based organization didn't have as high a standard of performance for its consultants because the consultants were judged only relative to the other employees in the area office and not across the entire organization, as was the case in the more practice-based organization. Rewards, of course, were focused on office, small team, and/or individual success.

The practice-based organization tended to assign consultants to projects regardless of where they lived. These nomad "road warriors" were typically "hit or miss" when it came to client relationships. They were measured and rewarded by members of their own practice, who in Darwinian style made sure that only the best technical problem-solving consultants remained in the firm. They didn't develop client relationships or client-relationship skills.

In assessing the two organizations, it was clear they got what their organization structure dictated and the reward program complemented. What might have happened if the reward programs were cross-administered? For example, the practice-based organization could have used the geographic managers' input to reward consultants who worked consistently with clients within the organization, and the geographic organization could have listened to the practice leaders more. This would most likely have produced a firm with great consultants *and* great client relationships.

## Process

When it comes to management processes, you must first identify the requirements for proficiency and then do a gap analysis against your organization's true capability. Reward strategy emphasis needs to be placed on the processes that require the greatest movement—those that you need to get better at.

Management processes influence the money dimension of TRS in several ways. First, because they define how a business is managed, the capabilities it requires, the things it needs to do well, and the accumulated competencies, management processes inform us about people markets and competitive levels. Equally important in this regard is the impact of the processes on where in the organization those capabilities reside (e.g., centralized versus decentralized decision making), further determining the focus of rewards. This is primarily characteristic of the surgical nature of the money dimension and decisions afforded in the mix dimension.

When considering mix vis-à-vis core process, a traditional risk/reward balance is assessed. Identify the requirements for speed, decision making, collaboration, supervision, and change, and ensure that you have afforded the emphasis those issues require in both the correct proportions (i.e., amounts commensurate with the weight of the requirement) and placement in the structure (i.e., how eligibility is actually affected).

Messages, again, focus the attention of your employees on the management processes that deliver the highest impact and/or those requiring the most dramatic improvement. When asked, "To what degree have expectations been met?" with respect to the five core management processes (see Chapter 3, Figure 3-19), most respondents indicated that results are generally "mixed" (three on a scale of one to five).[2] Improvement in this regard is a function of focusing key messages.

## Culture

Culture most closely approximates an organization's personality by defining the attributes of the business that are required for success. This is all about Total Rewards Strategy and its dimensions—money, mix, and key messages. Most important here is the need to be purposeful; define the culture and direct rewards toward the attraction and retention of the people who will personify that culture (money and messages) and motivate those people to behave in ways that define it (mix and messages).

Culture is becoming more intense.[3] Cultural emphasis isn't so much shifting—moving from one set of attributes to another—as the requirements to be better at more things is intensifying. This trend has significant implications for key messages. First is the requirement to increase the amplitude of the message being delivered. Consider that few companies are delivering more in terms of rewards—instead they are saying more about what's important while keeping the same value in total rewards. And they have to deliver more information through the same medium.

### THE POWER OF CHOICE

A research and development–oriented company was looking to initiate a new research arm in science for which it was not very well known. To be successful, the R&D company would need to attract top scientists from the best schools and facilities. To be successful, it would have to break the mold!

Although this was an R&D arm of a global company, it built the research facility's TRS from the ground up—starting with the critical roles. The initial crew of scientists and human resources staff formed a design team. Using a whiteboard, the team tackled the question: "What will it take to attract, retain, and motivate the caliber of research required for success?" Here is what they decided and why:

- *Base salaries would be at the market median for scientists in the field.* The team recognized that salary was not a battle worth fighting—the parent company was a median player. This is not where the team members believed they could effect any real differentiation.

- *Short- and long-term variable pay should emphasize phantom ownership.* The team's decision was based on the need to link the R&D area to the commercial viability of its ideas through the shift of short-term cash incentives to longer-term objectives.

- *Core benefits (H&W and retirement) would be directly aligned with the parent company.* The team decided on this so it could capitalize on their leverage.

- *Other noncash compensation would be customized.* The team decided to implement a single, paid, time-off bank to replace all holidays, vacations, and sick days so that the facility would be accessible 24/7. When and how a person worked wasn't of consequence. If a person wanted to work on December 25, why not?

- *Personal development would include education benefits.* Scientists would thus be able to stay current in their fields and the offering would be personalized.

- *The opportunity to pursue personal research would be encouraged.* This was decided on because of the interest of researchers in satisfying their intellectual curiosity, and because it was a significant differentiator as compared with other R&D labs.

Second is the requirement to deliver more "bang for the buck"—that is, to deliver more value at the same cost. This suggests personalization of rewards—or "flexible rewards." Just as flexible benefits that were introduced a decade ago allowed organizations to realize more value from the same benefit costs, the next generation of rewards will be personalized. It's all about mix and messages.

The mix dimension is defining culture going forward, and it may need to be rewritten on a person-by-person basis. This is not to say "let's make a deal" will prevail and the spoils will go to the highest bidder; it means, however, that a deeper commitment must be made to identifying what is important to the people you are working to attract and retain while building plans around those offerings. This work may be done by employee category—for example, to accommodate scientists in an R&D-focused organization (see the case study titled "The Power of Choice")—or on an individual basis, where the company sets standards for reward categories (i.e., noncash rewards, training, and development) and then allows individuals to choose.

The relationships between organizational culture and TRS are outlined in Figure 4-10.

## TRS Considerations and People Strategy Critical Success Factors

How organizations leverage and value expectations is in the realm of the messages delivered and the mix of elements. Accordingly, what you want people to do is communicated through reward messages; orienting the delivery of rewards provides the exclamation point! Most notable are the degree of unionization and the specialization of employee skills—two factors that most dramatically influence both the degree of freedom to design and the types of designs deployed (see Figure 4-11).

As people strategy critical success factors (PSCSFs) translate well to specific metrics (i.e., the objectives to accomplish), it is easy to use them to tie employee outcomes to business objectives. It is for this reason that PSCSFs have the greatest impact on the delivery of key messages and the mix of elements.

Figure 4–10. Organizational culture and its impact on TRS.

| Reward Strategy Dimension | Linkage | Organizational Culture–Based TRS | | | |
|---|---|---|---|---|---|
| | | Functional | Process | Time-Based | Network |
| Money | • Reward levels are tied to the key part of the organization | • Executive – above<br>• Management – market<br>• Professional – low<br>• Other – lowest | • At market (for all levels of employees) | • At market<br>• At market<br>• At market or above<br>• At market | • At market<br>• Below market<br>• Above market<br>• At market |
| Mix | • The mix is a function of freedom to act versus process controlled | • Low freedom to act translates to high base, low variable, and few benefits | • Key positions that control the processes are given approprite short- or long-term variable pay | • Employee groups near the customer are rewarded for success | • Key contributors along the chain are rewarded for success |
| Messages | • The messages reinforce the critical attributes of the culture | • Critical aspect is the strategic apex<br>• "Do your job right" | • Critical aspect is the staff group that creates the regulator<br>• "Get it right" | • Critical aspect is the operating core and its ability to adapt to customers<br>• "Get it done" | • Coordinating personnel throughout and special contributors<br>• "Get it done and disband" |

Figure 4–11. Employee knowledge requirements and their impact on TRS.

| Reward Strategy Dimension | Linkage | Employee-Based TRS | |
|---|---|---|---|
| | | Employees Highly Specialized of Knowledge | Employees Not Highly Specialized of Knowledge |
| Money | • Attraction or access to employee population<br>• Retention of employees | • Employees tend to be paid above market<br>• Nonkey employees paid below market | • Employees are paid at or below market |
| Mix | • Variable rewards tend to reflect the degree of system control versus employee control | • If highly specialized employees have high degree of control, then variable pay is high for them<br>• All other employees have low variable pay | • Variable pay is low, if control over output is low<br>• Variable pay is high, if control is high |
| Messages | • Organizational level or measure<br>• Rewards and recognition<br>• Timing (short- versus long-term) | • Specialized employees receive high individual reward programs | • Organization performance-based pay<br>• Variable pay is moderate and short-term |

## ROLE REDESIGN AND BEHAVIOR CHANGE AS A STRATEGIC PROCESS, BY DAVID BROWNE

Our client, a regional grocery retailer with above-average profitability and a super-high quality service and merchandise reputation, was beginning to face a major threat from a new concept competitor, the Wal-Mart Supercenter. Concurrently, the risk of mass-migration of customers to Internet-based home grocery shopping was on the horizon.

The executive team reached a strategic decision to further differentiate itself (from both home and Supercenter shopping) by adding value to the "sensory and human interaction–centered" in-store shopping experience. The transformation would be led by reshaping value-critical employee behavior.

With the client team, we identified value-critical roles in the seafood and prepared foods/deli departments. It was in these categories that knowledge-based suggestive selling could most enhance loyalty to the in-store shopping experience while increasing profitable growth of these and related merchandise categories. As the traditional career paths of these seafood and deli employees had been in production jobs (especially meat cutting), where they were *doing*, not *selling*, the change was to be more than superficial.

We began the transformation process by developing new role designs, including new modes of customer observation and interaction. We then articulated targeted, objectively observable behaviors for each job or role. This was quickly followed with knowledge tools for seafood and deli employees' easy commitment of key merchandise facts to memory (geographic source of seafood, taste description, suggested portions, preparation, accompaniments, aisle location, etc.). The behavior change process then identified unique behavior change "action priorities" for each individual employee and supported each with frequently delivered feedback on the effectiveness and productivity of his or her learning and behavior change efforts.

As a result of this role-driven strategic transformation, the client increased shopping loyalty, transaction size, and department profitability. By year three of implementation there were minimal incursions by home shopping. Moreover, the Wal-Mart Supercenter's success was coming mainly at the expense of other competitors.

*David Browne is an organization effectiveness consultant with Buck Consultants.*

Chapter 3 introduced the balanced scorecard as a means for translating business strategy into people outcomes and as an approach for communicating strategy and organization capabilities. As defined in this book, people strategy critical success factors are the specific things a company wants people to do to achieve strategy. Again, because PSCSFs translate well into metrics, they create a good framework for further discussing the balanced scorecard in this context.

As you might expect, sophisticated users of the balanced scorecard have evolved beyond the traditional perspectives defined by Kaplan and Norton. This balanced view of success is depicted in Figure 4-12. It points out that today companies start by customizing the perspectives that make the most sense for measuring their business. This process often starts with some overall view of the company's culture and values, includes some financial measurement, and is then translated into a personalized view of one to three other perspectives. Regardless, the result is a range of metrics for people beyond financial measures.

An organization's ability to link employees to a breadth of metrics is at the foundation of PSCSFs. In Chapter 5, exercises are provided to assist in the development of these critical metrics. Before moving on to the next chapter, let's conclude by defining their impact on the three dimensions of Total Rewards Strategy:

- *Money.* This dimension of TRS defines elements and timing that reflect the breadth of your PSCSFs. If it is purely financial, this is not an issue, but typically you can look beyond the financial. Attach rewards to the metrics by demonstrating a causal relationship (e.g., "We need to be better at this, therefore we provide development rewards at X level."). Purposefully identify the value of the various PSCSFs and perspectives across a time frame, and link short- and long-term rewards to each, as appropriate.

- *Mix.* This dimension defines the pay-for-performance orientation in the PSCSF context. What are you prepared to pay for (e.g., results other than financial), and exactly how much leverage can you provide? In a balanced scorecard framework, designers must clearly define which of the perspectives the organization will pay for. It is very possible to have metrics and compensable metrics. The former define success; the latter, the specific successes to be compensated for.

- *Messages.* Herein lies the greatest opportunity to link and leverage. A balanced scorecard framework provides a means for delivering messages

Figure 4-12. A balanced view of success.

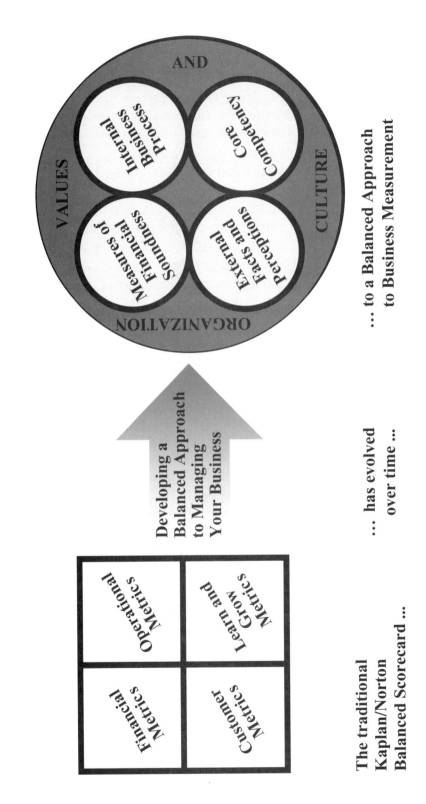

about what is important across a broad spectrum of the business. Because it pushes the user to define how strategy is executed, the balanced scorecard orients the organization toward the specific requirements for success by perspective and organization level. It demonstrates to the user what must be done to win. Accordingly, using a balanced scorecard to identify the PSCSFs and communicate their value in organization success allows the user to customize the reward plans to the unique demands of the company. For example, every company may have a variable pay plan—few specifically articulate what unique behaviors and outcomes need to be achieved; demonstrate how each eligible participant exhibits those behaviors and impacts those outcomes; and specify how successful employees get remunerated.

## Priority Setting

Many very smart people have spent their careers developing and thinking about the strategic deployment of rewards. There is a belief that the secret decoder ring, which would allow us to align all of the factors that influence rewards and come up with the exact right answer, exists. If there is a means for deriving the single most correct answer, it is an incredibly complex multivariate equation. The dynamics of business and the environment have competing directions, where one factor will point to one response and another the opposite. Regardless, it is important to align all of the factors that affect your design and consider them against one another. It takes experience and instinct to resolve conflicts, although tools can help.

Although there are different factors affecting each of us, both individually and in the aggregate, those factors account for 100 percent of the considerations. Accordingly, it is possible to rank and prioritize the factors. Doing so will allow you to place emphasis where it belongs while eliminating factors that do not have a significant influence.

Certainly there are aspects of business beyond those identified here that influence the design of a Total Rewards Strategy. In fact, they may be infinite. Yet research and experience suggest that the aspects defined and developed here represent nearly 90 percent of what must be considered. There are diminishing returns to further analysis. So, with this as a backdrop, it is time to begin the data gathering, organizing, and design process.

Before exploring how to do this, review the phased communication plan and be sure that:

- Design process roles and responsibilities are clearly communicated and participants know what is expected of them.

Figure 4–13.  Efficient frontiers.

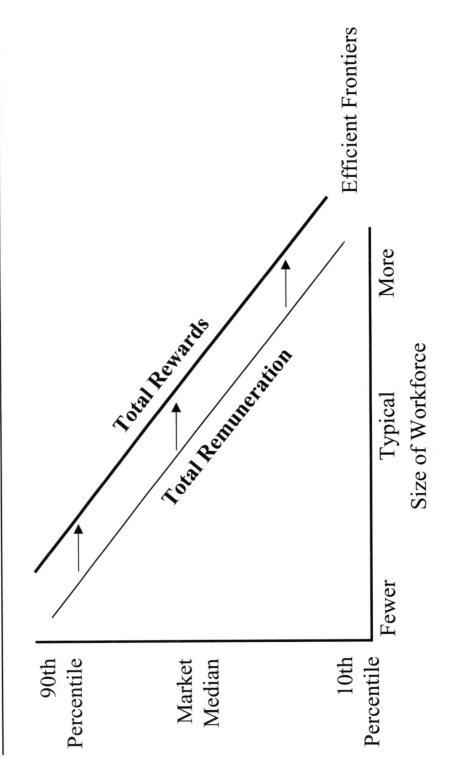

- There is a foundational understanding of the aspects of business that influence the process and how to interpret those aspects of business within the context of the company.

Don't rush yourself or your team; take the time to ensure a solid foundation. Remember, the master holds three pebbles in his hand; the grasshopper cannot leave the monastery until he can take the pebble from his master's hand.

Figure 4-13 illustrates that employee costs cannot exceed some point where it becomes inefficient for the organization to pay more. Efficiency can be achieved by hiring fewer people who work harder to achieve the same productivity, or more people who are willing to trade working less for earning less money. In other words, at every point along the efficient frontier, hard costs to the employer are equivalent.

Adopting a Total Rewards perspective has the effect of enhancing the frontier. Total Rewards provide for a more efficient means to deliver value and to differentiate the employee/employer relationship. It creates a more engaged workforce without raising cost.

## Chapter 5

# LEVERAGING PEOPLE— CREATING THE TOTAL REWARDS ARCHITECTURE

PREVIOUS CHAPTERS HAVE ORGANIZED THE process, defined the critical dimensions of your business, and articulated the linkages between each dimension and Total Rewards Strategy (TRS). Chapter 5 focuses on the completion of the first half of Phase II of the design process, by building the Reward Architecture. To do so will require you to organize the information collected, interpret it, and articulate the key messages. Money and mix will follow suit. This establishes the foundation to move forward with detailed plan design as described in Chapter 6.

Reward Architecture is a plan for the design, development, and delivery of reward programs in a manner that supports Total Rewards Strategy. Whereas strategy provides the framework for how resources are to be allocated, architecture is the detailed plan for doing so. Any skilled plan designer can follow an architecture (e.g., the blueprint) and build the programs that support it.

The analogy to building, say, a home, may help. Suppose you own some land on which you want to build a house. First you would assess the characteristics of your lifestyle, the size of your family, how you plan to use your home, personal preferences, and so on. You would also consider the lay of the land—the way the plot is laid out, the environment, and the topography. From this information you would define the characteristics of your desired house—say, a ranch or a colonial—and the resources required to build it (e.g., how much money is needed). This is your Total Rewards Strategy.

With the general direction identified, you would develop a blueprint for the house: a detailed plan for actually creating the structure. Any knowledgeable builder can follow the plan and build the house. The blueprint is your Reward Architecture. Of course, to actually build the house you would hire a variety of experts, from plumbers to carpenters to electricians. The same holds true with your Total Rewards Strategy. You also need to deploy experts—experts in executive compensation, broad-based employee compensation, variable pay, finance, human resources, and related subject matters—to build programs that execute the strategy.

Chapter 5 is dedicated to process. It will describe how to collect information and then take this information and use it to create the Reward Architecture and Total Rewards Strategy. It starts with a discussion about "operationalizing" business strategy to define the extent to which it is understood and embedded in the organization. Then, it describes the process for developing key messages (the foundation of the TRS). The money and mix dimensions finalize Reward Architecture.

## Collecting Information for Analysis

The previous chapters defined what information to collect and why; this chapter will define how to collect it. The requisite information is typically collected through two parallel processes: document review and stakeholder input.

### Document Review

In today's information-rich world, the insights available to the design team are limitless. Information regarding human resources programs, company financials, and industry and analyst reports are readily available. Existing reward programs are a good place to start. With these, as with all current plans and processes, ensure that the design team members have a common understanding of your current reward programs and human resources processes that support those programs.

Market perceptions and industry knowledge can be gleaned from a wide variety of sources, including analyst reports from Value Line and Standard & Poor's, market analyses, Bloomberg news service reports, and other trade news. A review of the popular press and current articles on your industry and company can help frame these issues. Company literature, too, allows you to understand where and how the company is positioning its products, how it views its offerings, and what value it adds to your customers. Any financial information, particularly that which is in the public domain (e.g., the annual report or 10K filing), is a must. Company web site information is also helpful, as well as advertising collateral that defines product and corporate positioning.

Market share can tell you where your organization fits relative to its competition. What is the business environment? Is it a mature business or a growing business? Within a given business sector, are you a mature company or a growing one? What is your peer group positioning, that is, how do customers see you? How do your competitors see you? And where do you position yourself relative to those competitors?

Industry and company history influences any organization's culture. Where does your organization position its products and brands? Are you, for example, number one or number two for every brand category? Or is your organization in the mainstream of your product's designs? What do your customers think about your products and about your company? And what are the popular press or analysts saying about your organization as well? What is the news coverage? How is the organization perceived within its industry by the public that it serves? To what degree do stakeholders (i.e., competitors, owners, customers, suppliers, and business partners) influence daily operations?

It is also helpful to understand the community within which your organization operates and how your company interfaces with that community. Are you, for example, a major employer in that community? What kind of the impact do your operations have within the community? Imagine a first meeting with a plant human resources manager in an industrial Midwest town, where the first words out of the client's mouth are, "Here's my problem. We operate in a community of 20,000 working-age people where unemployment is 2 percent. I know all 400 of those unemployed people and I don't want to hire any of them. How do I retain my current workforce and attract new people?" This is a very different problem from, say, what a manager would face in Newfoundland, Canada, where the unemployment rate is 30 percent!

Finally, but certainly no less important, is the competitiveness of your current reward programs. You cannot begin to design a new reward program without understanding where you are positioned now. This kind of analysis should assess both the competitive level of reward and programmatic comparisons of reward delivery. This analysis:

- Values the company's total cash, total direct cash, and total remuneration
- Assesses the impact of total rewards
- Compares reward to key drivers of retention

Although the extent and depth of information that can be gleaned is virtually limitless, a systematic review of the following items will provide the information necessary for design:

- All the influences described in Chapters 3 and 4 as related specifically to your organization
- Financials
- Products and/or services
- Current reward plan designs and competitiveness

### Stakeholder Input

A stakeholder is anyone with a vested interest in the designs of any elements of the Total Rewards Strategy. This book and the accompanying CD-ROM provide specific tools and techniques for collecting information from employees, executives, and others. Stakeholder input comes from executive interviews, employee input (through focus groups and attitude surveys), and interviews or surveys with other relevant parties, such as owners, customers, and the community at large.

■ *Executive and Management Interviews.* Your executives provide several key inputs into the process. First, executives tend to have the clearest understanding of the strategy and the vision, mission, and values of the organization. Second, executives commonly have predisposed notions about the design process and outcome. It's important to understand these ideas so they can be addressed through the process. Use the interview process to capture your executives' understanding of the organization; then flush out any predisposition or sacred cows and challenge those against the potential linkages between business strategy and TRS. Equally important, spend time educating the top tier of management about the process. The "Executive Interview Guide" sidebar provides a simple framework for questions. The *Business, People, and Total Reward Strategy Alignment Questionnaire* provided on the CD-ROM can be used to collect insights into reward influences.

■ *Employee Input.* Employees are a source of input on the design team; however, they must also provide input through focus groups and/or surveys. The value of employee input is threefold. First, if you want to understand what motivates employees, ask them. Second, employees will be very candid about their perceptions of existing reward programs. These insights into their perceptions are very valuable, particularly if they are not supported by facts. For example, it is not uncommon for pay programs to be market competitive, and for organizations to go through painstaking analysis to determine that. Yet employees may feel undercompensated. Armed with the facts, the company can often address those employee perceptions. Third, employee input is key to developing a communications strategy. Asking employees to comment or review programs does not mandate that you make change, but rather that you either make change or openly communicate the business reason for not doing so. In other words, put the information in one of two contexts. Either say, "Hey, we hear you and we've made changes based on what you've said," or, "We hear you and here is why we cannot make the change you are requesting." Ultimately, reward offerings reflect a business decision driven by the economics of your business. If employees don't understand those economics, educate them appropriately.

> **Executive Interview Guide**
>
> - How do you want the market to view this company?
> - Define the company's business strategy. What are the strengths that you possess that will facilitate its accomplishment?
> - What are the three to five things you must get right, or what must you be able to do well (internally) to achieve this strategy?
> - Who are your market competitors? What are the greatest weaknesses for this company in facing them?
> - What does this company value?
> - Describe the corporate culture.
> - What assets in this company will make it successful? How and why?
> - What are your views about the compensation programs?
> - Who owns the compensation plans? What aspects of the existing plans are effective?
> - What aspects of the plans are ineffective?
> - What are the core management processes that drive this business?

Employee focus group facilitation is typically highly customized to match both the design effort and the company's culture. Two rules always apply, however. First, the facilitator needs to assure the participants that their input will be kept confidential. Ensure that each participant respects the confidentiality of his fellow participants. Second, the facilitator needs to get input from all participants and not allow any one to dominate. The sidebar "Focus Group Facilitation Guide" on the next page provides a general framework for questions.

- *Input from Owners, Customers, and the Community.* The design team should consider the extent to which it wants to reach out to other, external stakeholders for additional insights. Most often this data gathering is done through one-on-one interviews, although questionnaires can be used as well. Typical sources include:

- Members of the board of directors (particularly the compensation committee)
- Customers
- Suppliers, vendors, and/or consultants

## Organizing the Information Collected

Focus Group Facilitation Guide

- Do employees trust management?
- Complete this statement from your perspective: "When the design team finishes its work, it will have done a good job if the new plans _____."
- How would you describe the corporate culture in this company? List three to five adjectives that you would use to describe your work environment.
- Would you recommend this company to a friend? Why or why not?
- Why do people work and stay at this organization?
- What is it like to work in this company? Pick three to five adjectives that describe what it's like working here.

Thus far, this chapter has been dedicated to the process of collecting the information you will need (both internal and external) to make educated decisions about plan designs. Members of the design team not only require a common understanding from those steps, they must also be able to share that information with other constituencies (e.g., steering committee members and executives) in a manner that allows everyone to understand how various factors influence plan design. In making sense of the abundance of information collected, begin with a simple process of organizing the inputs. It is best not to debate facts while putting the perceptions in perspective. Figure 5-1 (which corresponds to page 42 of 99 on the CD-ROM) is a matrix that's broken into four boxes; it's a useful tool that allows for the consideration of both the type of input (fact or perception, by column) and the source of the input (internal or external, by row). This is not to minimize the importance of perceptions, because sometimes they are more meaningful than facts. Figure 5-1 is purely a means of organizing the input for interpretation.

Figure 5-1. The fact/perception matrix.

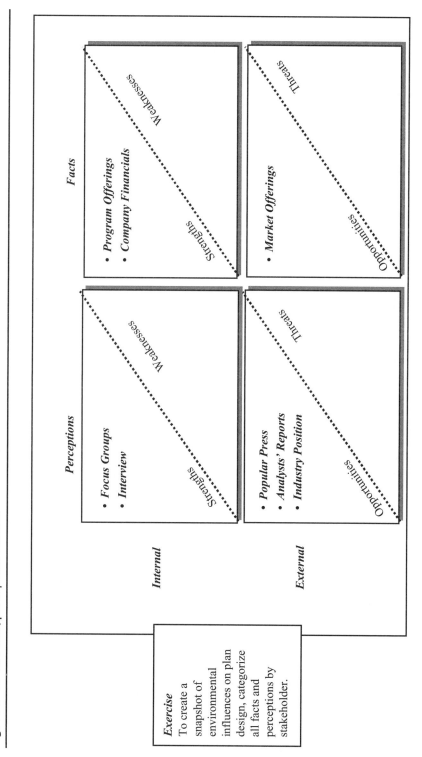

One method to organize the knowledge gained is to assess all facts and perceptions based on the various stakeholders.

## Therefore Statements

In order to transition from the building know-how phase into the architecture and plan design phases, you must create transitional statements of understanding. Such transitional statements of understanding are part of the "therefore statement" analysis. For each input that has been developed from the fact and perception matrix (Figure 5-1), it is possible to create one or more actionable plan design statements. This exercise requires a fair amount of judgment and can lead to some interesting insights into possible alternative plan designs. At this point it is more important to be inclusive rather than exclusive; creativity should be employed as much as possible and statements should be as open-ended as tolerable. This exercise, as demonstrated in Figure 5-2, involves taking each fact/perception and determining a course of action. The result is a lengthy "wish list" of desired outcomes for the design team. The "therefore" statements can also be used to validate the gap analysis conducted in scoping the project (see Chapter 2). Comparing the wish list to current programs verifies the redesign effort.

For example, a possible internal fact statement may be that the average employee's seniority is less than five years. Accordingly, a possible actionable plan design feature may be to include employees in some retention plan that begins after the first year, in an attempt to try to retain them past the second year (the average termination date) and into the third and fourth years.

Many external influences represent possible opportunities for "therefore" statements. The deregulation of the telecommunications industry was a fact that many telecom organizations had to take into account when designing employee reward programs. The Telecommunications Act of 1996 was intended to increase competition, and as a natural consequence, it put pressure on the cost of providing telephone service. As the price of a telephone minute began to come down, the most successful telephone companies reconsidered the impact on employee-related costs by rethinking Total Rewards Strategy. For one large Baby Bell, this cost of labor

---

**Definitions of Total Rewards Strategy, Architecture, and Detailed Plans**

*Total Rewards Strategy (TRS).* This is a plan for allocating reward resources to positively affect business outcomes. TRS is defined in a concise set of statements that articulate money, mix, and messages.

*Architecture.* This is the blueprint for building the strategy. It defines in detail the types of plans, their mechanics, and how they work together.

*Detailed Plans.* These plans deliver the rewards to the employee. They represent the plan document and implementation.

Figure 5-2. Therefore statement tool.

*Creating Therefore Statements*

Because

_____

Enter a learning from the Fact/Perception Matrix

Therefore

_____

Actionable Plan Design Feature

To process learnings, take every fact and perception and turn it into an actionable feature of plan design.

review focused on what behaviors and results were rewarded and at what level. Gap analysis revealed that existing plans had a significant degree of flexibility, a feature that on the surface might have seemed positive. However, what were required were significant changes to the reward programs in terms of money and mix. Competitive levels of reward had to be reduced and variable pay had to become a larger portion of the reward program. Ultimately, plan flexibility was reined in as the company delivered more focused messages about pay for performance and individual contribution.

## Transferring Know-How: The Building Knowledge Phase

Whenever you decide to evaluate potential changes to reward plans, you need to make certain decisions about communications, the first of which is determining the message. Your group will want to create messages about its efforts that it delivers universally and continuously. Team members should discuss and agree on the message, how much information is to be shared, and what the rules for confidentiality will be. These decisions need to be evaluated constantly as the process moves along. The message also needs to be tailored to the various audiences—executives, management, and employees.

In communicating with executives, ensure that team members understand how they want to be kept informed and how they will provide feedback. In one successful effort, each member of the design team was assigned an executive to keep updated about the design process, and was directed to bring back to the team that executive's reaction. Management is, ultimately, your client group since the objective of the design effort is to build management tools that facilitate performance enhancement. Management needs to be a step ahead of employees and understand the evolution of your messages. In this way managers will understand the ultimate design more thoroughly as they will have insight into the underlying thinking of the design team.

How pay is delivered is of critical importance to the recipient. The minute the team is formed word will get out. Be preemptive by communicating your message before rumors form. There is a simple rule of thumb for communicating a message: Do it until employees tell you they've got it, then do it one more time.

In the beginning communicate what you are doing, what you aren't doing, and why. Share information about which programs you may be considering changing, the sources of input, and the process. Inform employees about the timing, and when they may expect any additional information and change.

The Employee Engagement Design Process is about knowledge transfer. Although we use rewards as the vehicle to deliver the messages about what is important, it is the business-based knowledge that provides the means to link employees to the business. Figure 5-3 outlines the continuous nature of the knowledge transfer phase—it threads throughout the entire process and carries it onward.

With knowledge building complete, the team should begin to communicate by:

- Thanking people who participated in the process
- Letting people know where the process stands
- Defining the next steps
- Sharing whatever information is relevant at the moment

## Making Business Strategy Operational

The purpose of the design team's efforts in this regard is to be able to say, "Given this business strategy, here are the reward strategy and plan design alternatives and processes that we need to develop in support of that business strategy." To do so, however, demands that two conditions be met. First, the fundamental basis of the strategy must be known. Several operational models exist (some of which were described in Chapters 3 and 4), and some organizations develop proprietary approaches, all of which are fine. Knowing the basis for organizational strategy allows the design team to define both what the company is and what it is not. (For example, is the company a low-cost provider, or a product/service differentiator?) Second, knowing the extent to which consensus exists about the strategy at the executive level is also important. It is not uncommon for a company to have developed its business strategy without having built consensus around it. This can be likened to blindfolding executives and then stationing them at different locations around an elephant. If each one were asked to reach out and feel the animal and then describe it, you'd get several and quite likely very different descriptions.

The design team should be able to assess both based on its data gathering. The team should be prepared to comment on the degree to which both conditions exist, remembering that:

- To the extent these conditions are found, the design effort will be much simplified and focused.

Figure 5–3. Knowledge transfer timeline.

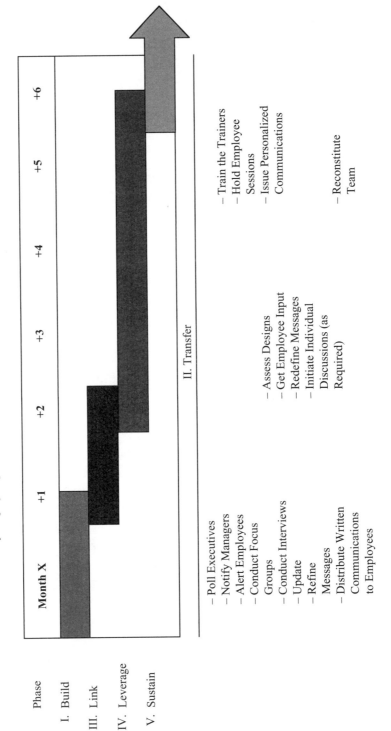

Use your project plan to deliver program knowledge throughout the process:

- An absence of these conditions should raise a huge red flag. If the basis of a company's strategy cannot be ascertained and executives do not have consensus regarding strategic outcomes, this effort will flounder.

## Understanding the Level of Knowledge of Organization Strategy

Furthermore, the level of knowledge penetration within the company—that is, the degree to which employees know the strategic plan and their role in making it successful—is important. Fundamental to your efforts to create an integrated Total Rewards Strategy is knowing the extent to which your organization's business strategy and its vision, mission, and values are developed, communicated, understood, and made operational. Is business strategy closely held within the confines of your business's leadership, or is it well articulated and understood throughout the company?

Understanding the extent to which business strategy has been articulated is a reasonable starting point. What you are trying to determine is the extent to which business strategy has been formalized and then communicated. Here's a simple way to measure the depth with which strategy is communicated in your company: Stop an employee in the hallway and ask him, "Where will this company be in three to five years?" Does the employee know the answer? If you asked a manager or leader in the organization, would she be able to answer that same question?

How well (or poorly) people in your company understand business strategy creates a starting point for the development of the communications plan in support of the business and its Total Rewards Strategy. Once reward programs are developed, for example, are employees questioning why, or, conversely, are they responding, "Oh yes, I understand that our strategy is toward increased efficiencies and therefore we need to do these things"?

If you understand the underlying operational basis of your company's strategy, you can use the techniques described in this chapter to conduct the analysis. Other business strategy models you might use include product life cycle, portfolio analysis (Boston Consulting Group/General Electric), organizational capability analysis (Gary Hamel), volume/cost analysis (Fredrick Taylor), and economic value added analysis (Stern Stewart, Inc.).

Because they have proven simple in their design and timeless in their application, Michael Porter's general business strategy and value chain models are useful tools to use when undertaking this analysis. According to Porter, there are three generic business strategies:

1. *Cost Advantage.* This strategy demonstrates cost leadership through the production of products or services with the greatest efficiency.
2. *Product Differentiation.* This strategy gives customers what they want, in the manner they want it, yielding a recognizable difference to the consumer that supports a premium price.
3. *Focus.* Focus directs efforts toward a specific buyer, segment, or geography through the application of one of the other two strategies.

Making strategy operational is the extent to which the organization has brought business strategy imperatives down to an operational level so that these goals and objectives can be understood and acted upon by employees. It is one thing to have communicated the organization's business strategy; employees may know what it is, but does each employee know what she needs to do to affect that strategy? As a human resources professional, for example, what is it that you do that allows this company to achieve that strategy? Your answer should come from a very specific, grass-roots level: What behaviors do *you* exhibit? What values do *you* support? How do *you* organize your department to best support the end mission? And what are the management processes and human resources processes that your organization needs to build upon in order for it to be effective?

Using Michael Porter's axiom, you must first understand where you are in these differentiation strategies. Each function within the organization—from the time raw materials are taken in to the delivery of the product or services to the customer—adds some element of value to that product and ultimately to the customer. Business strategy led us to defining the organization capabilities—those things the organization must do well to succeed. They are accomplished through properly structuring functions, departments, and people; creating the appropriate processes; and defining the correct attributes of culture. These are further refined into people strategy critical success factors—the core people strategy competencies that must reside in your employees. These relationships lead us to the question, "What is it that employees need to do to properly execute that strategy?"

Figure 5-4 (corresponding to page 21 of 99 of the CD-ROM) uses the value chain to assess specifically which employees within which functions

Figure 5-4. Value chain behavioral analysis.

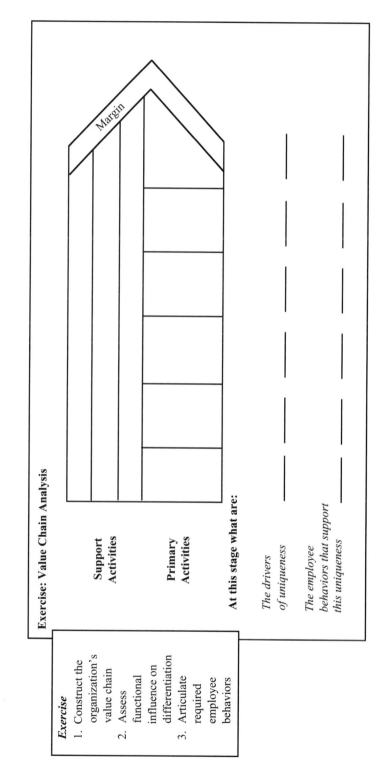

**Exercise: Value Chain Analysis**

*Exercise*

1. Construct the organization's value chain
2. Assess functional influence on differentiation
3. Articulate required employee behaviors

**Support Activities**

**Primary Activities**

**At this stage what are:**

*The drivers of uniqueness*

*The employee behaviors that support this uniqueness*

Margin

Assessing an organization's ability to sustain competitive advantage depends on how well it maximizes opportunities along the value chain.

and processes using which cultural attributes drive the organization's uniqueness. This value chain behavioral analysis allows each function's process and role to define the specific drivers of this uniqueness and demonstrate what each employee must do to support and build additional and unique elements of your product. Those "to do's" are very different if your strategy is of the cost-advantage or product-differentiation variety. Either way, the exercise still develops a set of specific behaviors and desired outcomes at each function and, ultimately, each role within the organization, allowing the entities collectively to execute the business strategy. Begin by developing the value chain for your organization. (You can use Figure 3-6, which is based on Porter's generic value chain model, as a guide.) For each function that's defined, identify the drivers of uniqueness/savings. Each function may or may not contribute equally. For example, you may be selling a better mousetrap, but the operation of manufacturing the trap is rather standard. Your unique qualities may be in research and development, engineering and design, and human resources, since you will require HR to be able to develop programs to recruit and retain the best engineers and research team.

A second valuable tool for determining the value/cost benefit is Figure 5-5 (page 18 of 99 on the CD-ROM). It is used to assess, from the customers' perspective, what is valuable vis-à-vis the ability of the organization to deliver on that value. Remember, decoding the business strategy requires introspection. This standard gap analysis tool is used to measure your company's ability to deliver on the customers' demands. Begin by defining the specific capabilities of your organization. Then list the attributes of your product that are most valued by your customers (preferably this information is obtained through actual customer interviews). In addition to asking open-ended questions about what they value and how your products add value to their efforts, ask customers about the value they place on your specific capabilities, using a scale of one to five for this assessment. Through interviews with executives and line managers, determine the extent to which you are able to deliver on those requirements. Where you "overperform," reassign resources; where you "underperform," build capability.

## Value Proposition

An organization's value proposition defines what it must do in the external market to serve its customers and achieve its strategy. It can be defined in terms of the few key accomplishments that the organization must achieve externally to achieve its vision. It requires that plan designers understand the focus of its customers' businesses, how it inter-

Figure 5-5. Customer/cost differentiation.

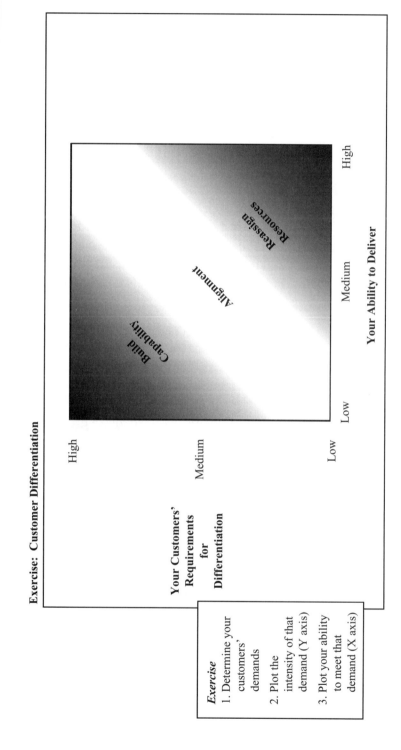

**Exercise:  Customer Differentiation**

**Your Customers'
Requirements
for
Differentiation**

High

Medium

Low

Build Capability

Alignment

Reassign Resources

Low          Medium          High

**Your Ability to Deliver**

*Exercise*
1. Determine your
   customers'
   demands
2. Plot the
   intensity of that
   demand (Y axis)
3. Plot your ability
   to meet that
   demand (X axis)

Assessing your organization's ability to sustain competitive advantage stems from how well it meets customers needs.

faces with its customers, and the value that its products/services add to them. It defines the company's position in the market and, ultimately, the key metrics that it needs to measure its attainment. Value proposition development is the domain of your executive team and is typically developed through a facilitated process. Ultimately, there should be three to five areas to focus on specifically. Figure 5-6 provides a framework for identifying value propositions and an associated set of metrics.

The first effort is just to list all potential requirements. The steering committee can assemble for a brainstorming session and use Figure 5-7 as a tool to create this list. Following that, you need to eliminate options that are outside the realm of the company or that can be combined. For the value proposition to become operational, however, each of the three to five items has to be defined in terms that can be understood by line management, in plain language. Figure 5-8 provides the framework for creating these definitions. The definitions can be further refined into high-level metrics using Figure 5-9 (note that each value proposition is numbered).

## People Strategy Critical Success Factors

People strategy critical success factors (PSCSFs) identify what the organization must do right, internally, to achieve its value proposition. For each value proposition you define there should be a unique set of PSCSFs (use Figure 5-10 to assemble this list). For this exercise, use a group that represents a cross-section of line managers and, in this case, have them define each PSCSF so that it is understandable to the rank and file who will actually accomplish the specified PSCSFs. Do not leave this exercise until you have each PSCSF defined in terms that the employees responsible for executing them can understand—so that when they come to work the next day they'll be able to understand what they need to do to effect this outcome. Again, each value proposition will be accomplished through a handful of PSCSFs; label the PSCSF using a number and letter (as shown in Figure 5-11), with the number designating the value proposition and the letter specifying the PSCSF.

For each PSCSF you need to develop high-level metrics that will determine success. Use Figure 5-12 to identify these internal measures.

## Metrics

Metrics are the foundation of every design. They tell us, very specifically, what the company intends to do and define, in actionable terms, how to

*(text continues on page 152)*

**Figure 5–6.** Value propositions and key metrics.

Understand the value proposition and how the organization measures success:

| Value Proposition | Key Metrics |
| --- | --- |
| Volume | Market Share, M &A, Growth |
| Efficiency | Margin, Costs, Processes |
| Specialization | Niche |
| Innovation | Product Development |
| Flexibility | Customer Responsiveness |

**Figure 5-7. Brainstorm value proposition.**

Activity 1: Brainstorm Value Proposition

*Setting Value Proposition*

- Is the domain of the leadership team

- Must flow from business strategy

- Starts with brainstorming all possibilities, then distilling them to a cogent list of three to five

- Defines market-based (external) achievements

- Will provide the foundation for measurement

| **Value Proposition** |
| --- |
| **What do we want to achieve in the marketplace?** |
| 1. |
| 2. |
| 3. |
| 4. |
| 5. |

**Figure 5-8: Define value propositions.**

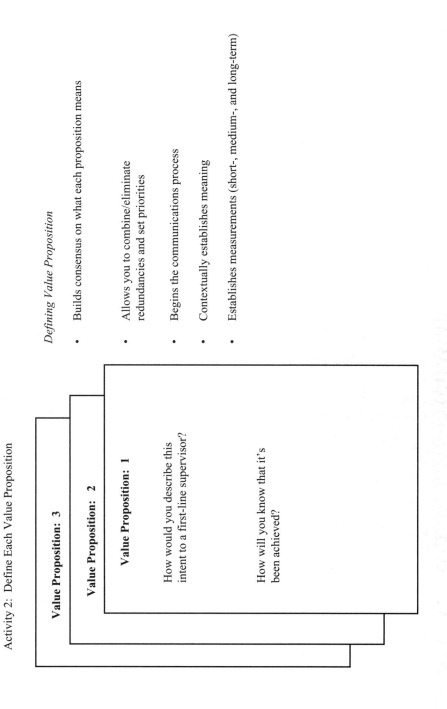

Activity 2: Define Each Value Proposition

Value Proposition: 3

Value Proposition: 2

**Value Proposition: 1**

How would you describe this intent to a first-line supervisor?

How will you know that it's been achieved?

*Defining Value Proposition*

• Builds consensus on what each proposition means

• Allows you to combine/eliminate redundancies and set priorities

• Begins the communications process

• Contextually establishes meaning

• Establishes measurements (short-, medium-, and long-term)

Figure 5-9. Value proposition matrix.

Activity 3: Create the Value Proposition Matrix (describe each value proposition and the outward-looking measures associated with it).

| Organization Vision Statement | | | | | | | | | | |
|---|---|---|---|---|---|---|---|---|---|---|
| Value Proposition | 1 | | | 2 | | | 3 | | | |
| Description | | | | | | | | | | |
| Measures | | | | | | | | | | |

Figure 5-10. Determining the critical success factors.

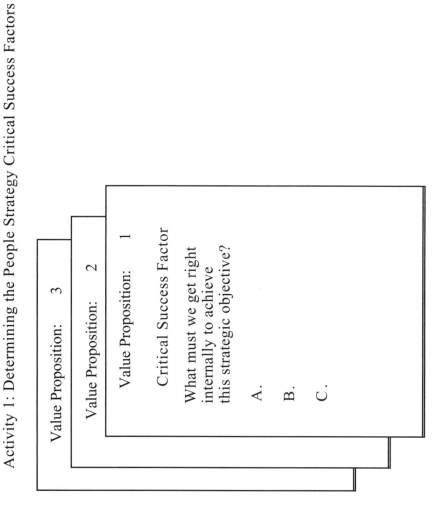

Activity 1: Determining the People Strategy Critical Success Factors

Value Proposition: 3

Value Proposition: 2

Value Proposition: 1

Critical Success Factor

What must we get right internally to achieve this strategic objective?

A.

B.

C.

Figure 5–11. People strategy critical success factors definitions.

Activity 2: Define Each Critical Success Factor

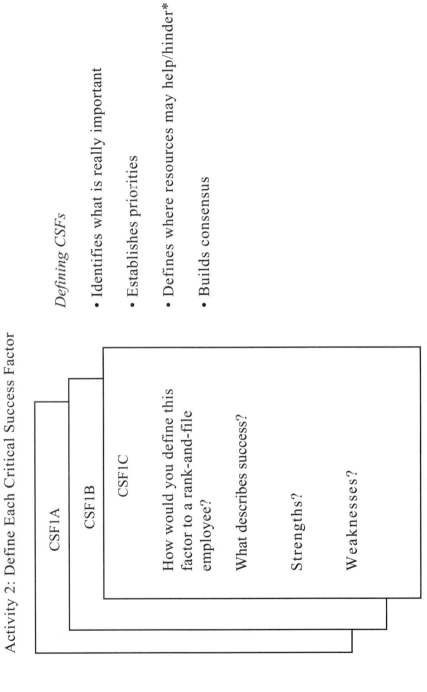

*Defining CSFs*

- Identifies what is really important

- Establishes priorities

- Defines where resources may help/hinder*

- Builds consensus

CSF1A

CSF1B

CSF1C

How would you define this factor to a rank-and-file employee?

What describes success?

Strengths?

Weaknesses?

*SWOT analysis is a parallel tool that can be used to make this assessment.

Figure 5–12. People strategy critical success factors matrix.

Activity 3: Create the CSF Matrix (define each CSF and identify the internal measures

| Critical Success Factor | Definition | Measures |
|---|---|---|
|  |  |  |
|  |  |  |
|  |  |  |
|  |  |  |
|  |  |  |
|  |  |  |
|  |  |  |

determine success. They must be:

- Measurable in a manner that is credible and defensible through some historic or predictive perspective
- Accountable to an individual or a team of people who hold themselves mutually accountable
- Attainable yet challenging
- Within the influence of those people and teams responsible for their accomplishment
- Time-based

Begin by organizing the value proposition and PSCSF statements, using the matrix format in Figure 5-13. The purpose of this exercise is twofold: to determine how strongly each PSCSF influences each value proposition and to prioritize the PSCSFs by assessing the degree of overlap. You can then use Figure 5-14 to further define the interrelationships between the PSCSFs and the value proposition.

At this point it is helpful to begin to assess the best means of organizing the measures (when you get to the plan design details you will better determine the level of measurement for each metric). Metrics are commonly organized by:

- Value proposition
- People strategy critical success factor
- Measurement type
- Metric owner
- Business resource applied to the metric
- Area of influence (e.g., financial, customer)

## Knowing Your Strengths and Weaknesses, Opportunities and Threats

Before discussing further how to collect information, let's review a proven business analysis technique known as SWOT analysis. SWOT is the acronym for strengths, weaknesses, opportunities, and threats. It is a simple model that organizes the internal references as strengths and weaknesses, and external ones in terms of opportunities and threats. Because the primary objectives of the Total Rewards Strategy are to attract,

Figure 5–13. Value proposition/PSCSF matrix.

| Critical Success Factor | Value Proposition | | | To what extent does each critical success factor drive the achievement of each value proposition?<br><br>1 = Influences<br>2 = Strongly influences<br>3 = Highly influences (critical)<br><br>If no influence, then leave blank. |
|---|---|---|---|---|
| | 1 | 2 | 3 | |
| | | | | |
| | | | | |
| | | | | |
| | | | | |
| | | | | |
| | | | | |
| | | | | |
| | | | | |

Figure 5-14. Value proposition/PSCSF measurement analysis.

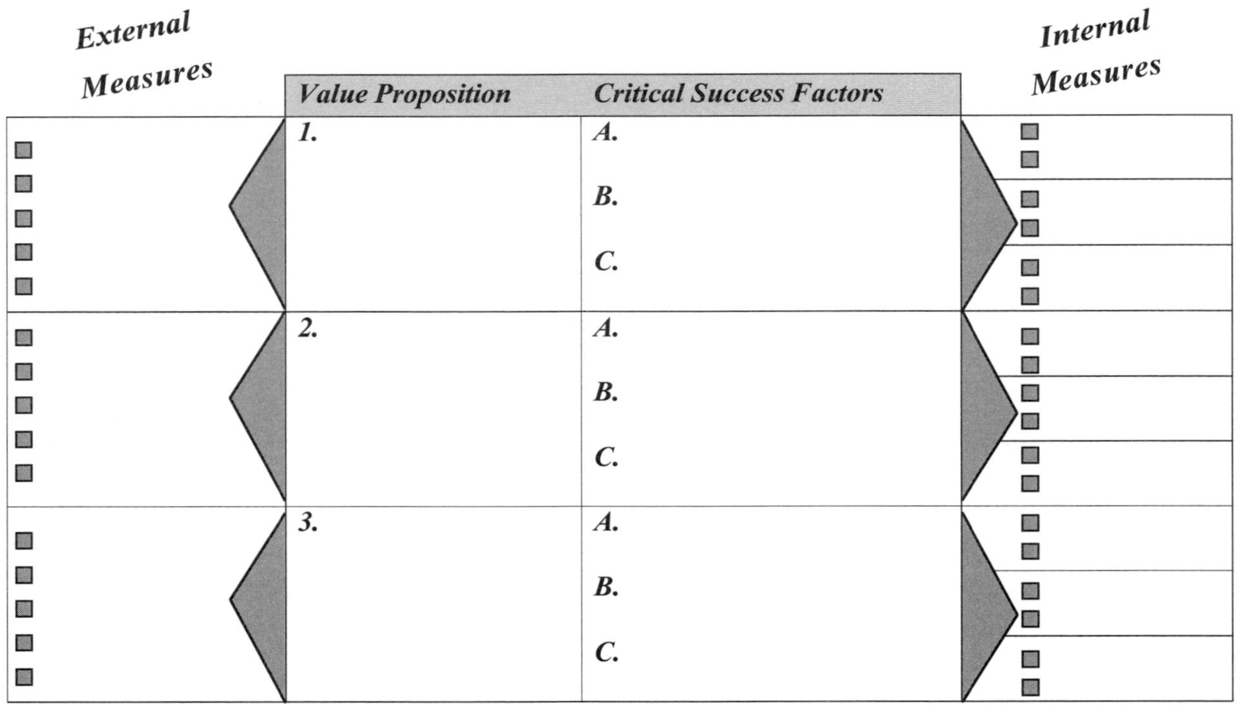

retain, and motivate talent, the SWOT analysis is applied to the rewards strategy as shown in Figure 5-15. The Total Rewards Strategy should allow an organization to increase its ability to attract its fair share of the top quality in the labor market; to motivate that workforce to achieve the greatest results given the reward dollars the company invests; and to retain those top-quality people over the appropriate period of time. Understanding where your organization fits in the context of the business environment is clearly important when determining how to achieve those objectives, affecting both your ability to pay and your need to pay.

From the internal perspective, consider tactics to attract talent, assessing and framing all of the differentiators that you offer as an organization. This requires introspection in order to analyze how each offering differentiates you in the market or makes you vulnerable. Assessment means that you have looked at each offering and compared it to the demands of high-performing, highly competent employee groups. This builds your organization's motivation tactics. Framing means packaging the offerings in such a way that it can be communicated to your employees in terms that demonstrate their value. Without communication, there is no value; it is the foundation of a retention strategy.

Total Rewards Strategy's ability to influence attraction, retention, and motivation is fundamentally influenced by the:

- Knowledge/perception of your industry and company by the investment community, customers, competitors, and general populace
- Positioning of your brands and products in their markets
- Competitiveness of your total reward programs (both programmatically and by competitive level)
- Positioning of your company's peers and their drivers of success

## Linking TRS Mission and Objectives: Key Messages

Key messages are the foundation of the Total Rewards Strategy's money, mix, and messages dimensions. They represent the purposeful statements that an organization wants to communicate to employees about values and its expectations. Key messages are used for several purposes and, most significantly, link the objectives of the rewards program directly to business strategy. This is most effectively done using metrics as a guidepost and key messages as a means for communicating how each employee's job is linked to business outcomes. It is also the most mean-

Figure 5-15. SWOT and the rewards strategy imperative.

Assess the reward strategy imperative using SWOT analysis:

|  | Internal | External |
|---|---|---|
| **REWARD STRATEGIC IMPERATIVE** — Attract, Retain, Motivate | **Strengths**<br>• What will attract people to our company? Do we have the right referral plans?<br>• Why will they stay? How do we continue to identify and reward key contributors?<br>• How do we direct their efforts toward desired ends? | **Weaknesses**<br>• Which of our offerings are not competitive with the market?<br>• What about our company will cause people to leave? Where will they go and why?<br>• Where have we not clearly established the linkage between desired outcomes and rewards? |
|  | **Opportunities**<br>• What is unique about our company? How will we attract our share of talent?<br>• How do our offerings beat the competition's?<br>• What is our profile in the community? How do we profile our people? | **Threats**<br>• What core skills will we have difficulty acquiring?<br>• Where are we vulnerable to losing talent? Where will they go? Why?<br>• Who has outpositioned us? What are they offering? |

ingful way to differentiate your company from the competition. A core component of rewards is demonstrating the difference between working at your company and anywhere else. This allows for a great degree of creativity in defining key messages. (Delivering on those messages is part of the money considerations.)

Messages define the organization's values and expectations. Any employee/employer compact or reward mission statement should work to define for the employees the offerings of the company, as well as the expectations of the company (i.e., what the employer is expecting from the employee in return for the fair value of the reward program).

Through key messages the organization can outline its unique approach to employee rewards and develop the sense of identity that differentiates it from other organizations. It is at this point that Microsoft becomes Microsoft and "B Co." becomes "B Co." This gives a company a lot of latitude in terms of designing the actual architectural mission statement.

In the end, it is very important to have the overall program speak to an employee compact. The balance is between what the organization is offering (in terms of the amount of reward and the mix of the various elements) and the key messages of the program about employer expectations. Reward programs are the most powerful lever an organization has for attracting and retaining the type of employees that the organization needs to prosper and for motivating those employees to accomplish the goals and objectives of the organization.

> **Total Reward Strategy in an Elevator Ride**
>
> McKinsey & Company first conceived the idea that you need to deliver your message in the course of a single elevator ride. The company teaches its consultants to have a message ready so that if the CEO gets on the elevator they can deliver it to him in the course of that ride. Given the speed at which business is conducted, you need to step up your efforts, as a designer, by a function of three. Get the requisite information, process it, and regurgitate it in that same span of time. This demands that you ask the right questions, have a methodology to make decisions based on the information you collect, and deliver that message in the form of specific management tools.[1]

## Key Messages Examples

Let's explore two organizations' key messages. The first is a global food company whose key messages suggest continual employment and treatment of employees with a great deal of respect, integrity, and purpose. Contrast that company with another—a fast-paced, high-tech company that openly communicates its expectation that employees work really hard and buy into the "deal" and the mission for "a finite period of time." This second company doesn't expect a long-term arrangement with its employees but one that is finite, frequently even short. In both cases there is even exchange of value; one can predict that the food company reward program accentuates job security while the high-tech concern focuses on short-term challenge and earnings. Though these key messages are at opposite ends of the spectrum, the program design provides the opportunity to articulate messages that are at either extreme.

Another example is the case of two companies attempting to develop a unique combined organization to deflect a very important competitive threat. One was a large company famous for making mainframes (let's call it "B Co.") and the other was a smaller personal computer company ("A Co."). In the early 1980s, both organizations were trying to come up with a team called the *Pink Team,* composed of a significant number of key software systems engineers. Human resources individuals from B Co. were attempting to select from both A Co.'s and B Co.'s reward plans those plans that were "best of breed" so they could move them together onto a common platform that generally reflected the best of both companies. The message to employees would have certainly been, "No matter whether you're from B Co. or A Co., you will have the highest base pay, the highest incentive, and the highest of the best-designed retirement programs and group insurance benefits." That message clearly would have said belonging to this unique software engineering group was a real privilege.

In this instance, though, A Co.'s representative was attempting to have as low a base pay as possible and a short-term incentive plan that reflected only average benefits and programs. The message that A Co. was attempting to force into the design of the reward program for the combined unit was that it was absolutely critical that software designers be successful in the short-term and that they develop a competitive open software package that would be an alternative to what was becoming, at the time, a direct competitor steamroller.

In addition, A Co.'s reward designer believed it was very important for the software engineers not to be able to return to either B Co. or to A Co. in the case of failure. In other words, the program would be designed to actually terminate the employees of each of the two organizations and to reenroll them in the new organization as if they were new employees. The key message was that there was no turning back, that the mission that they were on was critical to both organizations' success and that it needed to be accomplished posthaste. There was to be a large amount of short-term incentive and stock equity as part of the resulting reward plans.

Those two messages—"best of both/best of breed" versus "high risk/high reward"—were at opposite extremes of the spectrum with respect to design and potential impact. It is obviously a challenge to develop the appropriate messages for any organization; it is particularly difficult to develop the right messages for organizations at unique points of time in their history or when they are developing unique initiatives, such as B Co. and A Co. were in the 1980s.

Key messages have to be well embedded in Total Rewards Strategy, particularly since it is important for the key messages to be understood by the various constituencies or stakeholders both within and outside the organization. Each key message should be reviewed for how the various stakeholders (e.g., the rank and file, management and executives, owners, suppliers, customers) will perceive its implications. It may even be important to look outside the organization at those who could be owners or potential strategic alliance partners. Companies often have to design an incentive plan that may or may not come into the hands of the public. For instance, incentive plans may encourage salespeople to sell additional, expensive high-profit margin services to clients, even if those products or services are not in the clients' best interest. Invariably, these designs come in return for high commissions. When the plan comes to the public light in the business press it can often create difficult public/customer relations problems. While these plans make complete sense to the company, they point up the need to have balanced key messages.

### ONLY AS LONG AS IT MAKES SENSE

A privately owned pharmaceutical concern was looking to define the compact between itself and its employees. Although company executives understood that a rewards policy delivered the messages about what it meant to work for the company, they knew that the words that went behind the strategy were equally as important.

The company presented an opportunity for people to contribute, learn, and move on, but it did not represent employment for life. The executives were eager to accentuate that employment model because it made them unique. Therefore, the executive team defined "the deal." A focal point of the deal was ". . . employment for as long as it made sense." While the team debated that phrase for hours, it turned out to work for them for years. This sole key message allowed executives to approach employees and employees to approach the executives to openly talk about what made sense in their relationship. Articulating the key messages in this way, and management's ability to exemplify those messages, created a very open and nonthreatening environment. While reward plans came and went, as did people, employment for as long as it made sense turned out to be a key message that made sense for a long time.

## Because Statements

Because statements create the linkage between key messages and program designs. They are a means for collecting information about desired outcomes, and they are used to establish key plans and specific plan detail design principles. During the data collection process, interviews, focus groups, or meetings, the design team should constantly ask line managers, employees, and itself the following question: "The rewards/design team did a good job *because*...?" In completing this statement the team will be developing key messages for the plan from each stakeholder's point of view.

Confirm the "therefore" statements and "because" statements with the steering committee since they typically have good insights and represent broad subject matter expertise.

Because statements are a tool for suggesting how the various learnings and influences from Phase I should manifest themselves in plan design. Emulate and reinforce the design aspects that are good about existing programs and HR processes and redesign the things that are not good or are encumbrances to ensuring a smooth execution of business strategy. A good place to start has always been with a group of executives within the organization. A structured brainstorming session on strengths and weaknesses of the various programs can be very informative. Many executives will express, in a frustrated way, that their business strategy "doesn't have any traction with employees." Force those executives to discuss why employees "just don't get it." Generally, insights will flow directly and profusely. Employees are also extremely insightful in terms of which programs work and which do not. So often, the easiest sources demanding the least analysis can deliver some of the most effective insights. Sometimes the facts are not as important to understand when reviewing the reward programs' effectiveness as the various stakeholders' perceptions and the resulting impact on the overall employee population (or at least key portions of that population). Once again, you can use Figure 5-15 to facilitate this discussion (see CD-ROM page 39 of 99).

The gap between the desired future reward program mission and the present reward program is probably going to be substantial. This process does not necessarily need to done in a "quantitative" fashion; it can be accomplished by reviewing each mission statement of the reward program. It can be done for different stakeholder groups within the organization. The gap analysis really allows you to see the difference between the overall reward program mission statements and how the existing reward program fulfills those missions.

## Curly's "One Thing" (The Key Message)

In the popular movie *City Slickers*, the cowboy character Curly goes through the movie telling his riding mates that only one thing matters in life. He dies before moviegoers learn what that one thing is.

Curly's "one thing" is a facilitation technique that is designed to get managers to articulate (before it's too late) what they want employees to do to support the business. Don't stop until the message is broken down into simple enough terms to be understood by the recipients. This is referred to as Curly's one thing for two reasons: First, these messages about what is important should be limited in number—certainly no more than three to five. Second, the communications should be made early!

The first step toward developing the Total Rewards Strategy is preparing a tight document, maybe two pages in length, that delivers a contextual definition of the company's offering and expectation to the organization. Money and mix will be used to deliver on the key messages. The document should tell employees what the company values (in terms of behaviors, results, and performance) and will pay for—that is, the types of rewards being offered (money) and how those rewards are delivered (mix). A tool is provided for guidance on page 69 of 99 on the CD-ROM.

Some rules apply. First, be creative. Much of the effort thus far has been around collecting information and then organizing that information. This book has provided a framework for both, as well as for understanding the context of that information within your company. Now it is time for the team to actually create something with it.

Second, these key messages are "the talk." Money and mix need to be there to have the organization "walk the talk." Accordingly, it is important that key messages developed by the team be validated by the appropriate organizational authorities. This is also a good time to step back to the transfer know-how phase. Consider how the team may get input about its key messages from stakeholders outside the design effort.

## Analyzing the Information Collected

Analyzing the information collected thus far, and developing the Reward Architecture to support the strategy, requires that you assess each input, determine the organization's readiness for change, and further the communications process. There are a myriad of tools available for conducting this analysis. This book uses two standards—gap analysis and SWOT analysis.

### Gap Analysis

Gap analysis is a simple technique for assessing how far from the desired state the existing programs are. To do this analysis, take the key messages and the "because" and "therefore" statements and assess your current designs against each; this tells you how much change is necessary. A scale of one to five is typically used. Figure 5-16 is a simple tool for facilitating this process. The focus is on identifying aspects of the current programs that are worth retaining or emulating, as well as those that need to be redesigned. It is a means for establishing priorities, as well as understanding the depth and breadth of the change required.

---

**Messages and the Art of Bicycle Assembly**

Any parent has experienced his or her fair share of toys and bicycles to assemble. After a while you come to realize that slavishly following the directions is almost as bad as ignoring them altogether. Here's a happy medium to settle on—read the directions then throw them away and follow your own common sense.

This same advice may prove effective for your design team. Try this:

1. Ensure that everyone has read and understands all of the various forms of input.

2. Build consensus, through dialogue, about what that input means.

3. Put it all aside and simply write out the answers to the following questions to get your key messages:

   - What does the organization want its employees to feel about working here?
   - What is required of us, as an organization, to succeed?
   - What are our expectations about performance, results, and behavior?
   - What do we value?

---

### Program Design SWOT Analysis

Earlier in this chapter the concept of SWOT analysis was introduced in assessing an organization's Total Rewards Strategy. Here the SWOT analysis is applied to the specific reward plans through the questions provided in Figure 5-17 for each reward element. (Of course, you can substi-

Figure 5–16.  Gap analysis.

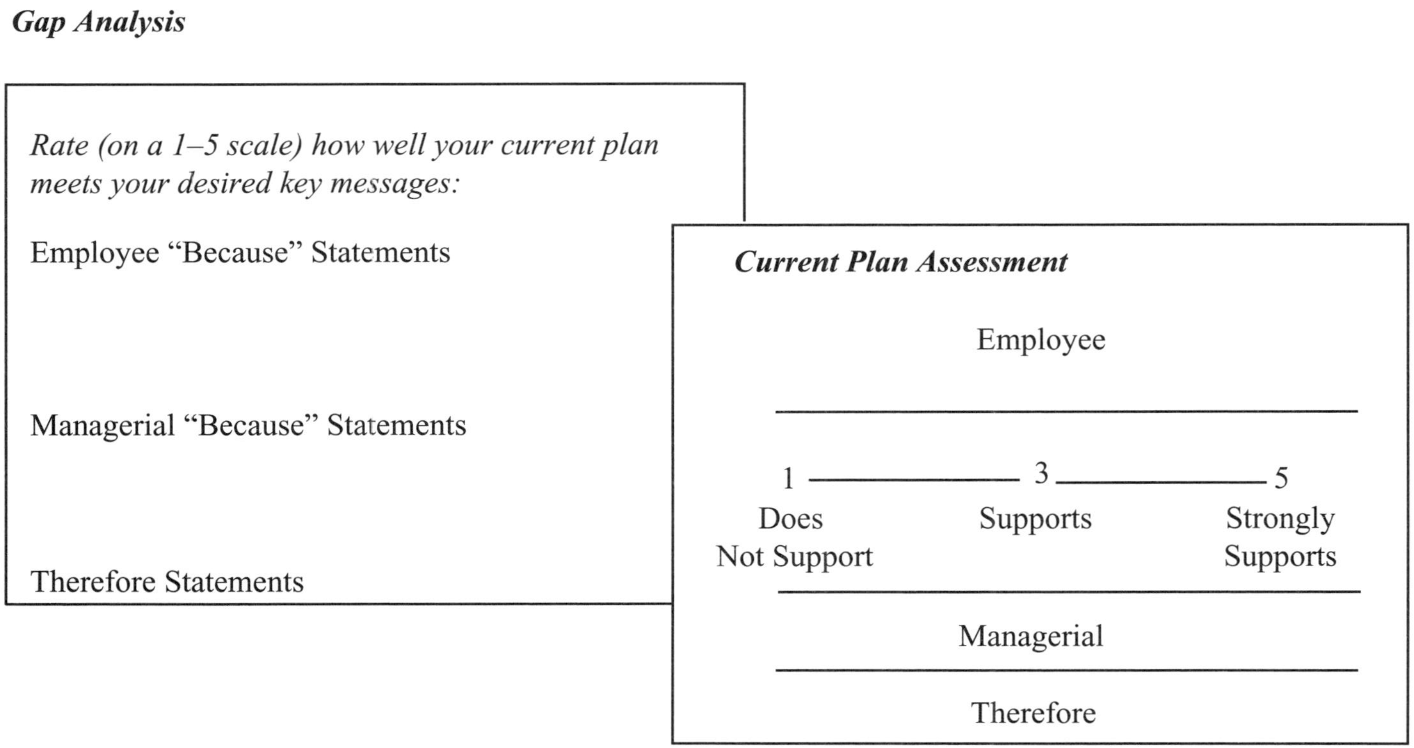

## Gap Analysis

*Rate (on a 1–5 scale) how well your current plan meets your desired key messages:*

Employee "Because" Statements

Managerial "Because" Statements

Therefore Statements

***Current Plan Assessment***

Employee

1 ——— 3 ——— 5
Does        Supports      Strongly
Not Support              Supports

Managerial

Therefore

Analyzing the "because" and "therefore" statements allows you to identify gaps as well as points to emulate.

Figure 5-17. SWOT analysis.

**SWOT Analysis**

*Exercise*
Based on the fact/perception matrix and the "therefore" statements, determine:

- Strengths
- Weaknesses
- Opportunities
- Threats

**Strengths**
- Which reward programs are effective today?
- What should we keep and/or emulate?

**Weaknesses**
- Which plans do not work today?
- How and how much needs to change?

**Opportunities**
- How can we best meet the demands of key stakeholders?

**Threats**
- What conditions threaten success?

SWOT analysis can be used to analyze program strengths and weaknesses.

tute other questions for your company.) For example, in the "strengths" category, the questions to explore are:

- Which reward programs are effective today?
- What should you keep, and what should you eliminate?
- What groups are these rewards particularly effective with?
- What impact are these programs having today?
- Is the base program effective at controlling costs?
- Is the incentive program effective in encouraging employees to behave in a particular way?
- Is the employees' suggestion program producing savings on key opportunities within the organization?

In examining each program, you need to be as granular as possible. Accordingly, you not only need to look at the program in terms of its ability to meet its objectives, but also in terms of its ability to meet its objectives with various employee populations. Although the suggestion program might work very well with your nonexempt secretarial staff, will it meet the objectives of your PhDs in research and development, for example?

A difficulty with this approach is that it is much easier to focus on weaknesses to the exclusion of the strengths. When conducting SWOT analysis:

- Know the facts.
- Stay away from personal feelings.
- Be diligent about balancing strengths and weaknesses.

Finally, consider the various stakeholders in the analysis, balancing the views of employees, owners, business partners, and customers in the discussion. Remember that traditional SWOT analysis always looks at strengths and weaknesses as internal forces and opportunities and threats as external. Therefore, in addition to looking at stakeholders who are either internal (e.g., employees, owners) or external (e.g., suppliers, community), look at the threats and understand the market conditions that infringe on the success of the program itself and/or the company's execution of its objectives.

One of the more creative aspects in developing an effective Total Rewards Strategy is to place it in the context of time. Strengths and weaknesses and opportunities and threats that existed in the past may or may not reflect future strengths, weaknesses, opportunities, and threats. This can be the result, for example, of changes to the external business environment, especially since certain environmental conditions may change rapidly (e.g., competitors' economic conditions or technology). When conducting SWOT to evaluate the various influences on design, the facilitators need to be mindful of how rapidly those influences are changing. To the extent possible, designers should consider how that change will orient the strengths, weaknesses, opportunities, and threats three to five years into the future. Total Rewards Strategy needs to be designed to be effective for years into the future, and in most cases, you should think about at least a five-year shelf life when you're developing SWOT analysis. Developing good content in the SWOT analysis and framing it in the context of time is critical for developing a shared sense of the design influences for the design team members.

### Readiness for Change

The design team should assess the organization's readiness for change in light of the facts and perceptions. Change may be evolutionary or revolutionary; it's up to the team to make a recommendation based on the information collected when building know-how, the gaps between the future and current requirements, and the appropriateness of the period of time when the program changes will take place. How much change is your organization ready, willing, or capable of taking? What is the speed with which it is prepared to invoke this change? And what resources do you need to make the change effective and long-lasting? The business demands, for example, may outstrip the organization's ability to change. In other words, the team may sit back and say, "The organization really needs to effect this type of change over forty-eight months." But four years may be too long, since you may not be in business that long if you keep doing what you are doing. If there is in fact a crisis, the organization needs to make change as quickly and effectively as possible. The imperative for making this assessment at this point in the project is that it will allow the design team to determine more appropriate future steps.

Existing reward programs need to be evaluated to determine which plan elements should be emulated and which need to be redesigned, and in what order of priority. Understanding the competitiveness of the organization's existing programs, in terms of level and design, is a key influence.

### Reconsidering the Business Case

You have new evidence and with it you should reconsider your business case. First, review the gap analysis to see if your plans are more directly supporting future initiatives than you originally expected. Consider the readiness for change and determine where you stand in one of three potential outcomes:

1. *You are worse off than you originally thought.* In this case, determine if additional resources are required and consider their allocation. Ask yourself: Is there a greater need for speed than originally expected?

2. *You are about where you thought; your choice of project scope is appropriate for the situation.* Take your team out for a beer and get ready to continue in the morning.

3. *You are not as bad off as you originally anticipated.* Free some resources. Leverage your communications.

### Transfer of Know-How

This is a good point to stop and reconsider your communications plan. Early on you let people know that you were undertaking this initiative. It's time for a status update now that more information has been processed.

Rethink the timing and the messages about when and how much change you will effect. Begin to communicate the key messages of the Total Rewards Strategy.

## Defining Reward Elements—Money

The money dimension defines three things:

> On September 11, 2001, I was working on this very section of this text, sitting in a hotel room in Boston at 8:45 A.M. The events that unfolded on CNN put this text in perspective for me.
>
> We are working hard to be efficient, to do things and introduce programs that help our companies operate more effectively. This is not life or death. Accordingly, we should take the license required to try new things and think differently.
>
> Let me neither overstate nor understate this point. Organizational rewards are a component of our lives; they transcend our personal and professional lives. Money is of critical importance to the recipient. Accordingly, it deserves study and analysis. However, it's not life or death. It's just doing our best to do the right thing. It does not demand paralysis.
> —Todd M. Manas

1. The competitive level at which you want to anchor rewards
2. The people markets that you are going to compete within

3. The reward elements that you are going to offer to meet that competitive level

It also represents a chance for the organization to complete a comprehensive analysis at both a micro level (by employee or position) and a macro level (in terms of its overall competitive level), and it allows us to look at the organization's overall macroeconomic model for employee rewards. The money axis is often defined in terms of a compensation philosophy. A company's compensation philosophy begins with a competitive assessment: What is the organization's marketplace for talent, and at what level within that marketplace is the organization going to position its reward level? Figure 5-18 (corresponding to CD-ROM page 57 of 59) plots this multivariate approach that addresses competitive level against organizational layers (e.g., senior management, middle management, exempt professional, and nonexempt). Chapter 4 defined value chain strategy that also is a means for varying the competitive level or money dimension by function or value chain step (e.g., purchasing, research, development, operations, logistics, sales, marketing, and customer service). Both are effective ways to view competitive level alternatives and can be used together.

The mission statement is used to do a gap analysis against existing plans and move into later stages of plan design. This is where the input from top management is critical. While other stakeholders can be considered, the initial Total Rewards Strategy mission statement should reflect key senior executives' opinions about what the reward program has to accomplish for them. If that is not done, then the other stakeholders' impacts on the plan's mission will probably be ineffective, and there will be difficulty getting the plan accepted; the ensuing program design underneath it will be either based on erroneous mission or equally as difficult to gain acceptance for (or both).

## Determining Which Elements to Include

The first decision is about what offerings you will include as rewards. Organizing and communicating those offerings comes next. Begin by being as broad as possible. (Use Figure 1-1 as a guide.) The team must answer the question: "What rewards plans will we use to deliver on our key messages?"

Figure 5-19 is a tool that can be used to effectively determine the best design. Along the column headers, indicate the future desired attributes as identified in previous steps. Row labels can be various program types

Figure 5–18. The money dimension.

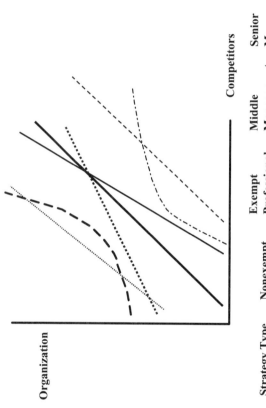

| Strategy Type | Nonexempt | Exempt Professional | Middle Management | Senior Management |
|---|---|---|---|---|
| Upside down curve | Very low | Below | At market | Below |
| Hi-low crossover | Very high | High | At market | Below |
| Off market | Below | Below | Below | Below |
| At market | At market | At market | At market | At market |
| Low-hi crossover | Very low | Below | At market | Above |
| Right-side up curve | Above | At market | At market | Above |
| Above market | Above | Above | Above | Above |

The money dimension can be defined by compensation philosophy and verified in the fact/perception matrix.

## Figure 5-19. Feasibility matrix.

***Feasibility Matrix***

*Because this organization values...*

*Therefore...*

| | Initiative Taking | Attraction/Retention of Top Talent | Team-Based Performance | Superior Performance | Uncertainty | Skills Development | Focused Objectives | Results Over Behaviors | Precision | Opportunism | Process Improvement | Decreased Cycle Time |
|---|---|---|---|---|---|---|---|---|---|---|---|---|
| **Gain Share** | Supports | Detracts | Supports | Supports | Detracts | Detracts | Strongly Supports | Strongly Supports | Strongly Detracts | Strongly Detracts | Strongly Supports | Strongly Supports |
| **Hybrid** | Supports | Detracts | Supports | Supports | Detracts | Supports | Supports | Supports | Detracts | Detracts | Supports | Strongly Supports |
| **Group Incentive** | Supports | Detracts | Strongly Supports | Supports | Detracts | Strongly Supports | Supports | Supports | Detracts | Detracts | Supports | Strongly Supports |

● = Strongly Supports ◒ = Supports ◓ = Detracts ○ = Strongly Detracts

***Exercise***

1. Place future desired attributes as column headers
2. Label rows with reward elements under consideration
3. Assess how each element supports desired attributes

In this exercise, balance most valued attributes against each element's ability to support desired outcomes.

(e.g., gain share, hybrid, group incentive). Rating the feasibility of each provides a systematic means for determining priorities.

Remember that *everything* an employee takes away from his relationship with an employer is a reward. It is up to plan designers to organize them as such and communicate their impact.

## Determining People Markets

Most organizations define people markets in an egalitarian manner—the same for everyone. It's not unusual, for example, for a large industrial company to compare itself to other large industrial companies. However, the marketplace itself may vary by level in the organization or, more specifically, by function within the organization, or both (i.e., by organization level and function). There's a clear trend toward employees who are more aligned with their functional expertise than with their employer. A more surgical approach may lead to both efficiencies and a more effective people strategy. Consider your various business strategies (GBS, VCS, and SBS) and make purposeful decisions about whether, because of where and how your business competes, certain key jobs or functions may be best recruited from other industries.

The process of determining people markets is best done by first identifying and defining all the possible differences, then prioritizing those differences to determine the key influences. Those differences include:

- Geography
- Functional expertise
- Organizational level
- Impact on business strategy

## Determining Competitive Levels

With people markets defined, the organization needs to define the level at which it wants to compete. Two primary considerations ensue:

- The general business strategy
- The level of talent required

Of course, you can balance the two—competitive level and people markets. In other words, you can achieve the same objective by selecting the right combination of either approach. You need to balance the two because decisions you make on both dimensions have cost implications. The key is to determine which is most palatable within your organization, whether the sources of external and internal data are available to determine and support it, and how your decision will reinforce your key messages. Also consider the extent to which specific industry experience is required. Figure 5-20 frames this debate.

The accompanying CD-ROM provides the user with several tools for defining the competitive level (money) dimension. It requires that the user determine the key influences on recruitment and selection decisions (e.g., geography, knowledge base, and expertise) whether functionally, technically, and/or by industry, and so on.

## Articulating a Mission and Objective for Each Reward Element

Underneath key messages come subordinate mission statements, or the objective statements of each of the elements of reward that you've decided to include. Remember, it's all about communication. These documents become the foundation not only of your plan design, but also of your employees' communications. For each element of rewards to be included in your design, develop a clearly articulated statement of how that program supports the successful accomplishment of strategy. It is intended to inform employees how they support business outcomes and how this program supports them. Once the mission statement has been developed, you should work toward a fair balance between what you're offering and your expectations. Fair balance suggests that there is an even value exchange between your reward programs and the work that is to be performed.

The program's mission statement needs to define how gaps will be closed by the reward elements. For example, if you are trying to eliminate a gap in terms of individual employee competencies, the base pay program may be designed to go from a time-based or merit pay program to a competency-based program with lump sum increases. (All of the individual program elements that will be redesigned or developed will be discussed in Chapter 6.)

Finally, most critical is to outline an effective implementation plan. Success in implementing change plans depends, to a large degree, on developing a unique sense of choreography for each of the plan design changes. That is to say, that if you want to replace a base salary plan that rewards for seniority with one that is performance-based, it may take

Figure 5-20. Overall competitive level and people markets.

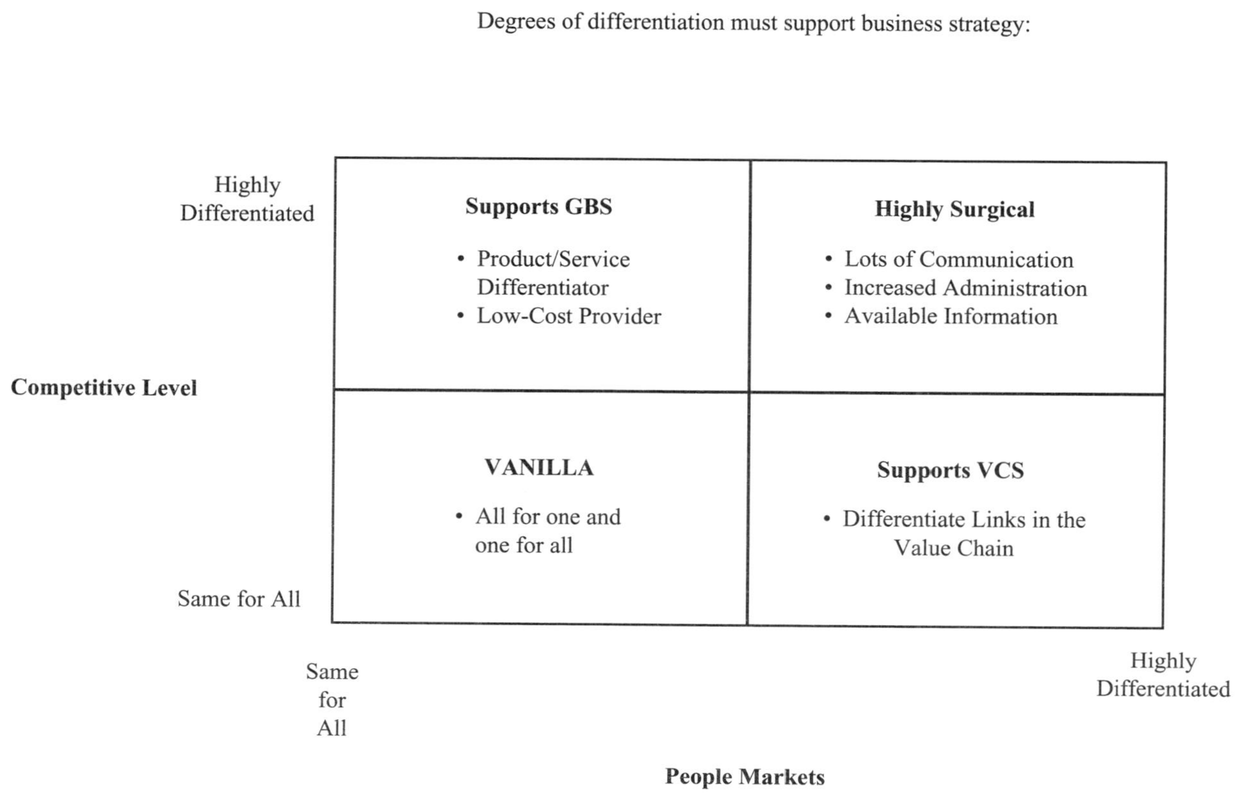

Degrees of differentiation must support business strategy:

**Competitive Level**

Highly
Differentiated

**Supports GBS**

• Product/Service
  Differentiator
• Low-Cost Provider

**Highly Surgical**

• Lots of Communication
• Increased Administration
• Available Information

**VANILLA**

• All for one and
  one for all

**Supports VCS**

• Differentiate Links in the
  Value Chain

Same for All

Same
for
All

Highly
Differentiated

**People Markets**

three years to implement the appropriate changes to bring the plan from one orientation to another. It is important not to rush these changes and to make sure that the momentum builds from the very beginning; that the success occurs early on in the implementation plan; and that the employees and the various key managers take ownership for the changes themselves. While the implementation plan doesn't need to occur over three years, in many cases the best timing may be anywhere between two and five years.

## Determining the Appropriate Mix

The mix, then, is how the design team utilizes the different elements of a reward program and causes them to work together to deliver rewards in the most efficient and appropriate manner possible. The mix defines how you deliver rewards, to whom (i.e., eligibility), and at what level (i.e., participation). Mix determines exactly which reward programs will be used and how the organization will deliver the various elements of a rewards strategy.

The decision here is far from trivial. While money may go a long way toward determining which league you play in—by defining the people markets and competitive levels—mix will do the most to determine the types of players you can get. Consider that the extent to which you shift compensation from fixed to variable compensation will alter the type of person who is attracted to your company and, in turn, dramatically affect your culture.

Focus is the key. The more you can allocate rewards in a more efficient means than cash, the better. Efficient in this context means both cost-effective and directed toward the desires of the recipient.

In making reward program mix decisions, consider the attributes of the workforce that you want and need, in terms of worker personality types, for example, in order to accomplish your business strategy. It may be very different from the one you have currently. Then consider what rewards will be effective at recruiting that workforce. This mix is illustrated in Figure 5-21. The conundrum that it portrays is that as an organization moves from a highly "aggressive" compensation mix, one that may be reflected by a straight commission sales force, to a highly "entitled" mix, it defines the personality of the people it attracts. As with any reward design, neither is inherently good nor bad; designers need to be aware of what the messages are, however, and be deliberate about choosing a mix of pay that defines the future desired culture.

Figure 5-21. Mix and the personality conundrum.

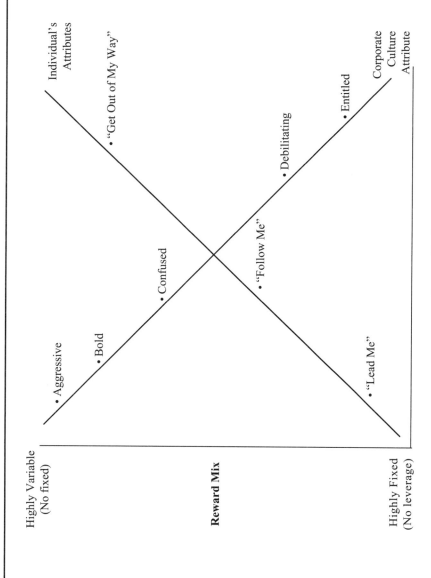

Mix is not just money. In fact, you may well be able to provide other rewards offerings that increase the efficiency of your plan design and drive your efficient frontier to a more rewarding position, but this requires an understanding of your organization's workforce.

There are organizations that are known as excellent training grounds in every profession. If, for example, you aspire to become a commercial pilot, there is no better way to achieve the training, hours, and credentials required than to join the U.S. military. This is a clear advantage in the recruitment process, and it is used to attract the caliber of talent the U.S. military demands.

Eligibility and participation are also plan design principles that should begin to be framed as mix decisions are made. Will there be short-term variable pay for everyone or just for specific categories of people? That is a mix debate that's both situational and a point to reconsider as your requirements change. (Eligibility and participation are defined at the strategic 30,000-foot level here; the discussion of these principles will be refined later.) The use of fixed versus variable pay and the use of training and development rewards may evolve as your business does. For example, if your company operates in a growing or changing business environment, it's advisable to increase investment in development rewards. In periods of cost reduction, leveraging pay may be more appropriate.

A company can organize reward strategy development by defining increasing degrees of freedom. The economic aspects and competitive aspects related to the business strategies (GBS, VCS, SBS) determine, to a large degree, the amount of money on an individual position basis, an individual employee basis, and on an overall organizational basis. How much money can actually be spent is heavily determined based on the competitive market position the organization has. Accordingly, the degrees of freedom of design on the money part of the mission statement are fairly limited inside the range of the organization's ability to pay. The mix, however, allows many organizations to become much more creative in determining whether they will use an incentive or variable compensation program (i.e., deciding how much of the overall program will be fixed, how much will be variable, how much will be short-term variable versus long-term variable, the portion of the reward program that benefit programs will provide, and how much of the program will pay for time not worked, etc.). These programs allow the organization a great deal of freedom to determine how the overall mix will be resourced, taking into account that the mix may be different for different types of positions or levels of positions within the organization.

# Confirming Objectives

Before turning the architecture into designs, you can confirm that your design objectives have been met. The designers should step back and review the proposed reward architecture and philosophy versus the design objectives articulated in the business case to confirm that the Total Rewards Strategy supports your objectives. You can also conduct a gap analysis to determine the extent to which the Total Rewards Strategy supports the overall human resources strategies. Figure 5-22 is one example, in a graphic format, of how this comparison can be done. The reward elements—such as base salary, pay delivery, team incentives, strategic business unit incentives, disability and health benefits, and welfare and pension programs—are aligned across the top. The desired human resources strategy is aligned along the left-hand column. Each current and desired program is then reviewed to the extent that it supports, somewhat supports, does not support, or even completely detracts from the desired human resources strategies. The proposed reward programs are the second row in each instance.

In Figure 5-22, the present human resources strategy is to attract employees, retain employees, provide income protection, provide future security, and develop a fixed workforce expense. The figure shows how each of the different reward elements that are presently designed for the organization either support or detract from those efforts. This is in the judgment of analysts and management.

At this point one must consider how to change or redesign the Total Rewards Strategy to support the new human resources strategy. It is natural to assess the degree to which various reward programs will support the new organization structure, processes, and culture that have been determined to be appropriate, given the organization's business strategy. To set the framework for creating or modifying each of the individual reward program elements and best support the desired change in the organization structure, process, and culture, it is important to review how each program element or a particular approach to base pay (e.g., competency base pay) supports the new organizational structure, process, or culture. Also, determine how that particular approach to a pay element may detract from the new people strategy. Consider a company where all of the decision making is accomplished at the strategic apex: There is very little middle management, and there are no staff employees to either support or regulate the actual operating core or the main body of employees. All decision making is centralized.

Figure 5-22. Future desired objectives.

| Desired People Strategy Critical Success Factors | Reward Element | | | | | | |
|---|---|---|---|---|---|---|---|
| | Base Salary | Pay Delivery | Team Incentive | SBU Incentive | Disability Benefits | Health & Welfare | Pension Program |
| Attract Key Technical Employees | | | | | | | |
| Have an Empowered Workforce | | | | | | | |
| Reward Team Results | | | | | | | |
| Eliminate Poor Performers | | | | | | | |
| Use Total Cost Average | | | | | | | |
| Assist in Income Protection | | | | | | | |
| Assist in Future Security | | | | | | | |
| Vary Expenses with Company Profits | | | | | | | |

■ Supports  ▣ Somewhat Supports  ☐ Doesn't Support  ☒ Detracts

Ultimately, present programs should be measured against the future desired human resources strategy.

If that organization were to evolve into a divisional/decentralized organization (where there is some staff freedom to make decisions and some guidance is given to the middle management and operating core employees to execute the actual business plan), then there clearly would need to be a rethinking of the strategy. This rethinking would take into account how to provide higher levels of reward for the middle management group of employees, since they would be taking on more authority and more decision making.

In addition, in terms of management processes, it would be important for the middle managers to begin to receive advice from the various support groups that are being created in the new organization. Cultures would need to change, too: Decision making would be shared, and the ability to take risk would probably be distributed throughout the organization. Planning and executing against longer-term plans would begin to develop further down in the organization than in the past, and the organization would probably need to develop a sense of change that was more continuous and less reactive than in the less hierarchical, more centralized organization.

The case could be made for the development of a reward program that would need to increase the amount of rewards for the middle management employees (money).

The mix would probably need to develop in such a way that the short-term incentive became an important part of the middle management groups' rewards. By contrast, a new longer-term incentive might be appropriate to make sure that the executives in the strategic apex do not continue to make day-to-day decisions, but are pulled consistently into the area of longer-term planning (with their awards, then, correspondingly becoming longer term). For example, the short-term incentive plan would actually pull the middle management group toward the new organizational structure, creating a sense of accountability and authority and a need for planning to accomplish the company's annual goals. It would also push the longer-term business requirements of the organization toward the senior management group. The senior management group would focus less on day-to-day operating issues that are best made by middle management, or staff groups, and more on long-term mission, vision, and values.

Many organizations today are trying to move their cultures from a functional orientation to a process-based or time-based one. If the base pay program is highly structured with traditional grades that are market-based, the resulting Total Rewards Strategy may call for a competency-based pay program, which would reward for the increase in the level of knowledge of employees. This would call for the redesign of base pay to rethink both the compensable factors and the organization of jobs into less traditional grades or potentially broader bands.

Another example might be in the design of benefit programs. Organizations that are typically functional or process-based need a longer-tenured employee. The corporate knowledge that the employee brings to the development of a particular process, or to a specific function in an organization, is necessary and valuable. Benefits rewards should deliver the message that long-term tenure is important. The retirement program should be a defined benefit program that rewards service. The opposite would be appropriate for a network culture where the organization is assembling various individuals and teams for specified periods of time, achieving a specific project, and then disbanding. In that culture, the portability of benefits is significantly more important, and although the amount may be the same, the retirement program should be structured more like a 401(k)-defined contribution plan. It would allow the employee to come, contribute, and then leave, and not have lost retirement program credit.

As you can see from the preceding examples, there are a tremendous number of combinations and permutations that can be developed when one focuses on the amount of the reward program and on the key mix between the various reward programs, and then manages the messages. The rewards programs can create a great deal of support for the changes to the organization's present people strategy (as manifested in its structure, process, and culture) and for the new, desired people strategy that will align with a new business strategy to enable it to perform well in its fresh environment. Once again, Figure 5-22 attempts to summarize and simplify the complexity of this process of reviewing proposed reward programs versus the desired people strategy critical success factors. In this format, it's clear that each actual reward program element, such as base pay, could be analyzed to determine whether it can support the desired PSCSF and/or the new general people strategy (the organization's structure, process, and culture). For example, the base pay program may have subelements to it—such as the level or the competitive strategy of the base pay program; the actual pay delivery of that base pay program; whether it was competency-based, skill-based, or performance-based; and whether it was a seniority- or time-based program. Also, whether the individual base pay program is heavily variable or predominantly fixed is a key design issue. Allowing employees to get paid for competency (and possibly receive discretionary lump sum merits for performance against key objectives) is a much different base pay program from one that follows steps from the beginning of the salary range (allowing employees to attain the maximum of the salary range merely by seniority). The base pay program alone in the previous example can represent a powerful set of messages to support the new people strategy. In the following manner, each program can itself be analyzed into subelements.

So far this book has explained how to interrelate plan design architecture to support an organization's move from its present to desired people strategy in support of business strategy. There are a tremendous number of combinations, and all plan design represents a balance between the desired program and messages and what is feasible to be administered, funded, and understood by employees. It is helpful at this point to review the architecture with various constituencies before going on to design.

## Architecture Constituency Review

First, it is important to be able to step back from the program design elements and, in the end, ask if the new reward architecture defines each element's objectives from the employees' perspective and articulates Curly's "one thing," or the one thing you want employees to do differently as a result of the change in reward structure. The key to the "one thing" is to put it in actionable terms that an employee can both understand and do. So, from the employee's perspective, you want to answer the question: "When I come back to work on Monday morning, what is the one thing I am supposed to do, or do differently, that I am not doing today?"

If the answer to that question is designed into the organization's reward program in as direct and straightforward a fashion as possible, then it is as good an acid test for the new reward program as there can be. This overall acid test for moving forward, based on what the employees will understand that their desired behavior should be in the near future, doesn't minimize the importance of detail plan design (covered in the next chapter), however.

While Curly's one thing allows the designers to consider the employees' perspective, it is equally important to assess the objectives of each reward element from management's perspective. This will demonstrate how each supports the overall Total Rewards Strategy. Step back to your business propositions, and define how employees add value to the company, as was done in the knowledge-building phase.

Additional acid tests would consider other key stakeholders' points of view. These key stakeholders include customers, owners of either privately or closely held firms, or shareholders of a publicly held firm. In addition to employees, management, and strategic partners, look at how customers may interpret new reward programs. All these stakeholders should be considered in the final review of the plan's architecture. In many instances, strategic alliances are critical to the success of organizations today. Many of the present reward programs do not take into account the effect of a particular incentive plan, or a particular benefit or base pay program, with respect to its impact or its ability to increase the success of any strategic alliance the company may have.

Occasionally key suppliers are considered in the design of an actual reward architecture, a trend that, while limited, may grow. Certain suppliers are critical to the health of an organization. Encouraging organizational elements such as purchasing, research and development, and even operations to work effectively with key suppliers may become an increasingly critical element of today's new organizational success given the high degree to which the organizations are outsourcing functions that aren't considered core competencies.

Finally, consider all the business-to-business relationships that exist between your entity and your business partners in your stakeholder analysis. This includes both suppliers and customers, representing relationships at both ends of the company's value chain. Plan designers will want to consider how reward programs might best support the interaction between the two businesses. Suppliers also make up a valued piece of the stakeholder chain.

By now your organization should have a fairly well defined plan architecture that has been reviewed for its impact on the organization's new business strategy and the way that new business strategy is interpreted through the new organizational structure, process, and culture. These critical acid tests should be accomplished before entering into the detail plan design phase of any overall reward strategy redesign effort.

## Field Testing

Before moving into detailed plan design, it is also helpful to solicit employee feedback about the plan's architecture. This feedback can often be obtained using challenge teams. A challenge team is a group of employees brought together to review and respond to plan architecture concepts. The point is to provide as much detail as your team is comfortable with—there need not be any commitment to alternatives. You are only presenting recommendations to them.

The value of employee input at this point is threefold: First, because your design team has been very close to the issues and influences, employee input provides an opportunity for the architecture to be reviewed by a new set of eyes. An employee challenge team is a good way for the design team to have the value of its work checked by its peers. Second, input from the challenge team is invaluable in taking architecture to detailed plan design. Remember, the team is not done. Collecting this additional input now is a good way to build toward the next phases of design and implementation. Finally, communications plans can be developed from the employee input. Clearly, you cannot change your design to satisfy the desires of your employees; there are still business considerations. You can, however, spin those changes that meet the commentary of your employees as designs intended to address employee concerns. Use the issues that you cannot change as a vehicle for educating employees about business requirements.

## Transferring Know-How: Leveraging People

The Total Rewards Strategy may now be ready, but it is not time just yet to move on to Chapter 6 and detailed plan design. First, reflect on what has been accomplished, what is to come, and what should be communicated to employees outside the design effort. Use the phased communications plan, and be ready to set up the process of linking and leveraging.

Begin with executive approval. The strategy will set the course of detailed designs; this is a natural point, then, to seek executive input before designing the reward elements. Be proactive. Bring the steering committee members both the strategy and the suggested communications materials. These materials should be short and informal, delivering the following:

- *The Key Message.* This message should articulate the intent of the TRS through its values and expectations.
- *The Process.* You want to demonstrate the thoughtfulness of the design process and the involvement of employees, subject matter experts, and the like.
- *The Next Steps.* You must describe what is to come and how the strategy may evolve.

To the extent that they are available, the following materials can be used to provide insight into human resources processes. You can use this list in making a data request from your own HR department.

### *Human Resources Processes*

1. Recruiting Materials
   - Recruitment locations (i.e., where recruitment takes place)
   - Sample recruitment ads
   - Interview and selection process
   - Recruitment training materials
   - Employee communications
   - Employee referrals

2. Training Materials
   - Curriculum
   - On-site training materials/off-site training materials
   - Continuation of training after initial employment date
   - Employee communications

3. Job Descriptions
   - Performance goals/objectives

4. Compensation Plan

5. Annual Incentive (Bonus) Plan

6. Long-Term Incentive Plan

7. Commission Plan

8. Benefit Plans
   - Medical/dental
   - Long-term disability
   - Employee life insurance
   - Dependent life insurance
   - Accidental death/dismemberment
   - Retirement
   - Tuition reimbursement
   - Others (e.g. flexible spending, workers compensation)

9. Employee Policy Manual
   - Paid time-off policy
   - Unpaid time-off policy
   - Holidays
   - Illness, injury, short-term disability policy
   - Maternity and adoption/paternity policy
   - Employee personal phone calls policy
   - Employee discounts

- Employee referrals
- Performance review/promotions policy
- Overtime policy

10. Schedule of Work Hours
- How is schedule determined?
- Preference of hours/days/holidays?
- Staffing by-product, hours, expertise?

11. Organizational Structure
- By store
- By department

## Chapter 6

# TURNING ARCHITECTURE INTO PROGRAM DESIGN

OKAY, SO YOU'VE GOT YOUR architecture done and approved and you are ready to move to the next step: designing the details for each reward element that you're going to use. The devil is always in the detail. However, herein lies the greatest opportunity to customize your plans to fit your organization's needs. This chapter provides design principles for each reward element. Consider these reward principles a guide—the design team should add to and/or modify them to fit its purpose.

## Standard Reward Design Principles

Whatever you do, however, should be founded on the broadest definition of rewards. Chapter 1 illustrated the need for satisfying varying tastes and preferences among a diverse workforce. Unfortunately, most organizations do not take this holistic view (see Figure 6-1), thereby diminishing the value of their offerings.[1] And if a company does not structure and communicate its Total Rewards Strategy as such, employees will easily consider rewards as entitlements.

Figure 6-2 lists the major reward elements of base cash, short-term variable, long-term variable, benefits, perquisites, and other noncash rewards. The program design you choose (see common examples column) will be used to communicate the people strategy critical success factors (PSCSFs) and how employees will be rewarded when these goals, objectives, and tasks are (or aren't) accomplished. That is why it is important to choose wisely. Design principles reflect guideposts that

Figure 6-1. Considering rewards broadly.

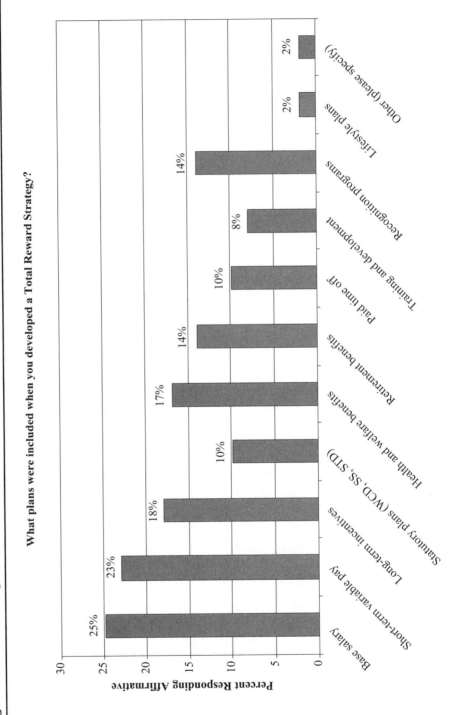

Figure 6-2. Total reward elements.

| Common Examples | Reward Elements | Definition |
|---|---|---|
| • Quality of Work & Life<br>• Affiliation<br>• Development | Other Noncash Rewards | TOTAL REWARD |
| • Cars<br>• Clubs<br>• Counseling<br>• Contracts | Perquisites | TOTAL REMUNERATION |
| • Retirement<br>• Health & Welfare<br>• Time Off w/Pay<br>• Statutory Programs | Benefits | |
| • Stock/Equity<br>• Cash<br>• Incentive (Long-Term) | Long-Term Variable | TOTAL DIRECT CASH |
| • Incentive (Short-Term)<br>• Bonus/Spot Awards<br>• Contract | Short-Term Variable | TOTAL CASH |
| • Base Salary<br>• Hourly Wage | Base Cash | |

Intrinsic

Extrinsic:

All things onto which we can assign a dollar value

Source: Adapted from Todd Manas, "Combining Reward Elements to Create the Right Team Chemistry," Workspan (November/December 2000), p. 47.

aid the team in determining the best orientation for each reward element. The balance of this chapter offers design principles that will aid you in selecting among the many alternative choices you will have. It will also guide you through the design detail your team will develop in its programs.

## Base Pay Design Principles

As illustrated in Figure 6-3, base pay design principles, and their use in developing fixed compensation reward elements, fall into four general categories:

- Work (the activities that define how work is characterized)
- People (the determinants of an employee's value to the company)
- Pay delivery (the reward for the characteristics of the job and the incumbent's value)
- Administration (managing information about pay and people)

### Looking at Work

How you document, analyze, value, and organize work is the first set of considerations for base pay. Since there is no legal requirement to do any of these things, it is important to consider the return on investment expected on time and resources. For example:

   - *Job Documentation.* Job documentation refers to how your company captures information about each job or role. The trade-off in this decision is between the requirement for detail and the allowance for flexibility. Be as detailed as your organization requires, but as flexible as it will tolerate. There is no requirement, legally, to maintain job documentation, but if you do, there are legal requirements that you must meet (e.g., the Americans with Disabilities Act).
   Figure 6-4 provides an overview of the four most common job documentation methods: job description; role descriptor; competency anchor; and level descriptor. In determining what format to use, ask yourself: "If I take the time to document this today, how often is it accurate?" and "What percent of time does the job actually describe what the person does?" This way, you can determine the required flexibility, based on how work is organized.

Figure 6-3. Base pay design principles.

| Design Principle | Program Aspect | Reward Aspect Defined |
|---|---|---|
| Looking at Work | Job Documentation | • How information about jobs is captured |
| | Job Analysis | • Collecting and organizing information about jobs |
| | Job Valuation | • The approach used to determine relative value of jobs within an organization |
| | Organization of Work | • The banding together of jobs of similar values into "value bands" |
| Looking at People | Competency | • The skills and knowledge individuals must possess to perform the work |
| | Results | • The accomplishments of the people |
| | Traits | • The behavioral conditions that exist within individuals that influence how they would attain results |
| Delivering Pay | Ranges | • The set of minimum pay and maximun pay rates that organizations use to manage pay costs |
| | Increments | • The various pay increase methods (e.g., merit, step, general) |
| Administration | | • Managing information about pay and people |

Figure 6–4. Work documentation.

Job Description: Detailed documentation* that may be:

- Task-based

- Responsibility-based

- Skill-based

- Competency-based (i.e., behavioral)

Role Descriptor: Provides documentation on a set of jobs that are defined by a role.

Competency Anchor: Define competency levels for various jobs or levels.

Level Descriptor: Document the organization's expectations of any job at a given hierarchical level; they may be function specific.

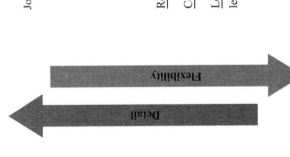

*Documentation refers to how your company captures information about each job, the format and level of detail.

- *Job Analysis.* Collecting the necessary information for job documentation is the process of job analysis. How much information you collect is, again, a decision along the continuum between the requirement for detail and the allowance of flexibility, as shown in Figure 6-5. Job analysis, however, is clearly necessary as you balance internal equity and external competitiveness, as you define your organization's compensation processes, and to start organizing work. At a minimum, you must define and describe a job, the abilities or capabilities necessary to meet the requirements of that job, and the application of the knowledge and skills that are ultimately required. For both job documentation and job analysis, the work that was developed in the earlier phases of the Employee Engagement Process will help designers understand the compensable factors and exactly what the organization values. That ultimately will define what it is you need to analyze and document.

It is also important to keep in mind the connection between job documentation and analysis, and other people processes. The information collected and analyzed here may impact training and development, staffing, and succession planning. This means that the decision regarding which method to use may not be completely within the influence of the rewards design team.

- *Job Valuation.* Job valuation is the procedure used to determine the relative value of each job within an organization and to ultimately create a job-worth hierarchy. A job-worth hierarchy is an ordering of jobs from those with the most to the least impact, based on the applicable compensable factors. It's about how a job fits within an organization (how an individual fits within the role is discussed a little later on in this chapter). Compensable factors create the linkage between the job value and how the job contributes to the execution of business strategy. The job-worth hierarchy sets a job's relative value within the organization. Figure 6-6 shows various forms of job evaluation methodologies.

- *Organization of Work.* If a job description is the organization of several tasks to form a job, then a grade or a salary band is the organization of several jobs to form a group of jobs that are of equal value to an organization. Traditional grading structures, or broad bands, in and of themselves are inherently neither good nor bad. The bottom line, though, is fit within the organization and the requirement (once more) for structure and hierarchy versus the allowance for flexibility. Figure 6-7 gives decision points in assessing the traditional grade, broad-band continuum. It uses your key messages to aid the designer in determining the

**Figure 6–5. Job analysis.**

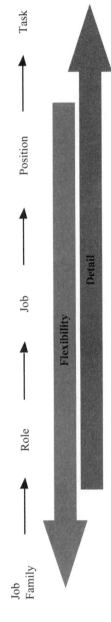

Collect relevant, work-related information with regard to a specific job:

Why collect this information

- Internal equity
- External benchmarking
- Compensation
- Work and organization design

What to collect

- The definition and description of a job and the abilities necessary to meet the requirements

How much to collect is a function of how people in your organization think about work

Job
Family      Role      Job      Position      Task

Flexibility

Detail

Figure 6–6.  Job valuation.

## Valuation Methodology

- Ranking

- Classification

- Factor comparison

- Point factor

- Market-based

**Compensable Factors** are those characteristics your company values that will help it achieve business objectives.

The valuation (or job evaluation) procedure is used to develop the relative worth of jobs within an organization in order to establish a job-worth hierarchy.

Figure 6–7. Organizing work.

The method for organizing jobs needs to reflect the organization's structure and work processes:

| Traditional Grades | Message | Broad Bands |
|---|---|---|
| More | Hierarchy | Less |
| More | Opportunity to Differentiate | Less |
| Diminished | Team Processes | Enhanced |
| Fewer | Structural Requirements | Greater |
| Less | Flexibility | More |
| Tighter | Cost Control | Looser |
| Redundant | Work | Fluid |
| More | Centralization | Less |

best fit. Of course, the decision need not be one or the other; any width of wage ranges can be developed to fit the specific requirements.

## Looking at People

The purpose of the previous section was to evaluate work irrespective of the incumbent in the job, and to place that job within a relative continuum within your organization. The question now is: How does each person fit within the wage range assigned to each job? To get the answer you have to first assess each person against the requirements of his or her job or role. Secondarily, it commands an equal requirement to manage pay using these factors.

This step looks at how employees measure up to those requirements in terms of skill or competency, their compensable factor attainment, delivery of results, or performance. A new reward program, new architecture, or new detailed design probably mandates the redevelopment of performance evaluation systems. If your performance evaluation is not in concert with the requirements of the jobs and the link of architecture to business strategy, then the performance evaluation is ultimately driving skills, competencies, or behaviors that are not in support of business objectives. In conducting the people assessment, it is helpful to look into the reward program mission statement (as developed with the Reward Architecture) and define what it is that you are trying to accomplish through the delivery of base pay.

Performance is an overused axiom. Ultimately, you must ask if you are really paying through base pay for performance or if you're paying for the application of compensable factors that may include knowledge, skills, or abilities (e.g., the ability to problem-solve or the application of specific skills and competencies). Base pay is fixed compensation and therefore a fixed cost to your company; use it in the same way that you would use any other fixed cost for a permanent process improvement. If, therefore, an employee were to accrue some human capital or some knowledge or process improvement that can be amortized over an extended period of years, that would be an appropriate use of increased fixed-wage costs. If, on the other hand, an employee applies that knowledge or skill in a single year to generate a single outcome, event, or result, that would more than likely be compensated for in a variable way. It would provide a one-time or variable product and therefore yield a variable cost.

Think of an employee's career as a production process. If you were to make a permanent improvement in a production process, you would yield a permanent increase in productivity over an extended period of time. If an employee therefore were to reeducate, retool, and reskill, that would provide a permanent process improvement. If, however, you just run the production line harder and in one particular year yield a greater throughput, the organization has not achieved a permanent process improvement. The organization may have achieved a one-year result and would realize a one-year payout, but in fact it may not have achieved a long-term, sustainable process improvement. If an employee were to work harder and apply better skills or competencies in a more thorough way in a particular year, then this should result in single-year payout in variable pay, but not an increase in fixed compensation.

## ATOMIC CAREER PATHS

A science and research–based government agency, experiencing significant turnover and lack of commitment by its workforce, sought—as many clients do initially and incorrectly—to increase the general compensation of its employees. Through the diagnostic phase, which included focus groups of scientists, it became clear that the driver of turnover was the lack of career advancement. The solution was not directly compensation related, although elements of the ultimate design worked to improve the overall competitiveness of the employees.

Keeping people at the agency was a matter of designing interesting jobs and careers. Accordingly, the solution was to improve the mechanics of making short- and long-term career decisions. The program was founded on a knowledge-based job analysis program. This design demonstrated both the job requirements and training necessary for a particular career. Then a process was developed to publicize opportunities and demonstrate both the requirements and the requisite learning for each position. This was job posting with two significant twists: First, as jobs were posted, employees could pick and choose based on whether that job got them the additional competency they required for the position they ultimately wanted, or it was the next rung on the ladder, or both. The second difference was that projects were also posted electronically with the associated knowledge to be gained, both technical and nontechnical (e.g., project management, presentation skills). Employees could bid on various aspects of the project in order to both contribute and learn the skill, knowledge, or competency required.

The results were both expected and unexpected. As expected, turnover went down. What was unusual, however, was that employees volunteered for extra work (in the form of the posted projects) in order to acquire skills and knowledge. The staffing problems evaporated, and while people did get raises associated with more frequent promotion, a general wage increase was deemed unnecessary. People wanted to learn more and wanted some control over that learning, much like they had enjoyed in a university setting. The effort became known as "self-directed learning and career pathing," or SDLCP; it allowed employees to influence their individual human capital and, accordingly, the value they delivered. The reward cost the company less than a traditional compensation program enhancement and generated additional savings in staffing.

## Delivering Pay

Once you have assessed jobs and people, you must deliver pay to bridge the gap between the organization's expectations and the employee's compensation. If you've come this far, you've got a collection of bands or grades, each with a set of jobs that are valued within the organization in a like fashion. You have defined the value of the work, the compensable factors, and the requirements you have placed on your employees to demonstrate that they meet job requirements. Therefore, if you take the collective set of jobs within each grade level and the midpoint or control point of those grade levels, you could ultimately define the "optimum payroll." With a fully competent, satisfactorily performing workforce, the payroll at that point should be equal to the number of people in each band or grade *times* the midpoint for each one of those band or grade levels.

By integrating compensable factors into the determination of base pay, the organization can ensure that it is rewarding what is valued. For example, if you are going to value certain skills and competencies, you may assess the organization's attainment of those skills and competencies collectively in the course of a year. So rather than use a traditional merit budget, which may reward based on how other organizations are delivering base pay, you would look at how you have advanced the competence of your people, relative to the optimum workforce, and set salary budgets accordingly. If the collective competency of your people has increased by, say, 5 percent, then you would determine that the collective compensation of your employees should also move by 5 percent. The key decision point involves the marketplace and the consideration of the increased cost of labor from year to year. The organization's ability to pay and the movement of people valued against organization compensable factors should be balanced.

In managing salaries, there are ultimately three decisions to be made:

- How are budgets established and maintained?
- What do you consider of value on an ongoing basis?
- How do you manage the incumbent's salary to a stated philosophy considering the unique value she adds?

The traditional approach to establishing and maintaining budgets is top-down, where the organization's management determines the ultimate merit increase budget and flows that down throughout the company. A bottom-up approach, where each line manager budgets an established amount for salary increases, is a second approach. This second approach is more inclusive and allows managers to influence employee compensation in a more direct way.

Whether to use a centralized approach or a decentralized approach to establishing and maintaining a budget is also a design decision. The fit within your organization should determine the methodology that is used. More and more, however, organizations manage to a "buckets o'cash" philosophy. Buckets o'cash implies that each line manager is given a certain dollar value based on the current payroll. Managers can then use those dollars however they think most effective. Line managers, however, should provide some fact-based input to the size of the bucket.

Buckets o'cash may, in fact, reward managers who staff, hire, and/or pay inefficiently. An organization's optimal design is an alternative approach to determining the size of the bucket. Taking current payroll and providing line managers with a specified percentage of that amount can reward for inefficiency. An alternative approach might be to look at your organization's optimum design to determine headcount and market references (or midpoints) and figure optimum cost structure and budget from there. This allows the organization to reward a manager who supervises a department that is understaffed. So, if a manager has fewer people in her department than she is allowed to have, her budget per person will be greater and she will be able to provide each employee with more reward, in percentage terms, than would be possible in an overstaffed department.

When and how you deliver pay to your employees is of critical importance to them. While the traditional means of weekly or biweekly pay-checks and annual assessments work in most organizations, applying creativity or "outside-the-box thinking" may be helpful. Again, look at the competency system. If the techniques at your disposal allow you to assess employee competency on a more frequent basis, then why not deliver pay increases more frequently, too, rather than doing it annually? New employees often have skill assessments at 90- or 180-day incre-ments. If you want to retain this employee, and he has in fact overcome the hurdle of the skill requirement, there's no reason, then, that you shouldn't deliver a pay increase commensurate with the increase in skill at the 90- or 180-day point.

---

### USING REWARD DESIGN AS A DIFFERENTIATOR, BY SCOTT WHITE

The telecom sector grew quickly and was deeply funded with venture capital in the late 1990s. A number of major start-ups converged on the same talent base. With their message of flexibility, innovation, and speed, these new kids on the block were employers of choice compared to the big, bureaucratic phone companies. But how would they gain competitive advantage in the employment market among themselves?

When two of these start-ups faced off in the same Midwestern city, bidding wars for key talent ensued. Determined to win its share of talent, and not compete solely with cash, one firm settled on an innovative reward design to position itself as a more desirable employer while at the same time controlling compensation costs. It adopted a broad-banded structure and market pricing methodology. Both were designed to be responsive and fast, although not neces-sarily painstakingly accurate. These tools were complemented with a simple, but meaningful, scale to assess the market value of each person. The one-page form was adapted for making both starting and annual review compensation decisions.

The message to the market was, "We'll pay you, not your job; you will have greater influence on your own earnings and potential." But unlike many broad banded systems with few internal controls, the individual market value scale gave managers data for managing com-pensation and careers; it also made each incumbent feel comfortable that his compensation was an accurate reflection of both the market and his fit within that market. Knowing when they had a "$60k person in a $75k job," had implications for staffing, development, pay, and performance management.

This reward design allowed the company to differentiate its people processes in two ways: First, it created an attractive image for luring talented people. As the profile of the individual being sought was more entrepreneurial, those people put a premium on being valued as individuals. Second, it balanced the organization's need for structure and flexibility, providing a cost-effective means for managing pay in an open system.

*Scott White is a principal of Buck Consultants and manages its Kansas City Office.*

Every time you consider the base or fixed pay of each of your employees, it gives you the opportunity to reassess what you value in the organization. If fixed pay is determined by the market and, again, the application of specific skills, competencies, or knowledge areas, then you must assess people against those values. Many organizations are working to separate the performance evaluation from the merit increase. Performance evaluation allows the manager to sit down with an employee and, in a very candid way, assess how she applied his skills, competencies, and compensable factors to his work during a given period of time. People assessment allows the company to say, "This is how we value your job, and here is how you are assessed in relation to those values." So whereas the organization may desire specific outcomes, it also values specific competencies or skills within a job and assesses those values to the market.

Finally, you have to determine the competitive "location" of an individual's compensation. This is a matter of managing the individual's pay around the state philosophy considering the individual's skills, experiences, performance, and so on. Options exist in the form of a control point, reference point, zone within a band, or some other form of midpoint or market assessment.

The need for administration never disappears, and with base pay design there are certain requirements that you must consider. These requirements predominantly fall under the headings of legal compliance and infrastructure, which should be kept in mind throughout the design process:

- *Legal Compliance.* There are mandates that you apply specific discrimination testing and that you meet the requirements of specific laws, including the Equal Pay Act and the Fair Labor Standards Act. During the design process, be sure to have all plans reviewed and evaluated by corporate counsel. Be certain to look at your organization's infrastructure during the process, too.

- *Infrastructure.* While often overlooked, infrastructure is also vital because an organization cannot function and manage its base pay programs if it does not possess the HRIS and HR personnel necessary to manage those processes. While you may be limiting yourself significantly if you allow infrastructure to drive plan design, you are putting yourself way behind the time and delivery curve if you don't consider it as you design your plan.

### Administration

The design team needs to be mindful of the requirements its design places on company resources. Specifically, the needs for information technology and people support are potential limitations on design. Ensure that the need for information and assistance can be satisfied.

## Variable Rewards Design Principles

Short-term rewards are those that come during any period of a year or less. Long-term plans measure periods longer than a year. Variable rewards, as their name implies, vary from one period to the next. A favorite definition for variable pay is attributable to Cotton Tyler of BASF in Freeport, Texas. He defines variable pay as follows: "One month you make your truck payment; one month you don't." Variable rewards are either:

- Incentives that have predefined criteria that yield a set payout (e.g., do X, get Y)
- Bonuses that are cash payments determined after-the-fact

Regardless of which category you are designing, the following reward concepts (see also Figure 6-8) should serve as a guideline. Those concepts are:

1. Eligibility (who)
2. Goals (what and how)
3. Line of sight (where)

Figure 6-8. Short-term variable design principles.

| Design Principle | Program Aspect | Definition |
|---|---|---|
| Eligibility (Who) | Participation | • The identification of which employees in the workforce will participate |
| Goals (What & How) | Goal Choice | • The selection of the goals to be included in the variable reward plan |
| | Goal Measurement | • How the goal will be measured for plan purposes |
| Line of Sight (Where) | Organizational Level of Measure and Goal Setting | • The level within the organization where goals will be determined and measured |
| | Sphere of Influence | • The groups/individuals in the incentive plan and their level of responsibility |
| Performance and Payout Relationship (Why) | Leverage/Share Ratio | • The ratio of performance and variable rewards throughout the performance range |
| Amount (How Much) | Funding | • The financial mechanism used to determine the total amount of variable reward paid |
| | Threshold | • The minimum level of performance where the variable rewards will be earned |
| | Target | • The expected performance for the normal amount of rewards to be earned |
| | Maximum | • The performance point where no more variable rewards will be earned regardless of performance |
| | Distribution | • The method to determine individual rewards |
| Timing (When) | Length of Performance Period | • The calendar period in which the performance periods are measured |
| | Frequency of Payout | • The calendar period in which the variable plan payouts are made |
| Administration (How) | Responsibility | • Who will be responsible for plan administration and their level of authority |
| | Conditions | • The events that will be determined within the administration |

4. Performance and payout relationship (why)
5. Amount (how much)
6. Timing (when)
7. Administration (how)

## Eligibility (Who)

Eligibility determines who's in and who's out. A starting point here is to define "all and only." That is, all of the employees in the organization who can impact on the end result that the organization is attempting to achieve and only those who can impact that result. "All and only" can be used to define variable pay eligibility broadly across the organization or within specific populations—for example, as team, function, or business unit–based pay.

It is also important to consider employees' eligibility in other plans and whether these plans are additive or exclusionary. For example, if you're developing a plan at a plant, you want to include everyone who might have impact on that facility's result. However, the management in that facility may already be in a variable pay plan that is linked to organization results. Consider allowing these plans to be additive or simply allow the management to have the best of each plan. The best-of-each option allows the eligible employees to receive the higher of the two plan awards only. As such, management, or any population in dual plans, would receive the cumulative effect without receiving the additive effect of the compensation.

If your environment is unionized, the eligibility question becomes even more complicated. On the one hand, eligibility should probably be extended to everyone who has impact on the outcome you are driving toward (remember, all and only). If that means negotiated union organizations, then they, too, should be included. The more typical position, however, is to implement the plan, allow it to become operational, and then use it as a negotiating point with the union at the next time of negotiation.

Be careful to consider, again, all those employees and employee groups that have an effect on the desired outcomes. Let's consider, for example, compensation plans for the sales force. Wouldn't a sales support staff or technical staff have an effect on a salesperson's ability to close a deal? In considering these supportive populations, don't forget where and how they affect the intended population's ability to get results.

Another example is in the instance of rewarding project teams or using team-based incentives. One often hears of individuals within a function who are left behind to do the work of employees who are taken from the department to serve on a special project. Those special project employees are eligible to receive incentives or project-based bonuses. But what about the employees who pick up the slack? They're doing more work but not receiving the benefit of serving on the team or the team-based incentive. Here, too, is an opportunity to recognize all of the employees who have some effect on the desired outcome. And while cash or a project-based incentive may not be the tool to extend to those individuals who are left to pick up the slack, you often can devise some tool or technique to deliver some value back to them. Just don't forget them.

## Goals (What and How)

There's an old total quality management (TQM) adage that says you get what you measure. As a compensation executive you don't get what you measure, you get what you pay for. Accordingly, plan measurement, and what organizational measures are linked to compensation systems, is by far the most important principle to be defined. Get this right or your plan will drive and pay for the wrong behaviors and outcomes. You'll get what you're paying for, but what you are paying for may be the wrong things. That is because plan measures translate objectives into actionable behaviors. This principal goal choice and number of goals is best understood by defining what to measure and how to measure it.

Goal Choice   Typically, in defining what to measure, you must first assess the forms of measurement that are correct for the organization. If you consider the work of Robert Kaplan and David Norton, those forms of measurement may be defined along the balanced scorecard continuum and grouped into financial, operational, customer, and "learn and grow" perspectives. Other forms of measurement are often defined based on key business strategy goals. Staying with the balanced scorecard example, the forms of measurement can further be refined into categories of measurement by asking specific subject matter experts (SMEs) what the important categories of practices are that must be accomplished, as defined by their function.

An example is typically found in managerial reporting. If you begin with the assumption that most organizations have some level of sophistication in terms of financial and operational reporting, then managerial and financial reports provide a good glimpse of what is important to a company from a financial perspective. Put it this way: If I walk into your plant and I say to the plant manager, "How you doin'?" And he responds, "We're doing good." I would say, "How do you know that?" In other words, how does any manager know whether he's doing good, bad, up/down, profitable/unprofitable? Analyzing managerial reports and assessing what is important to management and leadership defines the categories of measurement. Ultimately, of course, you have to decide how you can actually do the measurement and determine the specific metrics to be used to evaluate organizational success. Keep track of the number of measures you are using, too. Here's a rule of thumb regarding measures:

- One is focused.
- Two is company.
- Three is a crowd.
- Four is overcrowded.
- Five is the absolute max.

Here is a quick way to test the dilutive effects of having too many measures. Generally, individual incentive opportunity is expressed as a percent of base pay. Divide that percent by the number of measures and you see that the awards get small quickly. As my high school English teacher used to say, "less is more."

Goal Setting/Measurement    Once you've determined the metrics, establish your goals as defined by target minimums and maximums. Establishing goals is much like driving a car: in addition to looking out the windshield you need to check the side-view and rear-view mirrors. Looking forward, you can set goals based on budgets or business plans, using target returns.

If you look in the rear-view mirror, then you are looking back; this is tantamount to setting goals based on beating last year's actual perform-ance. Historical performance is a good indicator of the potential future of any investment. Accordingly, you can look at five- and ten-year per-formance, particularly in seasonal or cyclical businesses, to assess the potential outcomes you might yield from some investments. However, avoid setting goals for incentives purely based on historical measures, as this, again, would be like driving your car and only looking in the rear-view mirror.

When driving a car, you not only want to look out the windshield and the rear-view mirrors, you want to look side-to-side. Looking out of your side windows is analogous a look-around incentive plan. Looking around allows you to set your benchmarks based on "the competition." Competition, of course, can be a peer group, another set of like companies, or benchmarks established within your own company (e.g., other manufacturing facilities).

### Line of Sight (Where)

Even the best-designed, most technically accurate incentive compensation programs will be totally ineffective if the eligible population does not believe that it can influence the outcome. Establishing this sphere of influence, or line of sight, as it is often called, is an important piece of the plan design process.

Two exercises that can help in establishing line of sight are the value tree and the learning map:

- *Value Tree.* The value tree quantitatively breaks down key measures into the critical performance drivers that are required by an organization to meet those performance measures. It further takes these drivers and assesses the specific core and collective competencies that the organization members must exhibit to meet them.

- *Learning Map.* The learning map then takes those core competencies and breaks them down into specific behaviors, which are defined on a functional level to further assess how individual employees can best assess plan outcomes.

Organizational Level of Measure    The previous sections have allowed you to define who is going to be eligible in your company for specific programs and what goals and measures will be used. Now you must determine at what level within the organization you are going to conduct the measurements.

The first step is determining the appropriate organizational levels within your company, as well as the various employee constituencies and how they might be defined through eligible populations.

"Communists and cowboys" is a tool (see Figure 6-9) for determining how much of any employee's variable pay or incentive is determined by specific organizational units or levels. The closer employees are to the organizational level of measure, the more they are all in this together (communists); conversely, as you move farther to the individualist side of measure, everyone becomes cowboys. When using this kind of exercise, it is not unusual to find that the closer the employee is to the main work

Figure 6-9. Organizational level of measure: communists and cowboys example.

| | Organizational Level of Measure | | | | |
| | Organization | Group/Division | Team | Employee | Total |
|---|---|---|---|---|---|
| Top Management | 60% | 40% | N/A | N/A | 100% |
| Middle Management | 40% | 30% | 30% | N/A | 100% |
| Professional | 20% | 30% | 30% | 20% | 100% |
| Nonexempt | N/A | 20% | 30% | 50% | 100% |

"Communists"          versus          "Cowboys"

stream of the organization, the more likely he is to have considerable portions of his variable pay determined by his performance and that of the team or business unit. Whereas the closer an employee is to the strategic decision making within an organization, the more likely she may be to have her performance reward determined by the organization as a whole, or by specific units within that organization.

Sphere of Influence   Ability to influence is not quite as easy to measure. It requires a true examination of the organization and how various employee groups, jobs, or functions influence the desired outcomes. For example, consider the value chain analysis exercise completed in Chapter 5, Figure 5-4 (also provided on CD-ROM page 21 of 99). If the value chain allows us to assess how various functions, and employees within those functions, add value to products, services, and customers, it provides a reasonable framework for defining how various populations of employees impact desired outcomes.

### Performance and Payout Relationship (Why)

The performance and payout relationship allows the plan designer to assess how the dollars generated by success in accomplishing the plan goals are shared between the company and the eligible employees. It is used to create the total bonus pool. The performance and payout relationship can most simply be developed as a line that depicts how various levels of performance on the X axis yield various levels of payout on the Y axis (see Figure 6-10). The share ratio, or the steepness of the line, determines how much of the financial fund (as generated from performance against the plan) is given to the employees and how much is retained by the company.

As a rule of thumb, the closer the employee is to her ability to influence the plan outcomes, the lower the required share ratio. So, for example, if there is a very close or tight sphere of influence, there is less of a need to create a higher or more leveraged share ratio. If, however, an employee feels that he has limited ability to influence the specific outcomes, then you want to share more of that outcome to encourage the employee to do more, even though more might be perceived as quite little.

Another consideration in determining share ratio is the difficulty of the objective. Many organizations, by manner of corporate culture or policy, establish their objectives as stretch or far-reach objectives. If that is the case in your company, then the share ratio may need to be increased to allow an employee to say, "Okay, so this is a stretch, but if I get there, I get a

Figure 6–10. Performance and payout relationships.

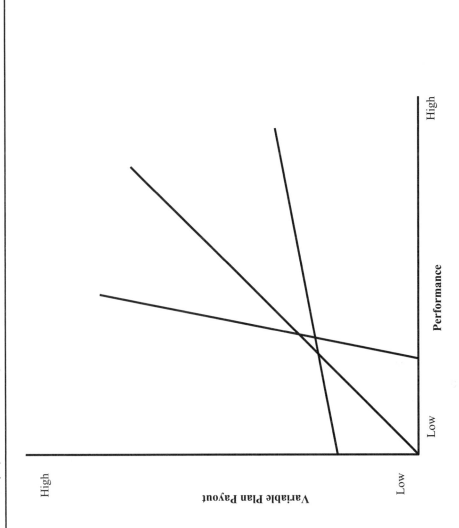

bigger carrot." The eligible population and its participation level are a good place to start, then, in assessing the share ratio. The organization can then decide (based on the cost of the payout) what types of revenues it needs to generate in excess of the need to pay in order to make this a viable return on investment. If you link participation level to the market and market competitive total cash compensation, the organization can then go backward from total cash compensation through eligibility through participation to share ratio. Finally, it is important to understand your management's willingness to share. Different cultures and organizations have different beliefs in how a share should be allocated.

### Amount (How Much)

Generally the key considerations for this design principle are funding, threshold incentive reward, target incentive reward, maximum incentive reward, and distribution. All five of these aspects can have significant impact on plan design since they are at the core of issues important to all key stakeholders. These issues are, of course, particularly important to the owners and the employees.

Funding    While funding seems like a very technical aspect of plan design, there are only three sources to funding:

- Self-funding
- Funding through foregone base pay increases
- Allocating of budget dollars

In self-funding, the most popular form of plan design, the pool of dollars to be allocated is generated by the creation of additional income—what you might call "excess income"—through the overachievement of financial or operational objectives. While certainly there is no such thing as excess income, you can consider the amount of income that exceeds management's expectation by defining the reasonable or required rate of return on a corporate investment and then asking the question, "If we achieve that rate of return or beyond, how much of that above-and-beyond revenue are we prepared to share with our employees?"

Foregoing base pay increases provides a second source of funding. First, however, you must define pay at risk. Pay at risk is any compensation that is variable. If you look at the total cash compensation equation (base pay plus variable pay), you can define pay at risk as any compensation below market-based pay that is moved into the variable side of an employee's total cash compensation equation. For example, if an employee could earn a $20,000 base salary, that's the market rate for him as a fully competent and satisfactory performer. In this particular employee's case, suppose you are going to pay him $19,000 and give him an opportunity for a 10 percent bonus. This makes the target total cash compensation $20,900. Here the employee has $1,000 at risk and an opportunity to earn an additional $900, or 4.5 percent above market total cash for a person in a similar position. Foregone base pay increases are, then, a method of diverting dollars from fixed costs to variable costs, as this can be done with either the entire amount of the base pay budget for a given year (or years) or some portion of an annual, merit, or base pay amount.

Budget allocation is the third way of funding a variable compensation program. This methodology, although not frequently used, can be seen as simply stating a cost of doing business. If an organization uses the market to assess its fixed compensation position, it is essentially saying, "In this market, for these employees, this is the cost of doing business. We have to offer this level of pay to get this level of employee." In shifting one's thinking from base pay position to a total cash compensation position, the same argument can be held. Clearly, if you are going to compensate at a given market position in total cash compensation, then that becomes a cost of doing business and a necessary budget item. Most practitioners are doubtful about this point, yet if you think about what you're doing currently in your variable compensation programs, maybe only in a limited population, it's true. Typically, organizations pay some form of variable compensation to their senior managers. If this compensation is budgeted as a target percentage of base pay and is not determined by a self-funding formula linked directly to a financial or operational objective, then essentially what your organization has done is budgeted this compensation over the years. This, therefore, is a budget allocation or "a cost of doing business."

In addition to the source of funding, a funding formula must also be established. Funding formulas come in a variety of types; the best type is dependent on your organization, the measures you've chosen, and the method of communication that is going to be used. Funding formulas may be algebraic, tabular, or graphic. A method called the combined performance metric (CPM) is an example of a funding formula. This method assesses performance on each critical axis of organizational level—that could be organizational performance, unit performance, team performance, or, again, even employee performance. By assessing each of these and weighting them accordingly (by the weighting assigned each employee), employees not only get a consolidated picture of performance at each level, they also get a reward that is weighted specifically for them or other employees at that level.

---

### WHAT FITS TODAY MAY NOT FIT TOMORROW

There is no such thing as a best practice. A practice is only best if it works best for you. But there is a matter of fit between the basic tenets of a design and your business. Here's an example:

The CEO of a financial services organization knew something was wrong with his program, he just didn't know what. It turns out that he had a rather simple and well-designed incentive compensation plan, with just one problem.

The plan was designed by someone who usually dealt with the industrial sector, so the designer had developed an approach that was distinctly industrial, based on a profit-sharing concept. In the industrial-products industry, the variability of profit is nowhere near the degree associated with the mutual fund industry. When the plans were originally designed, the assets under management were approximately $3 billion to $5 billion. It was determined that the mutual fund managers would share in the profits above a reasonable rate of return to the parent organization. As luck or fate would have it, the mutual fund managers were very successful and new money to invest gushed in. The assets under management ballooned to $50 billion. The difference between incentive plan design in the industrial-products and financial fund management industry became clear to everyone. The difference was leverage. The incentive plan payments (uncapped) ballooned to $30 million rapidly. Corporate management became concerned, justly. The plan paid an increasing percentage of an index (dollar profits) without a cap or a factor for size.

Although this is a story about lack of fit, the design flaws became apparent only when the fund under management grew so significantly. Even the "wrong" design worked at the time it was designed; the growth of the fund managers' coffers caused the dramatic inequity. The moral of the story is: Name and date your plans, and continue to periodically reevaluate them for fit.

**Threshold Incentive Reward**   The threshold of a variable reward plan is a function of many issues, including the degree to which the employee collects fixed base cash rewards. If the employee has little or no fixed compensation (typically sales and executive personnel), then the threshold for the variable compensation should be low relative to the target performance. If the fixed base cash reward is high, then the threshold where variable pay plans begin can and should be higher or close to the target level of performance. The message that should be inferred from the level of the threshold is the degree to which an employee is already compensated for her performance in her fixed base compensation.

**Target Incentive Reward**   The target variable reward is normally directly equal to the target required performance on the selected goals. This presumes that goals were set with sufficient knowledge to incorporate factors such as the overall economy, competitors' actions, and internal company contributing factors (e.g., production, distribution, marketing).

**Maximum Incentive Reward**   Variable compensation plans have always created the need to take a position on the issue of "When is enough too much?" The employees within a plan can rarely understand the logic behind a maximum "cap," as it is called in the profession. Plan designers and administrators always feel that caps tend to be necessary to ensure that a "windfall" amount is not paid out for performance on goals that are not the result of employees' direct efforts. Always consider the messages. (See the "To Cap or Not to Cap?" sidebar.)

**Distribution**   Award distribution is the method of paying individual awards, and it is best determined by your desired key messages. You can distribute the funds in the pool by:

> ### To Cap or Not to Cap?
>
> . . . That is the question and often the debate. Consider the message of a cap: Regardless of how well this organization performs (or how hard everyone in it works), this is the most you can possibly earn. Organizations will typically try to avoid a cap, unless it's absolutely necessary to protect themselves. This is a particularly good idea in a sales organization.
>
> But consider the experience of one product development–oriented organization. The commercial viability of its patents was of paramount importance. Accordingly, it created a variable pay plan that compensated the developer over a period of years on the profitability of any product. It put a cap of $1 million on that earnings opportunity! The message here was clear: "You can earn a million dollars for your efforts here."

- Equal dollar amounts for each eligible employee
- Equal percentages of either base pay or midpoint
- Some combination of the two methods

In determining the method for distribution, consider the extent to which base pay is a proxy for the value contributed in accomplishing the variable plans goals. Base pay, if done accurately, represents any job's value to the organization. If you are prepared to pay a certain position $100,000 and another position $20,000, you've made a statement, as an organization, that the value placed on that one position is greater than the value placed on the other. If, in fact, that value translates to results on the variable pay measures, then it is reasonable to pay the award based on an equal percentage or some other percentage of base pay or some proxy (e.g., a midpoint). If, however, everyone contributes equally, regardless of position within the organization, then a more likely distribution of rewards is based on an equal dollar amount for all participants within various populations.

## Timing (When)

The timing of reward payout is of critical importance to the recipient of the reward and is a function of the plan's key message. Figure 6-11 is a useful index for determining the timing of plan payout. A standard axiom, of course, is to pay as close to the event as possible. In terms of spot awards or bonuses, this is appropriate. In incentive pay design it is often impractical and sometimes even inappropriate. If, for example, your business is seasonal or cyclical, it is more important to stress the need for payment over a measurement period than the proviso of immediate recognition for specific events or actions.

## Administration

Virtually anything can be designed on the drawing board; it's important to be able to build it. Within this context, the design team needs to be cognizant of the company's ability to make the plan operate. Team members must consider:

- The human resources information systems capabilities to ensure that incumbent-level data is available and can be managed
- Human resources people capability to manage plan information

Figure 6-11.  Distribution timing.

| | Measurement Period* | | |
|---|---|---|---|
| **Payout Period** | **Monthly/Quarterly** | **Annually** | **Long-Term** |
| **Monthly/ Quarterly** | • Extremely short-term<br>• Yields immediate gratification<br>• Maintain a reserve fund | • Drawn against annual target<br>• Atypical, except in sales force<br>• Maintain a reserve fund | N/A |
| **Annually** | • Yields increased communication about results<br>• Very typical | • Business outcomes follow "standard" cycle<br>• Most common approach | • Used for overlapping periods<br>• Used for executives only |
| **Long-Term** | • Retention tool | • Retention tool | • Strategic outcomes only<br>• Typically for senior executives |

*The measurement period and timing of the award distributions send a key message.

- How information about measures and performance will be collected, organized, and evaluated
- How award decisions will be either centralized or decentralized
- The manner in which decisions about individual awards will be made and how those awards will be paid

## Long-Term Incentive Plans

Compensation professionals label any program that measures in periods of a year or less as short-term. The impact of shortening that term to something less than a year can clearly drive behaviors that will yield results in only a very specific period of time, such as a month or a quarter. As the financial and business communities measure on an annual basis and look at "an ongoing concern" as a viable business over the long-term, it can be dangerous to break down measures any finer than annually. In fact, one of the key advantages to the balance between short-term and long-term pay is to keep employees from thinking about outcomes in any period of a year and sacrificing long-term sustainable advantage. Again, driving metrics more frequently than annually can be dangerous unless the situation clearly dictates.

Long-term incentive plans are those reward plans that pay employees rewards for accomplishing goals and objectives that are longer than one year. Historically the long-term incentive plans were limited to executive groups. In the most recent decades the plans have seen extensive increases in eligible employees. Many organizations now provide long-term incentive plans to all employees.

There are many reasons to introduce long-term incentive plans to an organization's reward strategy mix. The most important reason is still, however, employee and organization goal alignment. To the extent that the employees reward program is dominated by rewards that are received for performance against short-term goals, the organization places its long-term viability at risk. The correct mix between short-term and long-term reward programs is one of the most difficult tasks for the organization to achieve effectively.

Long-term incentive plans can be extremely effective at recruitment retention and motivation. In addition, some long-term incentive plans can create tax benefits that are not available in the typical short-term cash incentive plans.

Long-term incentive plans can be broken down into three major types:

1. *Equity Plans.* Such plans provide the employee with rewards in the form of stock options, restricted stock grants, or stock purchase plans. Over the long term, these types of plans have been very successful in aligning the interests of employees with shareholders. Many stories exist that directly show a much greater concern over key drivers of stock price when employees own substantial amounts of stock. Designers must bear in mind that these plans are oriented to the long term; today's short-term downturn, while putting pressure on these plans, is no reason to stay the course of a strategy that includes them.

2. *Phantom Equity Plans.* These are cash bonus plans that use the price of the company's stock as an index with which to measure the performance of the organization. Phantom plans are simple to design and easy to understand, but have drawbacks for both the employee and the owner/shareholders. Generally the employees do not have voting rights and do not receive dividends, and the company receives no special tax advantages.

3. *Performance (Cash) Unit Plans.* As variable reward plans, they have the same characteristics as short-term cash plans but are for performance periods that are longer than one year—usually two to five years. Performance unit plans have the same design principles as the short-term variable plans (with the exception of administration). These include eligibility, goals, performance and payout relationship, line of sight, amount, and timing (see Figure 6-12).

According to a recent survey by iQuantic Buck, the following equity program practices prevail: First, certain historical trends continue. Most notably, participation in equity programs across executive, middle management, and nonexempt populations continues to rise. Moreover, industry still matters. Equity programs continue to be prevalent in some industries but not others. Second, certain historical trends are changing. Whereas options used to be delivered unilaterally to employees at a specified organizational level, recent data demonstrate that value creators are being identified and rewarded with options. This surgical approach is being deployed regardless of level. Finally, the market downturn has forced organizations to redouble their efforts to communicate equity as a long-term reward.[2]

Many organizations use combinations of plans to recruit, motivate, and retain employees. As always, each of the plan alternatives communicates a message to employees and other key stakeholders. All the spe-

Figure 6–12. Long-term variable design principles.

| Specific Reward Concept | Program Aspect | Definition |
| --- | --- | --- |
| Eligibility (Who) | Participation | • Identification of which employees in the workforce will participate |
| Goals (What) | Performance Measurements | • The selection and measurement of the goals of the long-term plan |
| Performance and Payout Relationship (Why) | Leverage Between Performance Measures and Payout | • The ratio of performance and variable rewards throughout the performance range and time period |
| Line of Sight (Where) | Organization Goals and Employee Accountability | • The goals and who within the organization is responsible for them |
| Amount (How Much) | Funding and Distribution<br>Threshold<br>Target<br>Maximum | • The overall funding of the plan and the method for individual award determination<br>• The least, target, and maximum amounts paid out from the plans |
| Timing (When) | Length of Performance Period<br><br>Frequency of Payout | • The calendar period for the long-term plan performance measurement<br>• The calendar period in which the plan's payouts are made to individuals |

cific reward concepts communicate loads of information to all stake-holders.

## Indirect Compensation Design Principles

The key strategic issues when dealing with the benefit component of Total Rewards Strategy are eligibility, participation, value delivered, funding (and cost), timing, distribution, and administration. These key issues are applied individually and in total to each benefit plan, and to all the benefits in total. The overall benefits program can be broken into key program groupings consisting of plans that have similar objectives. These major groupings are:

1. *Income Replacement Programs.* These benefit plans are the ones designed to replace an employee's income when he cannot work due to an illness or accident. A complete system of plans provides replacement for an employee's income if he or she is injured while at work or at home for short or long (up to age 65) periods. This grouping of benefit plans includes the following:

- *Sick Pay.* These are the individual sick days that are accumulated for an employee to use at his discretion when he suffers an illness that makes it inappropriate to be at work. Depending on the employee group, most employers provide a small number of paid sick days off (oftentimes based upon an employee's seniority) when an employee cannot or should not work.

- *Workers' Compensation.* These benefit plans provide for an employee to receive a portion of her income when she is injured while at work. Generally this benefit is statutory and paid by the company. Benefits can last up to age 65.

- *Short-Term Disability.* These benefit plans provide for an employee when he cannot work because of a non-work-related injury. These plans generally pay benefits up to twenty-six weeks.

- *Long-Term Disability.* These benefit plans provide for an employee when she cannot work because of an injury or illness as a result of non-work-related illness. These plans generally pay benefits from a minimum of twenty-six weeks to a maximum of age 65.

2. *Income Protection Programs.* These benefit plans are designed to protect an employee's income from unforeseen expenses, which would be difficult or impossible to save for as an individual.

3. *Future Financial Security Programs.* These benefit plans are designed to provide for the future financial security of the employee and her family. They are otherwise known as retirement programs.

4. *Pay for Time Not Worked.* These benefits plans are designed to provide for holidays, vacations, and sabbaticals; they give the employee a chance to enjoy the fruits of his labor.

---

### BREAKING DOWN THE ENTITLEMENT MENTALITY WITH PERFORMANCE-BASED BENEFIT PLANS, BY HOWARD FINE

Are benefits a form of compensation, or are they solely programs for managing employee risk and pooling purchasing power? One client took the position that making benefits a component of Total Rewards, and allowing them to vary with company performance, was instrumental in breaking down its entitlement culture and replacing it with a pay-for-performance orientation. It further believed that the change strengthened the concept of Total Rewards within its culture as employees became more aware of the value of the compensation and benefit offerings.

To achieve the advantages of increased awareness and alignment with company performance, the company introduced a profit component that flowed through specific benefit plans and reinforced the link between company performance and individual compensation. Under this new program, company profitability determined the level of a companywide cash incentive, the level of the match in the 401(k) plan, and *the level of credits awarded to each employee in the flexible benefits plan.* These benefits credits could be used for purchasing benefits or taken in cash. Linking the full suite of benefits to profitability and treating benefits as a part of its total rewards program effectively aligned employees' interests with those of the company.

*Howard Fine is a managing director with Buck Consultants.*

---

There are many design considerations when structuring the overall and individual plan designs for your organization. When it comes to income replacement plans, statutory requirements are the threshold. These requirements vary by country, state, and local government entities. Many are "experience rated" and have few design degrees of freedom. There may be more freedom to design the funding of the plans than there is to design the benefits themselves. After statutory benefit requirements are resolved, there is substantial room to design an effective set of individual plans that can give an employer a competitive advantage (often with fewer costs).

The second group of benefits, the income protection benefits programs, have undergone the most severe restructuring of any corporate expense related to employees in the last fifty years. Most companies have gone through the process of designing flexible benefits programs, including managed care, for the purpose of reducing costs and increasing the perceived value of the program by employees. These programs have been reasonably successful.

The third group of benefits programs that falls into the standard pile of programs is the retirement program. This three-headed program is a combination of company contributions, employee contributions, and government contributions (which are really employee and company contributions, too). The company program usually consists of either a defined benefit plan and/or a defined contribution plan. Both have similar objectives but work quite differently. The *defined benefit program* sets the benefit as a specific function of the individual's pay and/or years of seniority. This program requires a determination of funding (usually provided by an actuary) necessary to deliver the benefit at the individual's retirement date. The *defined contribution plan* is a plan that simply provides a specific contribution to an individual's retirement savings account. Generally there are individual and company contributions. There is also usually a range of available investment funds from which to choose. The government contribution to this family of future financial security benefits is Social Security. Social Security benefits are contributed to by both the company and the individual.

These programs are very expensive and have mixed value at the employee level. For example, it is difficult to get younger employees to be interested in Social Security (except for the wage deductions, which seem unreasonable). Older employees value retirement programs that are developed to help them fund retirement. The best way to think through the strategy of retirement program design is to emphasize the key stages of life and determine the degree to which the company feels it appropriate and/or good business to assist the employee in funding those life events. They include, but are not limited to, the purchase of a primary residence, major education goals (e.g., the tuition to send children to school), and the retirement of the employee.

By most estimates a full thirty- or forty-year career of savings is not required to fund a retirement program that replaces 60 percent to 80 percent of preretirement income. With respect to the three strategic dimensions of reward strategy design (money, mix, and messages), future financial security benefits programs will provide a critical battleground for the next twenty years. There is no individual-company control of the Social Security component. The money is going to continue to be determined by the politics of the "third rail" (i.e., the politician who touches it will get electrocuted). The mix of the Social Security plan itself is predetermined in most ways (e.g., the funding of the program is already split fifty-fifty between the employer and employee). And the messages are direct and clear: This program is for subsistence living and serves as a low-level security blanket. As the future rolls along, the portion derived from the company-designed system will likely become more and more significant to the overall future financial security program. Of the various benefit program groups, the future financial security program is also the most highly regulated and, in most cases, the most difficult to make commitments to employees about, since those commitments are expensive to fund. With all that said, it may be best to begin design work on this group of programs first.

Benefit plan design initiatives should challenge historical benefit plan design principles. In the past, key company officials designed benefit plans based on what they believed was in the best interests of the employees and the company. The assumption that the design experts could create the best benefits for a population of employees went unquestioned for a significant period of time. In fairness to these designers, the workforce they designed for was the workforce of *Ozzie and Harriet*: a male employee with a non-working spouse and 2.3 children, who was going to spend thirty years with the organization. Today that concept seems strange, but it did make for simple plan design. Then the workforce was homogeneous. (Or thought to be!) Today the workforce is anything but homogeneous. It is this diversity that has brought to the fore the creation of flexible benefits. And this trend is expected to continue.

The best way to begin the development of the benefits portion of the Total Rewards Strategy is to dissect the current workforce and determine whether it is the workforce for the company's future. If the workforce needs to change in some particular ways, such as increasing the number of technologically adept employees, increasing the global orientation, or increasing the diversity, then it would be appropriate to design the programs based on the workforce of the future and not on the workforce of today. Once the workforce demographics have been understood, then you can set in motion the same three-prong approach to the process of strategy by:

1. Determining the relative level or "money" to be spent in each benefit group
2. Setting up the mix of the various programs
3. Establishing the key messages

The development of criteria for the selection of the program's main themes should be a direct reflection of the organization's people strategy and the organization capabilities necessary to implement the business strategy. The most effective approach is to initially determine the overall cost of the benefit program (e.g., as a percentage of base salary). Then determine how those costs would best be divided among the key benefit groupings: future financial security, income replacement, income protection, pay for time not worked, work/life benefits, and employee perquisites. The next step is to determine the mix between the major elements and then within the major groupings. The last step is determining the overall messages and various layers of submessages. Each of these steps in the process are taken in conjunction and in full integration with one another. It is this integration that makes the development of a total benefits strategy so challenging. In addition, most organizations have existing benefits programs that were designed under a set of circumstances that no longer exist in either the organization or the workforce in general. The difficulty of developing a successful benefits strategy to support the people and business strategy is extraordinarily complex. It requires a redesign of already existing programs that employees have viewed as entitlements. Because of this sense of entitlement the redesign will be difficult, especially if benefits will be reduced in part or in total. The additional difficulty has to do with determining the costs of a benefit's program. Future financial security benefits have to provide a promise that needs to be paid and funded in the future.

Figure 6-13 is a summary view of the program aspects and definitions of the major benefits programs discussed so far.

## Perquisites

Programs that address specific needs of all or some employees are often called perquisites. Originally these programs were for key members of management. The word itself conjures up images of stretch limousines, drivers, and golf courses. These images are as out of fashion as the "three martini lunch." Certainly there are some corporate executives who still get driven around in stretch limos and play golf at resorts as one of their company perks. However, today's perquisites programs are predominantly

Figure 6–13. Indirect compensation design principles.

| Specific Reward Concept | Program Aspect | Reward Aspect Defined |
|---|---|---|
| Income Replacement (pay for time not worked due to illness) | Sick Pay | • Provided for absence due to short/individual illness |
| | Workers Compensation | • Provided when an injury is incurred while at work |
| | Short-Term Disability | • Provided for injuries incurred while not at work |
| | Long-Term Disability | • Provided for injuries that are long-term (over 26 weeks) |
| | Paternity/Maternity | • Payments for absence due to child born of either spouse |
| Income Protection (benefit payments made to protect the base fixed rewards) | Health & Welfare | • Medical and hospital benefits for illness |
| | Life Insurance | • Payment for income lost due to death of policy holder |
| | Vision | • Payments for reimbursement of vision correction costs |
| | Dental | • Payments for dental correction costs |
| | Dependent Care | • Payments for costs associated with invalid dependents |
| Future Financial Security | Social Security | • Payments made by the employer and the company to fund social retirement and medical programs |
| | Retirement | • Payments made to employees after their working career with the organization that have been funded by either the company or the individual |
| Time Off (pay for time not worked for holidays and rest and relaxation) | Holiday | • Payments for national/state/local celebrations |
| | Vacation | • Payments for periods spent at rest and relaxation |

designed not for prestige but for organizational purpose, risk avoidance, and tax benefits.

Perquisites can be grouped into four general categories: transportation, special facilities, special risks, and work assurance. Figure 6-14 shows the general concepts, program aspects, and definitions for these categories (known as "company cars, clubs, counseling, and contracts"). In each case the perquisites are designed to meet both the specific needs of the organization and of individuals.

Today employees need to be mobile in a world where physical movement is increasingly difficult. An executive once expressed it as "mobile in a hostile environment." Company cars and planes reduce the risk of personal injury and reduce the time required to travel while increasing the effectiveness of those employees who must be on the road. (When large groups travel together, the travel time can be utilized for meetings. Most corporate planes can actually reduce costs when used appropriately.)

In addition to mobility, special facilities are often required or are beneficial to promote either the organization's goals or the individual's health and welfare. These "eating, meeting, or recreational" clubs are normally provided so that individuals can grab a bite to eat while still conducting business, have a place to meet on confidential subjects, or get in some recreational or social-level activity also while conducting business.

Other perquisites fall into the category of special risk protection. These are financial, legal, or psychological benefit/risk reduction programs. Most organizations provide funds for individuals to have counseling when it would be beneficial for the employee or, more important, when it reduces the risks associated with the different life exposures individuals have today. These exposures are substantial for certain employees. The complexity of compensation arrangements, mobility of many executives, and variety of tax laws by state and country increase the risk that an employee will not pay appropriate taxes in all of the locales required. Oftentimes, the employee's failure to do so places a burden on the company, which may be obligated to assist. Financial counseling and tax preparation help can reduce some of this risk. Legal advice reduces the risk that the employee's personal issues may become a distraction for the employee or, worse, a legal issue for the organization.

The work assurance perquisites are an increasing phenomena that are a result of a major trend toward the use of contracts by powerful groups of employees (unions) and powerful employers (executives). Not only are more and more employees covered by contracts, but there are also a greater number of issues that are included within the contracts.

Figure 6–14. Perquisites design principles.

| Specific Reward Concept | Program Aspect | Reward Aspect Defined |
|---|---|---|
| Transportation | Company Cars and Planes | Leasing, reimbursement, or outright use of company- or employer-owned transportation as required by the organization |
| Special Facilities | Clubs (eating, meeting, or recreational) | Reimbursement for meeting and recreational costs incurred for the purpose of furthering the organizational goals |
| Special Risk Protection | Counseling (financial, legal, or psychological) | Funds (provided for the benefit of the employer) that increase the value of the employee or reduce the risk of distraction due to financial or legal issues |
| Work Assurance | Contracts | Benefits provided to employees for certain specified events (e.g., acquisitions, plant closings, death, or disability) |

## PARKING PERQUISITES

While considering a Total Rewards package, the managing director of a company reacted strongly to the request of several senior people for designated parking spaces. He responded quickly that he felt there was no need for designated parking because there were always covered parking spaces close to the building that were available when he arrived at 6:30 A.M. If people wanted specific parking spaces, they should arrive early enough to get them! In this case the message on values was hard to misunderstand or misinterpret: The managing director wanted to reward those who exhibited the behaviors of working the hardest, not those who were employed the longest.

Generally, the key to determining whether and how to design and install perquisite programs is to balance cost, risk, benefit (to the organization and employee), complexity, and communications.

### Other Noncash Rewards

For the purposes of understanding the design principles of this group of programs they have been grouped into the following three concepts: development, recognition, and lifestyle/work balance (see Figure 6-15).

■ *Noncash Rewards: Development Rewards.* These noncash benefits are grouped according to the individual's:

1. Present role
2. Future role within the job family
3. Future role within the organization
4. Future role with other organizations
5. Self-actualization

All organizations require employees to be trained for the specific jobs that they perform. That training can come from the formal education system of high schools, vocational schools, or colleges. In addition, there are thousands if not millions of training and development programs for individuals to choose from. The key design principles to be used for development rewards involve costs and benefits (to employees and organizations).

Figure 6–15. Other noncash rewards design principles.

| Specific Award Concept | Program Aspect | Reward Aspect Defined |
|---|---|---|
| Development | Present role | Investments made to train and develop employees so as to increase their value to the organization |
| | Future role (within job family) | |
| | Future role (within organization) | |
| | Future role (in other organizations) | |
| | Self-actualization | |
| Recognition | Nonfinancial | Rewards for various accomplishments that do not fall under the other reward programs and are generally individual- or team-based |
| | Financial | |
| Lifestyle/Work Balance | Role-based | Accommodations for the individual or organization that increase the effectiveness of each |
| | Organization-based | |
| | Individual-based | |

## TRAINING AND DEVELOPMENT AS A REWARD

Have you ever calculated the cumulative cost of training in your organization? It's virtually certain to be significantly higher than you think and even higher than any estimate you have of the total cost. Consider for a moment the hidden hard costs of training being done at the departmental level—for example, professional seminars, associations, and courses. Add in the soft costs and the final figures are astronomical. At one superregional, independent phone company, managers were amazed to be able to capture nearly $200 million in hard-dollar training costs, and they knew that a lot more cost remained unaccounted for. Like most organizations, training and development had become a hybrid of different programs at corporate, divisional, and team levels.

This firm was the eighth largest training and development organization in the United States. On the one hand, it is easy to say that it's great that the organization spent so much money training and developing its workforce. On the other hand, there were substantial and unique trends in the company that raised the question: "If it was your money, would you spend it this way?" One of the consulting trends was toward holding training programs in southern resort areas during the winter months and in the northeast during the summer months. Many of the same courses could easily be found in local colleges and institutions. In some cases the corporation even offered the training at the work site.

Some department heads were asked questions regarding their approval of the company's training and development program. Their replies indicated that while one part of their approval hinged on the need for training of the subordinate, the other part of their approval indicated the need for unscheduled perquisites for extra hard work or something of a similar nature. In other words, though their approval was about training and development, it was also about extra perquisites for the masses.

This in and of itself was not bad; training should be considered a "good deal" for the recipient. The problem was that the company was paying for a $200 million reward for which it got no credit. That is, the employees benefited from the training they received, but at best they appreciated it—at worst, they considered it a job requirement.

The solution was to codify the process into a formal development rewards plan. The program provided every employee with specified guidelines about what the company would and would not pay for, the amount of time away from work, and so on. Managers were authorized discretionary accounts from which they could enhance an employee's development rewards to demonstrate the company's appreciation for a job well done. The result was the same in terms of spending, and maybe even in results; however, employees appreciated the training more and were more committed to the organization.

- *Noncash Rewards: Recognition Rewards.* These can be financial and nonfinancial in nature. The best recognition award programs reflect the organization's mission, vision, and values, but in addition they complement or directly reinforce the organization's people strategy critical success factors (PSCSFs). In addition, recognition awards are often used as "gap fillers" and "legend makers." They are gap fillers because no matter how thoughtfully the major reward strategy programs are designed, and no matter how many messages are embedded into the general code of fixed cash, variable cash, or benefits, there will be behaviors and results that are appropriately in need of reward. Those behaviors and results are the ones that will be the target of the recognition programs. They are legend makers because an organization's culture is built on the stories that reflect its success and history. It needs heroes who embody its accomplishments. The legends of those heroes are best broadcast through recognition. There is no better example of a culture of recognition—where legends are created and exemplify performance—than the U.S. military.[3]

- *Noncash Rewards: Lifestyle/Work Balance Rewards.* These programs address role-based, individual-based, or organizational-based aspects of the employment compact as rewards. Casual dress, for instance, is predominantly an individual-based program. Little proof has been rendered (although much has been suggested) that casual dress is required for a job or to make an organization more effective. (Some organizations believe, though, that casual dress does make them more effective at recruiting and retaining today's employees.)

More important than casual dress are reward policies on job sharing, telecommuting, flexible work schedules, elder/dependent care days, and general employee assistance programs. The design principles for these types of programs should be governed by cost, benefit, and message-carrying capacity (i.e., communications value). In considering these types of plans, designers must take into account both the demographics of the desired workforce and industry norms. According to Buck Consultants' *2000/2001 Compensation Budget and Planning Survey,* significant differences exist among industries with respect to alternative work arrangements (flex time, job sharing, telecommuting). Meanwhile, casual dress is uniformly accepted across industries.[4]

---

### VIRTUALLY GLOBAL

A $1 billion division of a U.S. consulting firm—one providing outsourcing information technology services within the energy industry—came into being when the firm won the contracts of two global oil and gas concerns. It immediately added 1,200 IT consulting professionals from two very different and strongly defined cultures to its own, equally strong culture. This acquisition was made more problematic as the consulting culture—defined by billable hours, sales, and customer service—clashed with the paternalistic cultures of the two energy companies. One statistic that illustrates the difference between the acquiring consulting firm and the energy companies is tenure: The average tenure at the consulting firm was 2.4 years; at the combined energy companies it was 11+ years for the IT people. Understanding the need for HR interventions to smooth the integration of the three populations, the organization formed a global rewards strategy team. The team functioned across three locations in the United States, one in Canada, and in four countries in Europe. Several lessons learned from this experience—about what made the team and the project work, and the resulting Total Rewards Strategy effective—are worth recounting here.

The team was successful because it established its purpose and the rules through which it would operate to achieve that purpose. Immediately, the team defined its primary objective: to collect, organize, interpret, and make design recommendations for the establishment of consistent reward and recognition processes across all locations. The team did the simple stuff, such as establishing weekly meetings (at 11 A.M. Eastern time, to accommodate as many participants on either coast as possible). Each meeting had a preset agenda and defined purpose—to ensure that every member had done what was needed and each member understood the next week's steps. Members would "attend" in person or by conference call, set ground rules for participation, make commitments to working together, and hold one another accountable for reaching deadlines. Even remotely, the team members' candid way of addressing one another and the issues worked to its advantage.

The team made the tough decisions, too. For one, the team members identified common processes for collecting, organizing, and analyzing information that transcended country and culture. They agreed, for example, to the level of input that would be required of employees and executives and the process tools for collecting that input. Locally, however, the team members decided the depth with which those processes would be deployed, the percentages of employees to involve, and the level and number of executives to include. All the team's data collection materials (including both facts and perceptions) were shared using a Lotus Notes database, allowing the members, regardless of location, to view, comment on, and jointly analyze inputs from every location. At one weekly meeting it became clear that the division was desperate for a spot recognition program; in one day the team designed a simple and effective plan and introduced it to the executive sponsors. The plan then got implemented within the week.

Of course, collecting and organizing information consistently is not the endgame. It was clear from the start that success would require promoting the high-performance culture of the consulting parent to stimulate the sense of belonging. Here, there were several keys to the team's success. First, the team was not afraid to make recommendations and get plans implemented. Its members understood that success in its culture was a roughly right solution that worked— fast—not an overengineered design. Second, the team stuck to its purpose of making fact-based design recommendations. It focused less on the process and more on the results. Finally, the team was open and honest with all its members. By working through a set of design principles that made sense for the company, the team was able to work across cultural boundaries.

What made the Total Rewards Strategy successful was its detail and flexibility. The team learned that the varied cultures, both across companies and countries, affected the timing of various program introductions more than the designs themselves. The team defined the strategic design orientation: For example, every employee on the account would have some portion of her total cash compensation tied to variable pay. Some cultures found that decision uncomfortable, but not unreasonable. The team would proceed to the next decision, working toward increasing levels of detail, through the defined design principles. Next, the team would define organizational level of measure. Throughout the building know-how phase it appeared that two levels of measure made sense: account and local team. In actuality, some countries wanted only account measures while others wanted to include yet a third level of measure—the individual. The result was a compromise and a phase in; the team defined three levels of measure, with ranges of awards around each, but it gave each of the country managers the flexibility to work with one, two, or three measures as it made sense for them, within the strategic framework. The team also defined a period of time over which the designs would be brought more into line (although it stopped short of dictating overall consistency).

The group defined the participation, or percent of total pay, that each person had "at risk." This, too, created compromises. Some country managers said they could not shift compensation from fixed to variable at all. The team soon came to appreciate that the issue was not whether pay would be put at risk, but rather how much pay and how fast. In the United States, for example, it was easy enough to say that there would be no increase to fixed compensation during the following year so that those dollars could be put into funding an incentive pool. In other countries—for example, in Germany—compensation was more negotiable. The changes in these countries had to be phased in over a longer period of time. The team still met its objective of having every employee tied to some variable compensation. (It just met the objective in varied timing and amount.)

## Where We Have Come From and Where We Are Going

This has been a long journey, and the progress your team has made is considerable. Figure 6-16 illustrates the process you have been through to get to the design of specific reward elements. Of course, you're not done, although this is a good point to stop, reflect, and gather input from various stakeholders before moving forward with implementation.

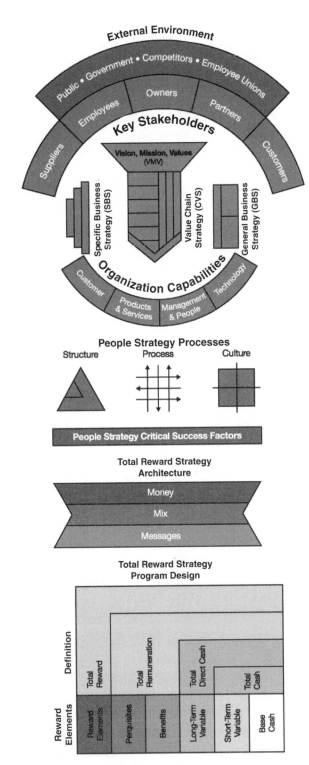

Figure 6-16. Total Rewards and the business environment.

The primary question you want answered is this: "Do you want employees involved or committed?" This stems from the old MBA paradigm about ham and eggs—the chicken is involved; the pig is committed. Figure 6-17 on page 238 lists examples of some field testing techniques you can use to make this determination, one of which is challenge teams.

Challenge teams present a good middle-of-the-road position. They allow the design team to go to various stakeholders with concepts and ideas and force them to be challenged. These facilitated sessions generate wonderful input to the design and implementation processes. Regardless, take the time now to collect feedback before going to full-scale implementation.

Figure 6–17. Field testing techniques.

To go from the drawing board to the boardroom, test design concepts using an approach that fits your corporate culture:

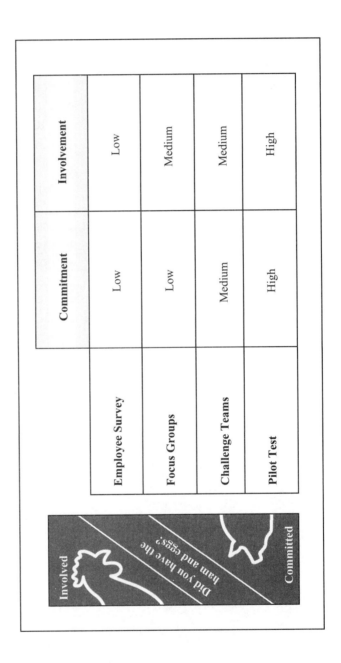

|  | Commitment | Involvement |
|---|---|---|
| **Employee Survey** | Low | Low |
| **Focus Groups** | Low | Medium |
| **Challenge Teams** | Medium | Medium |
| **Pilot Test** | High | High |

## Chapter 7

# DELIVERING THE DESIRED KEY MESSAGES

PHASE IV OF THE PLAN design process, leveraging know-how, requires that you introduce the new Total Rewards Strategy, and its supporting program elements, throughout the organization in a thoughtful way. This is where it all matters; nothing that you have designed through this or any other process will have any traction without smooth communications. Informing is not enough. The objective is to build understanding and to engage and energize employees through the power of rewards. Consider that any good benefits or compensation person can develop a technically sound plan; the intent here is to ensure that the plan achieves its objective of linking employees to the business outcomes they help deliver.

Implementation requires four steps, as shown in Figure 7-1. First, plan testing at the macro and micro levels. This is done both for the purposes of reconsidering any designs and for knowing what you are up against in terms of communications. Second, plan for success and contingencies by identifying barriers to success and quick wins for implementation. There are potential upside contingencies and downside risks to everything; this effort is no exception. You will want to have contingency plans for potential downside risks; you also want to leverage upside contingencies to make the most of every opportunity. Implementing the plans, and communicating changes to reward plans, needs to be both thoughtful and deliberate. Compensation transcends our personal and professional lives—change requires careful consideration. The detailed implementation plan, including training, communications, and learning activities, needs to support the desired key messages. Finally, delivering the plans requires focused messages.

Figure 7-1. Implementation for superior performance.

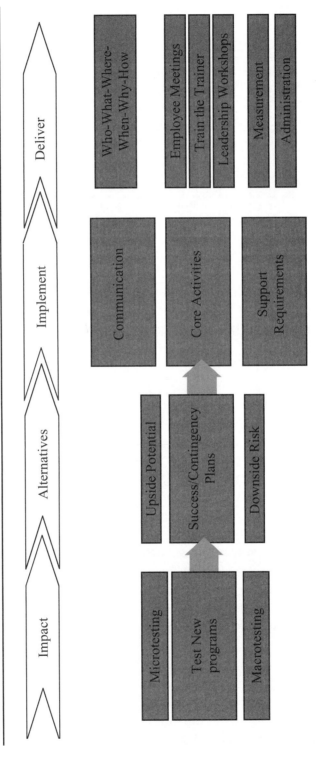

Implementation Planning defines the appropriate timing of, staging of, and approach for implementation for all stakeholders impacted. Key to the implementation is the communication of the changes, training to ensure correct application of the changes, and any support requirements to reinforce the ongoing success of the changes.

## Impact Testing

Testing, of course, demands that you look at various constituencies and stakeholders to assess the impact from the perspective of owners, employees, management, customers, suppliers, and business partners. Accordingly, assess the value delivered (i.e., the "bang for the buck") as well as the cost of delivering that value. Always assess the impact—costs and benefits—in the aggregate and individually.

Accordingly, look at testing programs from both the macro and the micro perspective. Macrotesting affects the organization as a whole and is often done to answer the questions, "What does this plan design mean to us? What does it mean to this company as a whole?" Microtesting, however, requires that you look at very specific audiences, answering the question (in many cases on a person-by-person basis), "What does this plan design mean to me?" Segment the market, just as you would if you were marketing a new product or a new service, which in a sense you are, to the broad employee population. For example, what does a person with twenty years of seniority, who works in the operations area, is paid $30,000, and has a particular family condition, want or think he wants from the new reward program? On the other hand, someone with five years of seniority, with no family, who is paid $150,000 to $200,000 and is in upper middle management, may perceive the program differently. Both of these audiences are appropriate to speak with regarding the key messages of the new reward strategy. Bear in mind that design changes, by their very nature, have winners and losers.

Recent activities in the world of cash balance plans illustrate this point. Litigation proliferates today, and it is the subject of articles almost daily about organizations that, because of potential cost savings, change their retirement programs from a traditional defined-benefit program to a cash balance plan. However, the negative impact of these plans, particularly on longer-service employees, has caused at a minimum significant ripple effects, bad press, and even lawsuits. The purpose of macro- and microtesting is to determine if design changes are required and to ensure that you are delivering the key messages. This requires being able to address both the masses and the individual.

Finally, testing must consider the plan's administrative requirements vis-à-vis the company's ability to manage it. Occasionally, it is a constraint on implementation that certain types of reward programs are either difficult or even impossible to administer because they cannot be programmed or administered by your human resources information system.

Financial Analysis

In building the business case for moving any design initiative forward, return on investment is always a consideration. Although the heavy lifting should have been done during the design phases, it is helpful to conduct this analysis in terms of fixed and variable compensation. There are three potential impacts of new designs that should be addressed:

1. *Aggregate fixed compensation costs will be going up.* In the first scenario, aggregate overall fixed compensation costs may rise as a result of the new Total Reward Strategy. This is most typically the case when your programs are less competitive than your stated or required reward strategy and/or you have made the decision to raise the money axis. You may be competing in different markets; competing at a higher percentile within those markets; and/or enhancing the mix of total rewards. Raising fixed compensation costs can be justified through future gains in productivity as achieved by stimulating higher performance from existing personnel and/or attracting and retaining a higher caliber of talent (see the case study on General Motors). This can frequently offset the incremental productivity increase, as measured through revenues per employee. Compare the key measures of employee impact at a top-performing company (e.g., one in the seventy-fifth percentile versus your company's) to establish both a baseline and a going-forward goal. What you should be able to achieve in revenue if you can acquire and retain seventy-fifth percentile talent, and have the programs in place to have them perform at that level, should clearly exceed the incremental cost increase. If not, it is not worth the change.

---

### THE GENERAL MOTORS PARADIGM

Roger Smith is credited with once having said, "If I double the salaries of every employee at GM, I would not increase the company's productivity." He was correct, sort of. His problem was he was focused only on the money dimension without considering how to either enhance mix or refocus the messages (or both).

Enhancing the mix would entail putting that additional two-times pay on a leveraged basis—making it variable and performance-based. Most rewards professionals would argue that this design would impact productivity.

Refocusing messages may take many forms. One would be to establish GM as the high-performing car company, attracting a higher caliber of talent by competing against a different set of peer companies—those achieving seventy-fifth percentile results in the industries. This would require GM to assess the performance level of its peer comparison companies to determine the impact of raiding the bar and hiring a higher caliber of talent. Essentially, Smith is right; if he paid a median talent workforce at seventy-fifth percentile, he would not impact results. However, evidence proves that if he acquired seventy-fifth percentile talent he would dramatically impact results.

2. *Some individuals will be considered to be overcompensated while others will be undercompensated based on new measurement criteria.* In this scenario there are individual "winners" and "losers." A winner would be any employee who would be considered "undercompensated" relative to her internal worth; losers are those who are overcompensated relative to some new set of compensable factors and/or internal worth. In the former case, an employee may expect more upside opportunity—but the converse will happen in the latter case.

For both individuals, it needs to be clear that the company's decision to adopt or change the reward strategy and programs is purely a business decision. Reward plans have value for a specified point of time in a company's development; not forever. Changes do not mean, however, immediate adjustments to compensation levels in either case. Those who are deemed undercompensated, relative to their job or grade, still need to demonstrate that they possess the newly valued skill/competency to do the job and can perform relative to the new standard. For those whose compensation is already above the expected new value, rarely would they have their compensation cut—in fact, that happens only in extreme situations. Rather, the message here is that relative to a current set of standards and requirements, their compensation is at a premium relative to the going rate.

## DRIVING SALES THROUGH LINE OF SIGHT, BY KRISTEN BUSANG AND TONI JACKSON

A national sales and marketing organization, with annual sales of $5 billion, had a simple broad-based incentive and sales compensation plan. The organization employed approximately eight hundred sales staff and an additional two thousand nonsales staff and management employees across multiple geographical locations. Every employee was eligible to participate in the same sales incentive plan, independent of job role or sales-related responsibilities. The design focused on driving sales volume within its retail and wholesale operations. During good years, when sales and earnings exceeded budget, the sales staff would reap the financial rewards of their efforts; meanwhile, nonsales staff would experience what amounted to a "windfall" based on the same set of sales performance criteria. When the company's earnings performance worsened, management realized that what it had gained in simplicity and focus on top line sales, it had lost on bottom line earnings.

The answer came in the form of enhanced line of sight and a more proportionate allocation of the company's limited incentive funds. To accommodate this, the new design had two very different foci: First, for sales staff, the plan encouraged more aggressive behaviors in uncovering and closing sales opportunities. Second, it made all nonsales staff eligible for a broad-based incentive plan that measured expense control (to drive net profit), and customer satisfaction. The new design reoriented the various employee groups toward business metrics that each could impact, increased new customer acquisition, and enhanced the company's ability to compete in a low margin business.

In the new design there was a redistribution of the incentive pool, essentially causing certain nonsales employee groups to "lose" while allowing sales employees to "win." To accommodate the lower target opportunity afforded the nonsales staff, the company redoubled its communications on pay-for-performance. By clearly demonstrating the enhanced line of sight, and connecting each employee's payout to personal efforts, the company averted employee relations issues.

*Kristen Busang and Toni Jackson are compensation consultants with Buck Consultants.*

3. *Your aggregate compensation costs are going to go down.* The third scenario suggests that the overall fixed compensation costs are higher than your stated strategy. As noted previously, one rarely reduces base pay at the implementation of a new program; this posture should be undertaken only if the company is in trouble. The most effective strategy in this scenario is to shift compensation costs from fixed to either variable (short- or long-term) or indirect compensation. This provides for the funding of other plans through the diversion of future base pay increases.

There are many advantages to variable pay over fixed pay, not the least of which is the opportunity to replace a fixed cost with a variable cost. This allows you to manage compensation expenses in line with business performance. As well, it enhances the organization's ability to deliver focused key messages.

In making this shift, consider the ancillary effects on budgets, including the impact on various employee costs (e.g., benefits, paid time off, retirement). There is no requirement to include variable pay in retirement calculations, but the decision whether to do so should be purposeful because employees will ask why it is or isn't policy. There is also the compounding impact of base pay, as illustrated in Figure 7-2. Base pay is an inefficient means for delivering rewards. Diverting this fixed cost into variable pay is a good way to minimize the negative effects of "freezing" base pay.

Variable pay changes are typically easier to address but need to be looked at from two angles. First, if you are "adding on" a variable pay plan (e.g., providing a self-funded plan that is above and beyond anything previously offered), the design should provide you with the business case for paying for incremental performance improvements. Shifting to a pay-at-risk position is an altogether different scenario. Here you need to create the balance between the foregone pay and the upside potential.

Remember, variable pay by definition is *not* pay at risk. To put pay at risk, your employee must be able to go someplace else and make that amount in base pay. If the company offers lower base wages, with the opportunity to achieve substantial upside, then the employee has put pay at risk. Most variable pay plans do not operate that way.

## Plan Objectives Testing

Understanding the financial impact of the programs is half the story, albeit a most important one when it comes to selling the plan to leader-

Figure 7-2. The compounding impact of fixed compensation.

**Baseline**

| Year | 5% Base Pay Increase |
|---|---|
| 1 | $30.00 |
| 2 | 31.50 |
| 3 | 33.08 |
| 4 | 34.72 |
| 5 | 36.46 |
| 6 | 38.29 |
| 7 | 40.20 |
| | $244.25 |

**Divert Half of Budget**

| | 2.5% Base Pay Increase | Variable Pool |
|---|---|---|
| | $30.00 | $2.54 |
| | 30.75 | 2.54 |
| | 31.59 | 2.54 |
| | 32.31 | 2.54 |
| | 33.11 | 2.54 |
| | 33.95 | 2.54 |
| | 34.79 | 2.54 |
| | $226.50 | $17.78 |

Variable Pool Equals 7.8% of Base Pay

**Divert All of Budget**

| | Base Pay | Variable Pay |
|---|---|---|
| | $30.0 | $4.89 |
| | 30.0 | 4.89 |
| | 30.0 | 4.89 |
| | 30.0 | 4.89 |
| | 30.0 | 4.89 |
| | 30.0 | 4.89 |
| | 30.0 | 4.89 |
| | $210.0 | $34.23 |

Variable Pool Equal 16.3% of Base Pay

Negative [Cash Flow] Positive

This example does not consider the effect of a lower base pay on other employee costs (e.g., overtime, differentials, benefits).

An example of funding from foregone base pay adjustments.

ship. The true test of its traction, however, comes in determining the extent to which the plan delivers on the desired key messages. Here you need to set out to test whether the plan meets and delivers on the objectives that you have set out to accomplish. There are three areas to test: plan objectives, key messages, and interrelationships of the plans.

Start with the plan objectives. As part of the design segment of this effort (Chapters 5 and 6), the team authored mission statements for each program. The mission statement identifies what you want to accomplish through the use of your Total Rewards Strategy holistically, and each program singularly. Go back and review those objective statements to validate that the plans, as they've now been designed, support the behaviors and outcomes that you want to drive. Figure 7-3 provides the tool for accomplishing this portion of the testing. Start by identifying the plan. Remember, every plan has a name; list the plans by name and the objective(s) for each. Understanding that the design process spans a period of time and that it reflects the collaborative efforts of many parties, the end result, in terms of the actual plan, may not be exactly what you set out to do originally. Now is the time to define the extent to which the designs meet their objectives. Essentially, this is "reverse gap analysis." Whereas the plan was designed originally to close gaps, now you are testing the extent to which that has been achieved. Rank the plans as you have before on a scale of one to five, one being to a significant extent, five being to a minimal extent, and three indicating it neither positively nor negatively achieves its objectives (neutral).

Next, test the key messages. You have identified specific key messages using exercises such as "because statement" definition and "therefore" designs. Have the design team assess how the existing program meets the initially stated key message and determine if it has the features built in to deliver those messages. Begin by returning to your original work product and identifying the articulated "because statements." (Do they still reflect your desired key messages?) Attach the appropriate "therefore" statements to each "because" statement—something you may have done already. Now ask yourself, What plan feature specifically addresses the "therefore and because statement(s)"? Ensure that you can make the connection by going one step further and asking, "How?" Use Figure 7-4 to assess the degree to which the team executed on those ideas and validate that what you have created actually delivers those key messages.

Finally, the interrelationships of the plans must be considered. Previously, you inventoried the existing reward programs to determine the effec-

Figure 7-3. Evaluating plan objectives.

| Plan | Originally Stated Objectives | Extent Objectives Achieved |
|---|---|---|
| List each plan in your TRS. | Describe the objective(s), for each plan in your inventory, as you originally defined it. What behaviors, results, or outcomes are you attempting to achieve, within what populations(s), over what time frame? | With the plan now designed, to what extent does it achieve the desired objective(s)? This is "reverse gap" analysis. You designed originally to close gaps—now you are testing the extent to which it's succeeded. Rank the plans as you have before, on a scale of one to five |
| Example: 2003 Profit Sharing Plan | • Increase employee awareness of financial objectives <br> • Share success | (2) Communications effectively define company financials <br> (3) Target 4% payout |

Figure 7-4. Analyzing "because statements."

| **"Because" Statement** | | **"Therefore" Action** | | **Plan Feature** | | **How Linked** |
|---|---|---|---|---|---|---|
| From the Design Stages of this process | → | Specific Feature | | | | |
| The program differentiates (e.g., pay for performance) | → | Broader use of variable pay | → | Eligibility down throughout the organization | → | Team and individual metrics |

tiveness of each one separately and then in aggregate. Here you want to review all the new programs that make up your Total Rewards Strategy, ensuring that they are holistic as a group and delivering the same messages together as one strategy. This is, for the most part, an empirical review.

## Barriers to Success/Easy Wins

There will always be business issues, events, and constraints that will hamper your ability to succeed. Conversely, there will be some fast successes, too. Manage both.

Start with the easy wins. Easy wins are mostly a matter of defining the items that can be addressed quickly and efficiently and that have the most significant impact. The easier they are to address and the bigger the impact, the faster they should be accomplished. Doing so means that you must communicate broadly about the positive change being effected; this is called "surfing the wave."

---

### CONSIDERING TIMING WHEN CREATING CHANGE IN A NOT-FOR-PROFIT CULTURE, BY MARTHA GLANTZ

Not-for-profit (NFP) organizations are typically mission-based, attracting employees who are committed to the ideals of the organization. In the case of one particular Catholic-based NFP, this was particularly true. Throughout its 185-year history, the organization was in the enviable position of being able to remain singularly focused and operate on the interest generated by its endowment. By 2000 this became a less feasible strategy as operating expenses had risen, investment income had declined, and the organization was challenged by its new board to expand its reach through outreach programs. To rely less on its endowment, the NFP refocused its strategy to increase revenues from other ventures and reemphasize the needs of its constituencies. It sought to encourage its employees, already dedicated to its mission, to participate in some active way to raise contributions.

Dichotomous to this new strategy was a compensation system that reinforced the entitlement nature of pay. The NFP knew that it needed to implement a pay system that rewarded results, redirected the energies of current employees, retained top performers, and attracted talent in many critical new areas. Of course, the plan needed to be simple, to reflect the NFP's ability to administer it and the requirement for demonstrating that it was fact-based and fair. As alternatives were considered, the degree of change became apparent. Although the designers saw the need for significant change, they also saw the risks associated with going too far too fast. This caused the team to appreciate the requirement for timing and phasing the introduction. It wanted to effect change to stimulate interest in new ideals—not cause a total upheaval. Accordingly, the design addressed fixed compensation first, leaving variable pay for the following year.

The result was a market-based approach to managing pay, where individual contribution and performance were measured relative to the market price for each role in order to determine an employee's compensation. A broad-band structure was introduced to facilitate lateral job movement and eliminate internal bidding. Individual movement within the band was linked to performance and continued contribution, eliminating the virtually automatic across-the-board salary increases.

The next step will be to introduce a variable pay system. The foundation of the design will be to link participants to the strategic goals of the NFP and rewards for team-based successes. The compensation redesign process has allowed the NFP to realize and communicate that as it continues to assess its strategic direction, pay will continue to be adjusted within the context of how it supports that new direction.

*Martha Glantz is a compensation consultant with Buck Consultants.*

The opposite of easy wins are barriers to success—the organizational attributes or business realities that may keep these plans from achieving their objectives. This is the stuff that may cause you to sink to the bottom.

The purpose of collecting employee input is to be able to go back to your employees and say, "You told us this, and here is how we are responding," or "For these business reasons, here is why we cannot make the changes you have suggested." Start with the items you are directly responding to and make sure you publicize them and take credit. Be deliberate about what might occur to bring your plans down and have contingencies. One exercise that's helpful to develop thinking in this regard is illustrated in Figure 7-5. Ask your design team to:

Figure 7-5. Surfing or sinking.

| Surfing the Wave | | |
|---|---|---|
| What may occur to cause us unplanned success? | Likelihood | Impact |
| | | |
| | | |
| What wins can be gained with little risk or effort? | Who will take the lead and how? | |
| | | |
| | | |

| Sinking to the Bottom | | |
|---|---|---|
| What factors may cause us to fail? | Likelihood | Impact |
| | | |
| | | |
| What stands between us and success? | Who will champion this effort and how? | |
| | | |
| | | |

- *Surf the wave.* What may happen for us, from an environmental, business, and/or corporate perspective, that in the future may cause unanticipated success?
- *Sink to the bottom.* What may happen, from an environmental, business, and/or corporate perspective, that in the future may cause us unanticipated failure?

In both cases, consider opportunities your company can capitalize on and/or contingencies to which to respond.

## Implementation

Implementation includes everything required to get reward programs to function together as a plan that drives productivity and performance. It is not enough for reward programs to be simply understood by employees (and other stakeholders); strive for *impact*, not just awareness. In contrast to the phased communications plan that was used to keep employees updated about design progress, it is time to turn attention to full disclosure. This requires a thoughtful communications design; planning activities for delivering key messages; and support for existing plans and programs.

## Communication

The process of transferring know-how was introduced in Chapter 2, and that theme has continued throughout the book. Here it is time to use the "who-what-where-when-why-how-how much" tool to develop the communication programs.

First, define the audience (the who), as well as the messenger. There are likely to be different types of communication for various audiences. In Chapter 5 we conducted stakeholder analysis; use that analysis to define the requirements for communications to these various constituencies.

Once you have determined the audiences and how those audiences are to be segmented, the next step is to concentrate on the messages (the what) that will be part of the implementation plan. Focus on changes to each individual reward element, as well as the Total Rewards Strategy (TRS), and all the work that was done throughout the process to create these new designs. Analyze the organization's competition and discuss its business plan to demonstrate the reason and the logic behind the chosen approaches to strategy and plans; demonstrate how the approaches you've selected are a function of the business strategy and each job's role in making that strategy work. Review your "because" and "therefore" statements, which you developed to articulate key messages, in order to link the design decision you made in relation to those points back to the employees themselves.

> ## COMMUNICATING PERSONAL IMPACT FOR INCREASED COMPANY PERFORMANCE, BY MARY HOROWITZ
>
> A large specialty manufacturing company created a series of special incentive programs for 150 key executives to support ambitious goals to double sales over a three-year period. Although the focus of this plan by itself was clear, at implementation it became apparent that these executives neither fully understood the value of their total direct compensation nor how they (individually and as a group) impacted the value derived of the combined programs. In other words, each executive understood each plan individually; they did not comprehend the combined effects or the consistent messages about increasing top line sales.
>
> The solution was to create a personalized "brochure" explaining the various plans and programs that made up an individual's total direct compensation, and quantifying and reporting individual participation and potential payouts from special plans. In particular, the link between individual and company performance was underscored, since many incentives paid in company shares. Qualified and non-qualified plans were included, as well as employment terms (including such arrangements as change-of-control provisions). Attention was focused on variable performance-based stock and incentive programs, indicating progress toward goals.
>
> The results became clear, in both intended and unintended ways. First, executive focus on key sales objectives was increased, improving top line performance. Additionally, quantifying the value of special compensation arrangements supported the critical retention of key individuals. Some unintended but wonderful results were realized when recipients were so pleased with the customized communications that they used them for financial planning and requested annual updates. And one surprise dividend: The consolidated database of executive programs and participation, including the various employment agreements, proved invaluable when, eventually, the company entered into merger discussions. Even through

the subsequent sales of the company, executive retention remained high, further supporting the success of that initiative.

*Mary Horowitz is Regional Director, Metro New York Communications Consulting for Buck Consultants.*

Location (where) and timing (when) are not trivial issues. Consider the difference between a salesperson learning about changes to a compensation plan through the Lotus Notes server (accessed from his desk at home) or in the annual sales meeting. In one case, the salesperson has the opportunity to interact with the messenger and his peers—in the other, he is remote. Likewise, there is a big difference between hearing about something once and receiving continuous reinforcement of a message. Timing requires at least three repetitions of message delivery:

- Here is where we are going (the plan laid out in the beginning).
- Here is how we are doing relative to that plan (communicated several times throughout the year).
- Here is how we did—and why—in order to learn from that for the next period.

### FILLING THE VACUUM

It is a commonly held law of physics: Nature abhors a vacuum. Information is the same. In fact, it could be said that "absent fact, rumor fills the void." Sharing knowledge is essential. Consider the story of a New York–based hedge fund of funds. In this fund, employee turnover had reached 80 percent on an annual basis. Customer service was suffering, account management was an issue, and funds were performing badly. This is an example of limited degrees of freedom, because the fund was co-owned by two wealthy investors. The two of them determined what, when, how, and how much to communicate. Needless to say, what made them brilliant investors did not make them wonderful managers and communicators; communications to employees was nonexistent, leaving employees to believe that decisions about compensation were arbitrary. With little communication from the owners and no structure, employees assumed the worst and became "free agents" as soon as they had their ticket punched and gained experience.

The company finally adopted a Total Rewards Strategy that was very financial services centric. While there was nothing unique about the programs, the designs themselves allowed for the free and open exchange of information. Essentially, by codifying mostly what they were already doing they eliminated the mystery, put some rules and processes behind it, and opened up the books. A communications program was launched, and employees were engaged in developing objectives; salary ranges were communicated to each employee as well. Within a short period of time, employee turnover had dropped to less than 10 percent. Relative fund performance has increased, and new clients have signed on as key stockholders. As it turned out, employees were actually paid well above the market to begin with. In other words, the turnover wasn't about the money; it was about the key stakeholders' willingness to share not more money but more information.

## Core Activities

Both the medium (how the messages are delivered) and the messenger (who delivers them) are of primary importance. The design process engages employees at several functions. Use design teams and focus groups, or challenge team members as communications allies. They can help communicate the plan by returning information back to employees, telling them, "Here is what we have said; here is what we have heard; here is what we took as information; here is how it was incorporated into the plan."

Do not underestimate the importance of communicating the plan design process. Too many organizations tend to communicate only results. Demonstrate that the reward strategy development and testing process took place in a very logical format, with a number of key stakeholders taking part.

The communications needs to be ongoing through the duration of the implementation. It is likely that the implementation of a specific element or change in certain designs will not occur all at once. Develop a sense of momentum and also a sense of progress by outlining future changes and expectations. After making sure that those changes occur, reinforce your commitment to key messages and communications. This is a "say, do, say" approach, and it is powerful in building employee trust in management and morale.

Should the communications for the project be handled as a special event or as part of a regular business process? To some extent, this decision colors the approach to communications. A "special event" that occurs once every three to five years and takes several years to implement will deliver a very specific message about how leadership views this effort. No better or worse, but certainly different, is a more business-as-usual approach. "Oh, by the way, we are accomplishing certain key business goals and one of those business goals is to have a Total Rewards Strategy that aligns our employees with the factors critical to the organization's success." The special event adds an element of formality while the other approach presents TRS as part of a normal business process. Since these two communications concepts are very different, their implementation needs to reflect those differences. To that end, the medium that the company uses to communicate is just as important as the message. Either way, be as strong about communicating your message as possible.

> **Choosing the Right Messenger**
>
> At one of the post-deregulation Baby Bells, a new Total Rewards Strategy was used to drive the organization from its monopolistic operating model to the new world of competition. To demonstrate the company's commitment to success, the senior line managers inside the organization announced the new plans. They could speak most directly to the business challenges and how the new reward plans would drive the organization toward the necessary ends. It was critical that management demonstrate awareness, commitment, and buy-in.
>
> In another situation the plan design team, which included individuals from all walks of the corporation, effectively provided communications first to the senior management and then to their peers and colleagues. The benefit of this approach was in demonstrating the simplicity of the programs. Through every step the executive sponsors made it very clear that any plan design would need to be simple and easy to understand. Therefore, having the design team communicate the plans was the first demonstration of the plan's simplicity.

Consider your company's communications norms to decide which norms you should emulate and which you want to deviate from. A high-impact medium that is new for your company can send a more powerful message. Or just to ensure the messages get across, using your standard communications processes will send a business-as-usual message. Consider mixing and matching delivery methods to get your point across and intensify the impact. Beyond the means of communicating, consider how the words and phrases you choose fit within the organizational context. Throughout the plan design process, and while putting the details together, it is imperative that the words, tone, and language reflect your organization's identity. The influence of your outside advisers should not overshadow your own language—do not substitute consultant speak, or the advice of a professional communicator, for your own words and language.

Finally, it is important that the people delivering key messages and communications have a thorough understanding of the programs and are respectful of how the audience will receive those messages. The messenger must anticipate the sensitivity of the audience. A person's pay speaks to personal emotion and the individual's place inside the rest of the organization (e.g., job grade). The heightened emotion that swirls around this subject may cause the audience to react differently than you intended. In addition, how messages are received may vary from one group to the next. Be prepared and alert for the subtle feedback that your audience is sending you and work extra hard to engage it in the process. It is easy to disburse information—work hard to test for awareness and use the communications to jump-start the link and leverage processes. Flavor the messages with the organization's regular philosophy, strategy, and approach to communicating to employees, but understanding that reward programs are a sensitive subject, go beyond those bounds. Remember, change has its advantages—capitalize on them. All these issues need to discussed prior to message delivery, in "train the trainer" sessions.

Define how much to communicate, too. Begin with the idea that you will tell employees as much as you can; overcommunicating is better than undercommunicating. Be extraordinarily direct, honest, and forthright with respect to the changes. Any attempt to covertly mislead or understate the pluses or minuses in the changes resulting from the new reward strategy will significantly affect the credibility of management and all the people that contributed to the design, and the design itself will not be vitally accepted by the employees. It's not that every negative or positive has

---

**Compensation Transcends Our Personal and Professional Lives**

Rightly or wrongly, a manifestation of our society is that we frequently measure ourselves by what we earn; therefore, everything we do in terms of compensation has both a personal and professional impact. You could have a disagreement with your boss, be passed over for a promotion, or experience any number of organizational setbacks or frustrations, all of which can negatively influence your career. You may or may not take those concerns home with you at night and communicate them to your significant other. But if you do not get a raise, or you do not get your incentive, that is something that your significant other would clearly know about. Everything a company does and doesn't do when it comes to compensation and rewards strategy sends messages to its employees. It is important to define those messages in very clear and purposeful terms.

to be discussed and explained fully, but understand that in every change effort there are winners and there are losers. Address the negatives head-on and, as always, accentuate the positive.

Where there are significant negatives, let them be talked about openly and explain the reason for the changes, especially where there are certain take-aways. Time communications in accordance with the implementation choreography of the various programs. Choreography defines how, when, and in which order of priority various programs will be introduced. In setting priorities, you need to look at the desired impact on the organization, each program's ability to influence change within the organization, as well as the ease of implementation. It may be very easy, for example, to implement a spot award program; therefore, you can do that quickly and effectively. Changes to base pay, while important, may be longer-term objectives, and therefore the implementation timing might be set out over a period of more than a year, even two or three years.

With regard to integration, consider how various human resources interventions going on at the same time both affect and are influenced by a new reward strategy and the ensuing programs. These programs will interact with one another, certainly; there's an interaction between base pay and variable pay and benefits and all the other elements of reward. However, they will also be influenced and have an influence on other human resources programs, for example, performance management. It is important to inventory human resources processes to determine how each will be affected, then integrate the communications of the various programs.

Finally, there is the issue of the frequency of the message. Your key message has to be delivered often enough and through enough varied media that each key constituency "gets it." A simple suggestion: Deliver the message three times; and use three approaches to ensure the message is delivered. When employees tell you, "Okay, we get it," you only need to tell them one more time. Adults have different learning styles; use different media to capitalize on them.

## Chapter 8

# SUSTAINING PLAN EFFECTIVENESS

BY THIS TIME YOU'RE PROBABLY thinking, "Yeah! I'm almost done." In fact, plan design is an ongoing evolutionary process. The journey toward Total Rewards Strategy is a journey that does not end, because once the plan has been developed and implemented, you must determine how, and in what time frame, the plan's effectiveness will be measured and assessed. Assessment leads to the process of evaluation and adjustment. Here, too, specific design steps can be undertaken in the measurement and follow-up phase, as outlined in Figure 8-1. In all walks of life, the speed of obsolescence is increasing—rewards are no different.

Plan assessment is critical for some very sound reasons. The dynamics of your business are changing at an increasing rate, and they need to be responded to in kind through plan redesigns. Just fewer than 60 percent of the organizations in the *Business, People, and Total Reward Strategy Alignment Questionnaire* indicated that they would be reorganizing in the next three years (see Figure 8-2). Substantial organizational change will be driven by changes flowing directly from the environment, the business strategies, and resulting people strategy interfaces and dynamics. Companies today in virtually every industry are competing with organizations that they could never have imagined as their competitors ten years ago—and ten years from now there will be more competitors springing up in even shorter time periods.

The most dramatic finding for Total Reward Strategy (TRS) is that there are more points of strategic differentiation, more strategic initiatives and core capabilities than before. According to the data in Figure 8-3, there

Figure 8-1. Considering plan effectiveness.

| *Steps* | *Phase Deliverables* |
|---|---|
| 1. Create a data collection plan | • Employee feedback |
| 2. Establish formal mechanisms to measure employee commitment to the plan design | • A living/breathing plan design |
| 3. Review annual business plans to confirm continued fit | • Ongoing metrics |
| 4. Reconvene design team to recommend adjustments, as necessary | |
| 5. Execute phased transfer of know-how plan | |

is no relief, either. The strategic objectives, critical capabilities, and cultural attributes required for success are becoming both more voluminous and more intense. To respond, the number and the amplitude of key messages delivered through rewards are increasing correspondingly.

Many organizations are becoming effective at the art of managing the changes that are required to be successful in today's ever-changing environment. The business changes are at all levels of the strategy spectrum: from general business strategy (GBS) through value chain strategy (VCS) and specific business strategy (SBS). While the average organization strives to maintain competitive advantage in three points along the value chain, in the future the average organization will expect to have competitive advantage at four value chain points. Those same organizations that have today indicated an average of four specific business strategy initiatives have indicated that the average number of specific business initiatives will be six in the future (a 50 percent increase).

These strategic shifts manifest themselves in a corresponding increase in the organization's requiring additional core capabilities. Organizations that do more need to be better at more things; the pressures that this places on companies' management and people are significant. Rewards—it can be argued—are the strongest linkage between what the organization aspires to accomplish and the people who make it so. The lack of focus, and in some cases the disparate direction setting, needs purposeful management.

There is a corresponding intensification of corporate cultures as well. The findings in Figure 8-3 (Focus on Cultural Attributes Column) are

Figure 8-2. Plans to reorganize.

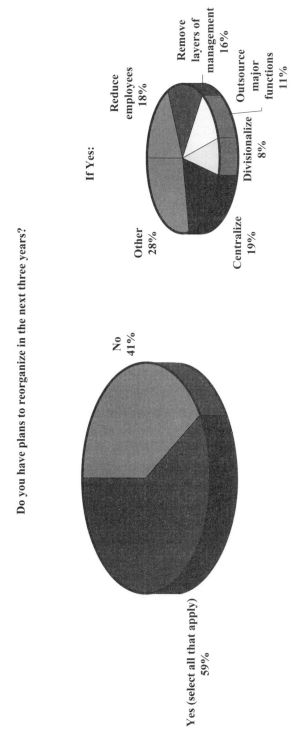

Do you have plans to reorganize in the next three years?

If Yes:

Reduce employees 18%

Remove layers of management 16%

Outsource major functions 11%

Divisionalize 8%

Centralize 19%

Other 28%

No 41%

Yes (select all that apply) 59%

Figure 8-3. The increasing dimensions of business strategy, core capabilities and cultural intensity.

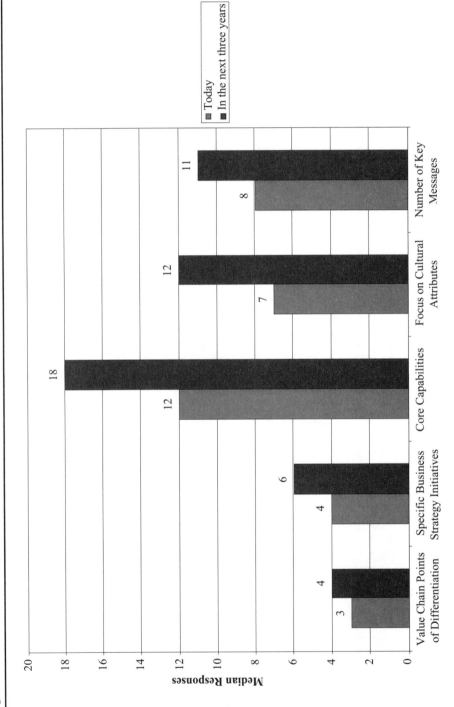

based on an assessment of fifteen key attributes (e.g., risk taking, speed, product or service orientation). In a cultural shift, some attributes gain in significance while others diminish; however, the findings from the data are that there is a cultural intensification—each of the key attributes of culture is becoming more significant to success. The need to manage the conflicting messages is key.

These findings manifest themselves in the growing amplitude of the messages being delivered through rewards. This suggests that there is a requirement for more varied reward tactics. As organizations need to do more with rewards, they need to have more specific reward plans to maintain that focus. That doesn't mean the organization has to pay more or deliver more rewards in total—rather, the company must focus the tools it uses to deliver those rewards. Managers need to have command of all the reward tactics required to run their business.

Consistent with the increase in the amplitude of the key messages, organizations are also using rewards to say more to employees. Figure 8-4 indicates the wide range of reward program key messages being communicated by companies. The variety of plans (not the total offerings or their payouts) and their customization is increasing. Two consistent themes are evident: There is a general shift in organizational level of measure from the individual toward the organization and from short-term to long-term performance. The clear message is that organizations and their employees are in this together for the long haul.

The demographics of the labor force are changing as well, making traditional forms of rewards ineffectual. The very makeup of the people who work for you today, and those you are actively recruiting, is changing in fundamental ways that need to be addressed. Failure to do so proactively will have far-flung implications—from ineffectiveness in attracting the caliber of talent you demand to potential lawsuits. Considering organizational requirements for variety and shifting demographics in concert with one another points up the need for more frequent plan design evaluation. Any design is representative of your organization at one point in time, but you must put those snapshots of your organization together and build a storyboard, responding to changes as they come along.

Let's step back for just a minute and match the future of business and organizational change with the fast pace of reward strategy revision. While business leaders (as represented in the study findings) are predicting massive increases in strategic, people, and organizational capabilities in the future, efforts to update reward strategies have been just short of dismal, historically. Figure 8-5 reveals that 35 percent of organi-

Figure 8-4. Reward program key messages.

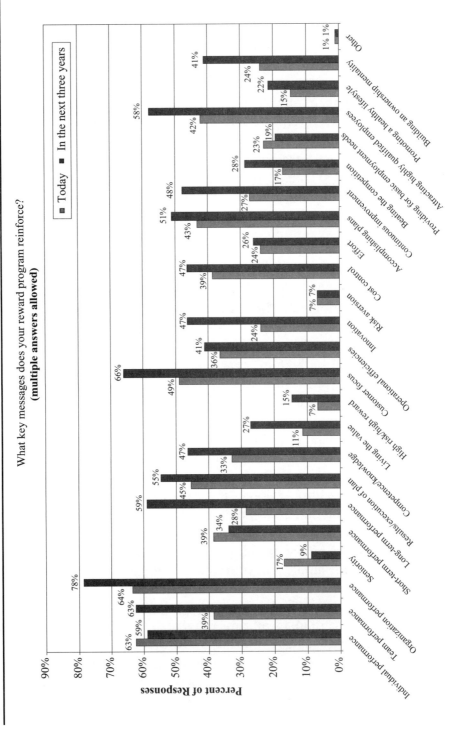

Figure 8–5.  Reward strategy change frequency.

**When was the last time you changed your reward strategy?**

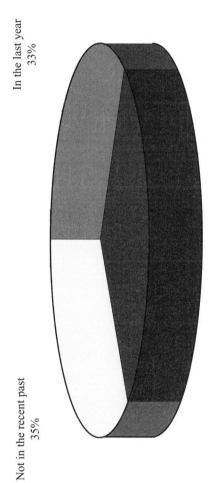

In the last year
33%

In the last five years
32%

Not in the recent past
35%

zations haven't revised their reward strategies in the recent past, and an additional 32 percent believe they have revised their reward strategies once in the past five years. People in the profession refer to this as "the train wreck between business leaders' requirements and human resources staff realities." The message to both is as Michael Hammer once said: "You are on the train or under it!"

More frequent change is not more extensive or more costly. Keeping a finger on the pulse of reward strategy designs, and their efficacy in your organization, can allow you to make more frequent, smaller adjustments, keeping them fresh and current. Oftentimes this practice relieves the pressures caused by more widespread change efforts.

Sustaining plan effectiveness stresses the ongoing need for inventorying plans and managing their interrelationships. Each year it is appropriate to inventory and validate all the plans and assess their performance on an ongoing basis. Remember, name your plans and begin each name with the year of its operation (e.g., "the 2002 . . ."). Chapter 2 outlined a technique to inventory plans and determine the return on plan investment (ROPI). That first analysis was used to build the business case for redesign. The techniques for impact testing, described in Chapter 7, can be combined with those earlier techniques and deployed here. The difference is that whereas previously you were testing for implementation, now you are testing effectiveness a year after the plans have been in operation (along with changes in the business environment) to assess potential design changes for the coming years.

## Data Collection

The measurement and follow-up phase begins by collecting the appropriate information and assessing how to measure that information against your plan design. You should be one step closer to it by now, however, because of the design effort you've been through already. The effort now is to determine how to reengage in the process to validate information previously collected and acted upon vis-à-vis changes in the business.

The first step in data collection planning is to establish the measures for success—that is, to determine the factors that will be used to decide whether the designs have met their objectives. These include:

- Employee commitment to plan ideals (i.e., buy-in and delivery of the key messages)

- Strategic impact between rewards and business strategies (i.e., building the measurements and connections between rewards and the business)
- Linkage between rewards strategy and plan designs (i.e., connecting people to the business through reward programs)

Figure 8-6 (see CD-ROM page 93 of 99) outlines the key business factors to be assessed and design implications for each factor. In formulating the data collection plan, assess the sources of information that you intend to use. This is a good opportunity to return to employees, managers, and executives who provided input at the onset of plan design and to evaluate whether the objectives that they had identified have been met.

Key stakeholders and business plans are other sources of information in assessing plan design and the ongoing fit of that design with the organization. Even a technical review of the plan design principles is of value as you look to determine whether there are any unintended effects. What's more, data collection can be both qualitative and quantitative—that is, you can assess whether the plan design process yielded a qualitative return on investment, but also whether there is a quantitative value yielded to the organization through the plan. The quantitative value is generally expressed in terms of the ROPI, calculated by dividing all of the costs associated with the plan by all of the economic gains. As discussed previously in Chapter 1, however, there are often additional benefits that may not be directly quantifiable. For example, the plan may improve employee morale or awareness of financial objectives, or it may reduce turnover. These benefits may be quantifiable—at least indirectly—but if they are not quantified, they should be captured contextually nonetheless.

## Plan Design Assessment

Take the defined plan success determinations and evaluate the plan's ability to deliver on them. Let's begin with employee commitment.

### Employee Commitment to Plan Design Principles

Figure 8-7 shows the variety of ways that employees perceive they are connected to the business, with rewards being the tool through which that connectivity is established.

As described and developed throughout this book, the effort is to link and leverage—that is, to get the most out of your employees' skills and

Figure 8–6. Business factors for reconsideration.

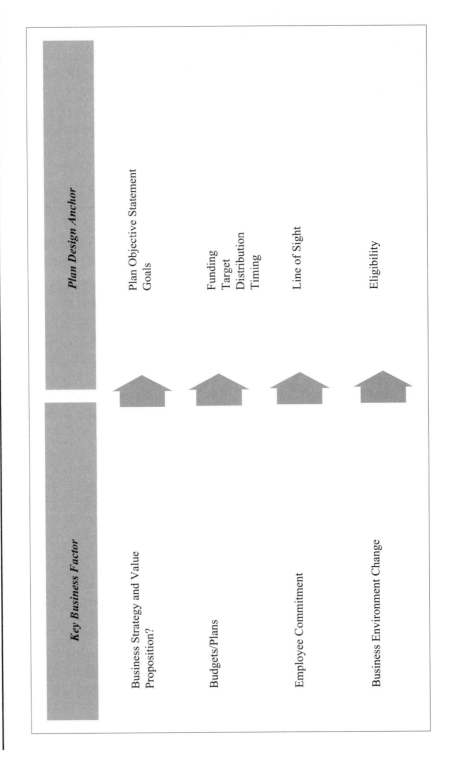

Figure 8–7. Measuring employee commitment.

| Measure | As Measured by | |
|---|---|---|
| | *This* | *That* |
| **Understanding** *I understand the plan's objectives* | I can see how these objectives affect business outcomes | I can understand your lousy plan |
| **Belief** *I believe that I can affect the outcomes* | I have the ability to influence the business | Corporate will tell me at year-end |
| **Action** *I act in accordance with plan objectives* | I behave in a way that affects my sphere of influence | Management, they... |

Employee commitment, the single most important criterion to evaluate, is a measure of understanding, translating into action.

capabilities by linking them to business outcomes and leveraging their combined capabilities. This is the point at which you are measuring the degree to which your design plan has been successful.

Ask your employees direct questions regarding the degree to which they understand the business and feel rewarded for their impact. Employee perceptions need to be directly explored and understood, and any disconnects have to be identified and addressed so as to magnify the effects of the plans. An employee focus group is one method for obtaining this feedback.

Management interviews can also assist in this data collection effort. The degree to which managers understand the various plans and utilize them in the appropriate situation is important in creating linkage.

## Fit with Business Strategy and Tactics

Total Rewards Strategy achieves its greatest impact when it is linked effectively to business strategy. (In Chapter 9, the Upstream Rewards Strategy Audit Process is presented as a tool for assessing how well that connection has been established.) It is important to review changes to the business strategy and plans that have occurred over the year as a baseline for deciding exactly where to begin—after all, business plan changes can easily command reward plan changes.

When assessing business plans and strategy, look for changes in strategic intent in the organization and the key metrics that are being used to address those changes. A popular approach to measuring business outcomes, and one that helps create the linkages between business plans and people, is the balanced scorecard. That methodology can be used to assess plan principles and their effect on business outcomes.

In their popular book *The Strategy Focused Organization*, Robert Kaplan and David Norton refined the balanced scorecard to demonstrate how organizations create a generic architecture for business strategy called *learning maps*. In this way a chain of events is illustrated, leading the user to specific people strategy critical success factors and metrics, as was outlined in Chapter 4.[1] Using this approach to assess the various plan design principles fast-tracks the process of creating linkage. This view is also helpful in determining where and how these changes affect your plan's design. Figure 8-8 illustrates this balanced view of metrics and the correlation to plan principles. At this point designers can assess the fundamental tenets of the designs, as was actualized through the design principles, to ensure that the right issues are focused upon in each business perspective. Accordingly, the designers validate that the plans have emphasized the correct behaviors

Figure 8-8. The balanced view of metrics.

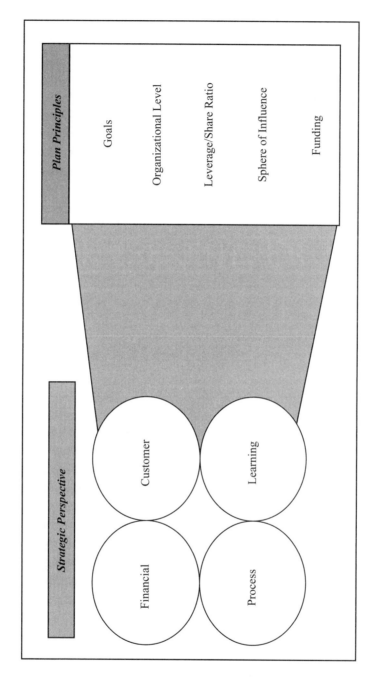

Changes in business strategies—short- or long-term—require adjustments to plan.

and results (in the correct proportions) through use of the appropriate measures; correct balance in the weighting of each measure; illustration of the individual's influence; and putting the money behind the message.

In previous chapters the balanced scorecard was used as a framework for executing strategy through people. As this connection is made through compensation plans, in the context of this book, that same framework can be used to test the validity of each reward design vis-à-vis strategy. This requires connecting the perspectives with associated design principles to ensure that the plans are effectively supporting the desired outcomes. Take, for example, the multimedia company that has a balanced scorecard perspective of "content." That is, the company measures the freshness, innovative nature, and how-to orientation of what it delivers using various media. The balanced scorecard is used to reevaluate plan effectiveness. In this case, the company has tested the extent to which each content developer has a measure of content freshness and each medium is sought for cross-utilization of ideas. The other plan design principles follow suit.

## Linkage and Leverage

The devil is in the details, and the details are the reward element tools that have been deployed to create linkage and get leverage. The Downstream Rewards Strategy Audit Process (which is covered in Chapter 9) is one method for determining the degree to which a plan delivers on Total Rewards Strategy. Those techniques can be applied to ensure that the connection continues to be made between the adjusted business strategy and the revised Total Rewards Strategy. Following the chain of connectivity—identifying the changes made to the business strategy, effecting change to the rewards strategy, and then adjusting reward plans accordingly—is how this process is completed. Use the inventory created through the data collection plan to identify how the aforementioned changes need to be addressed in program design adjustments.

## The Need to Adjust and Communicate

To sustain superior performance, the steering committee or detailed design team should be reconvened so it can assess the information collected against the current plan design. Many tools used in development of the plan architecture (e.g., the gap analysis) can be used here, too, to assess how the current plan fits with future desired outcomes or changes that have been implemented in the business strategy.

Finally, you will need to communicate the changes. This can be done through an annual communications process, such as an open enrollment, or a separate and parallel process. A phased communications strategy, which this book recommends at the onset of reward strategy development, should also be used for any revisions. Although most organizations communicate "what" has changed, few communicate "why" the change was made in relation to a changing environment, different stakeholder configurations, or new general, value chain, or specific business strategies. Fewer still (in fact, almost none) elect to translate those changes to needs for new or revised organizational capabilities, people strategies, or critical success factors. Amazingly, while employees have a great desire to understand the strategic level impacts, few management teams feel it is appropriate or necessary to share this information.

The research on employee culture and organization performance reveals that the single most highly correlated factor differentiating high performance is management credibility. Some people refer to this simply as "say, do, say" (otherwise known as "walk the talk"). One of the most important subjects that management should be involved in communicating is the rationale for any changes in the reward strategy of the organization.

---

### GETTING THE GREATEST PERFORMANCE BANG OUT OF AN INCREASINGLY LIMITED RESOURCE, BY JEFF MILLER

In order to continue its record of success in an increasingly competitive financial services industry, this southeastern superregional knew it had to raise the performance bar—dramatically. For the newly appointed chief human resource officer, a key indicator of the need to build a more performance-based culture was the dichotomy of ratings between the company as a whole and its people: Although financial results were sluggish, a sweeping majority of employees were rated "outstanding." In addition, annual merit reviews had begun to resemble general cost-of-living increases. Managers did little in differentiating pay based on performance or market.

Senior leadership delivered a mandate: Create a new rewards strategy to help drive a stronger performance culture and improve business results. The foundation of the new strategy was a base pay design that offered improved flexibility to reward employees based on contribution, retention risk, and current pay versus market. No longer would a traditional "merit matrix" be used to determine pay increases. Clearly, this strategy would only be as effective as the managers executing it.

### Creating High-Tech Tools and High-Touch Training

To enable managers to take advantage of the flexibility of the new program, an electronic pay-decision system was developed. The Excel-based tool enabled managers to:

- Make preliminary pay decisions and monitor salary budget used
- Sort market gap, retention risk, and ranking based on performance rating
- Access market data
- Upload pay decisions
- Receive necessary approvals

The pay-decision system gave managers the analytical tool they needed to make solid pay decisions. However, to change their behavior and help them feel confident in making and communicating pay decisions, high-impact training was needed.

The training was designed to enable managers to fulfill two critical roles—that of making sound, defensible pay decisions and that of communicating pay so that employees would clearly understand "why they are paid what they are paid, and what it will take to earn more."

The cornerstone of the training was a scenario-building/problem-solving exercise where managers could tackle complex pay and performance issues and collectively create solutions. The exercise was a catalyst for transforming managers from "pay administrator" to "pay manager." It made them the stewards for the performance culture. The impact of the new rewards system was manifold:

- Postimplementation surveys underscored that managers felt better equipped to drive and reward performance.
- Employees "got" the message about raising the performance bar and the impact on rewards.
- Managers got more bang out of their compensation dollar. In one business unit, they were able to award 7 percent average

increases using a 4 percent budget, simply by more effectively "picking their spots."

- And most important, the organization's financial perform-ance and total shareholder return have far outpaced industry averages.

In retrospect, while there was nothing revolutionary about the reward system design itself, it was pure. That is, the program was built on pure market pricing without any of the complication, bureaucracy, filtering, or other imperfections that often make a company's designs more generic. Accordingly, individual pay and performance decisions could be made without any organizational interference. A thorough implementation and training program delivered to line managers the market data necessary to make fact-based decisions; tools to run their businesses; and training in the human resources impacts of having pay- and performance-related discussions (both reinforcing and developmental). Ultimately, the new system allowed the company to place accountability for performance enhancement and return on compensation where it belonged—with line management.

*Jeff Miller is a Pittsburgh-based compensation consultant for Buck Consultants.*

Who should be responsible for determining the need for revision in an organization's reward strategy? Ultimately the chief executive officer is the individual most responsible for determining the need for review and mod-ification of this very important management tool. To the extent people con-tribute to the success of the organization, that accountability should not be delegated to staff individuals. If people are not key contributors to the orga-nization's success, then the accountability can be delegated to the head of human resources or the head of compensation and benefits. There are, of course, few organizations in today's world where people are not key con-tributors. For that reason, reward strategies are a chief executive responsi-bility. Many revised business strategies have failed because the existing reward strategy communicated messages that were at cross-purposes with them. CEOs frequently complain, "The new business strategy does not have any traction with employees!" It's somewhat surprising, then, to learn that there's been little or no revisions made to the reward architecture (i.e., via the money, mix, or messages dimensions) or the reward strategy pro-gram design itself. You have to ask those CEOs, "What did you expect?"

## That's Not All, Folks

You are nearly done—with this book, that is. But you've taken a long first step in the journey of a thousand miles. Reward strategists know that their work is never done. You will need to continue to test and adjust your plan as your business experiences the inevitable changes.

The challenge presented in this book is to drive knowledge of the business as deep into the organization as possible and tie people to it through rewards. To keep that message fresh you have to keep the reward plans themselves up-to-date and refreshed; this book has provided the tools to do that. Next and last—Chapter 9—provides several approaches to customize your approach and ensure that it continues as a systemic process.

But there is more. Through the Employee Engagement Process your organization now has a team of designers who have lived through this design and development and have put a structure in place. As such, you've begun to create an army of employees who "get it." They know how their efforts directly impact organization success and the role of rewards to support it. You must continue to recruit and to see that army grow throughout the organization. Don't stop delivering the message until every last man and woman is engaged!

## Chapter 9

# APPROACHES TO HELP CONDENSE THE PROCESS

FREQUENTLY, TODAY'S BUSINESS ENVIRONMENT DOESN'T afford us the luxury of time. Besides, as organizations strive to achieve more—in terms of productivity and results—they are less likely to put resources toward the development of HR processes. The key is to define the scope of the effort so as to meet the unique needs of the company. Accordingly, this chapter provides three methods for customizing (and, as appropriate, condensing) the Employee Engagement Process. In using these condensed processes the designers sacrifice some level of employee involvement. The goal, however, is still the same; reward plans that engage employees in business outcomes. You should consider these alternatives in any of the following circumstances:

- *Time and resources do not permit a more involved process.* Many of the ideas presented come from organizations as they worked through deregulation and other massive changes to their business environment. Likewise, organizations in extremes, like turnaround situations, benefit significantly from speed.

- *Jump-starting the initiative.* Even if the plan is to utilize an Employee Engagement Process for aspects of the detailed design, the conclave or expert panel approaches can be used to move quickly through the front end of the process. In environments where degrees of freedom are limited—for example, in privately held organizations—you can use the condensed process to get through the owner's articulating of the strategy quickly.

■ *(Re)consider current design effectiveness.* The speed of business change dictates the requirement for more frequent reviews of reward plans. These condensed approaches can be used a year or two after the Employee Engagement Process to validate the designs. Alternatively, the audit can be used before initiating a design process to establish need.

■ *Building a business case.* In the event that the extent of change is uncertain, or that management has not bought into the requirements for redesign, the condensed methodologies allow for the input into a business case and/or the demonstration of current plan shortcomings.

---

### INCREASING EFFECTIVENESS THROUGH EMPLOYEE INVOLVEMENT, BY ANTOINETTE PETRUCCI

A manufacturer of construction machinery implemented a new, lean manufacturing process that required significant behavior change of production technicians and consequently a change in how they were paid. Historically, each technician was hired and trained for one job, and all the techs, regardless of position, were paid about the same amount. The new manufacturing process required technicians to "flex" up and down the line. This meant learning new skills and working very differently. Career and pay growth needed to reflect individual contribution to the business. This was a fundamental change to the employment contract that was grounded in an egalitarian culture.

One of the first steps in the design process was to develop an involvement strategy. The organization wanted to ensure that everyone affected by the program changes had an opportunity to provide input about their concerns and issues regarding the lean manufacturing process. The need for speed, efficiency, and high involvement resulted in the use of various approaches for including employees in the process. A combination of surveys, interviews, and focus groups was used with various constituencies to gather information and test concepts. The approach used for each workforce segment reflected a balance of line scheduling and the type of information needed.

To help expedite the process, the organization asked an expert third party to gather and analyze the situation and develop a straw-model design. Leadership served as a challenge team for the straw-model design and actively participated in its further refinement and development. To test the design, leadership held a two-day summit with first-line supervisors who provided additional input that helped to finalize the plan details and shaped the implementation process.

The outcomes were very positive in terms of the business results achieved as a result of effective design and implementation. The entire process fostered the right degree of involvement that provided ownership of the outcome at all levels in the organization. In particular, leadership and first-line supervisors became real change agents in facilitating program implementation and ongoing involvement for renewal of both the manufacturing and compensation plan. Within a year, the workforce embraced the new manufacturing process through demonstrated behavior change resulting in improved business performance; exceeded productivity improvement goals; and higher profitability and return on asset performance requirements.

*Antoinette Petrucci is a principal with Buck Consultants.*

## The Conclave Approach to Total Rewards Strategy Development

The term *conclave* may conjure up visions of men in robes, locked in a dark room and not emerging until white smoke billows from the chimney, indicating that they have elected a new Pope, but this book's approach uses all the modern conveniences—including meeting rooms, whiteboards, and flipcharts. The most significant benefit of the conclave approach is speed; executives are brought together and put through a scripted facilitation where consensus is built and decisions are made. The second most significant benefit is that the products or outputs can be implemented immediately, because the participants are corporate decision makers. Here is how it works.

First, this approach needs an executive sponsor. Human resources is engaged to facilitate the process—not own it. The sponsor's role is to identify the appropriate executives who will participate and gain their support for the process. Further, the sponsor will manage the logistics and facilitation.

When selecting executives, determining who participates and who does not is imperative. The process has been done with intact executive teams or executives who represent various departments and functions. Begin with the premise that you are developing a strategic plan. Whom would you want? The session works only if the executives selected are indi-

```
+--------------------------------------+
|        Executive Conclave Agenda     |
|                                      |
|  Day One                             |
|                                      |
|  Icebreaker                          |
|  Reward strategy background          |
|  Environmental scan                  |
|  Business response                   |
|  SWOT and gap analysis               |
|                                      |
|  Three-dimensional reward strategy   |
|  Money, mix, and messages communi-   |
|     cations                          |
|  What's next?                        |
|                                      |
|  Day Two                             |
|                                      |
|  Architecture 101: blueprints        |
|  Who-what-where-when-why-how-        |
|     how much                         |
|  Because/therefore                   |
|  Upside/downside                     |
|  Implementation planning             |
+--------------------------------------+
```

viduals who possess the influence to make solid recommendations that have a high probability of acceptance. Typically, the sessions do not include the CEO. Recommendations are made to the CEO, but the bulk of the design is left up to the executive team. It is the top-level officers who have the authority, responsibility, and accountability to implement the decisions. Because key information lies with these top decision makers, executive selection is a key aspect of this process' success.

Although this approach can be abbreviated to accommodate the availability of your executives, the optimal approach is to have selected executives participate in two non-contiguous facilitated days of exercises to assess the key influences in reward design and then develop a reward strategy based on inputs from their assessment. (See the sidebar for the two-day agenda.) Between the two sessions, the facilitators organize the inputs from day one and structure the appropriate design foundation for day two. This process is designed to maximize the use of management's time by focusing the exercises on the most important aspects of their business as it relates to its human assets. Along the way they set priorities, organize inputs, and develop a plan. There are five critical steps to this process.

## Step One: Prework

The more the team can initially organize key influences on reward design, the easier the facilitation process will be. This requires that the facilitators identify the reward influences and then organize them in a way that allows participants to make design decisions. Typically, this takes the form of a document review, but selected executive interviews are also helpful in framing what is and isn't up for consideration. Tools and techniques to identify the influences are both detailed in Chapters 2 and 3 and are provided on the CD-ROM.

Interviews are often conducted with senior executives, some of whom will or will not participate in the conclave process. For nonconclave participants (e.g., the CEO), their input is required for defining the scope of the effort and any preconceived notions about rewards. For conclave participants, you may use the interview time to educate them or discuss issues they do not want to bring up in the group. While the prework does not directly create the finished product, it is a vital first step in the process. The prework sets the direction of the two facilitated days. Without it, the process would lack focus and integrity. Increased effort here will translate into larger gains during the two conclave sessions.

As part of the prework you will want to develop a reading package for the participants. This material should provide background information to the participants in order to speed the effort. It should include technical subject matter (e.g., articles on rewards and rewards strategy) as well as insights into the organization and the influences on reward program design.

Finalizing and gaining approval on the agenda is the final part of prework. Participants need to arrive at the session with an open mind and ready to work; make sure you prepare them for it!

## Step Two: Day One

The purpose of day one is to establish the overall goals for the process and provide the selected executives with the information that they need regarding Total Rewards Strategy, the key influences, and relevant company information derived from the prework. This facilitated session has fundamentally three parts: education, environmental evaluation, and gaining input into the design of architecture and philosophy development. Of course, this agenda can be effective only if the ad hoc team can work efficiently together. Accordingly, you should begin the session with an exercise to get the participants to open up and get comfortable with one another. An icebreaker can be used for this purpose.

With the stage set, the first part of the day is designed to provide the participants the information they require in order to build a common understanding of the key influences on reward designs. Review reward plan fundamentals and the business context with the participants. This information assists in defining the critical environmental factors that determine the best strategy design. You need to ensure that the participants have enough knowledge to make informed choices. Plan fundamentals and the business context typically include:

- *Fundamental Knowledge of Reward Programs.* This covers the definition of Total Rewards, the framework of a rewards strategy, and types of plans and how they work together. Executives have already been given articles in the prework; for context, build your information around these articles.

- *The Key Influences of Reward Program Design.* These influences (defined in Chapter 3) need to be presented and understood within the context of your organization. Accordingly, this discussion establishes the foundation for the environmental scan.

With this information serving as a foundation, the second part of the day's work is dedicated to analyzing the company, its environment, and the key influences on reward strategy design. The objective is to build understanding, insight, and consensus. Establishing both a common understanding of the various influences on design and of the consensus response requires that the facilitators develop the lens through which the participants view the pertinent topics.

Environmental evaluation and consensus building is facilitated through the environmental scan, business response, and SWOT analysis processes. Facilitating the group through the environmental scan is a matter of taking the information shared in the education sessions and assessing how to interpret it. This is the subject of Chapter 4, which gives insights into how the various influences on rewards drive designs. This discussion is designed to focus on your company's specific orientation with regard to those influences; the tools provided on the CD-ROM to identify and define internal and external influences (Phase I, steps 2 and 3) can be adapted to the team's requirements.

With the influences defined, the lens through which to view a response is set. Business response provides the exercises that allow the executive team to create reward plans that fit your company's specific situation. This session is built on brainstorming and allows the executives to "try on" various alternatives.

An important advantage of the conclave approach is that it is fast. Its speed, however, is valuable only if a path forward can be identified. Accordingly, it needs to provide the executives with the opportunities for building consensus and getting the job done, and for this you should use the standard tools of SWOT and gap analysis. These tools are provided on the CD-ROM and explained in Chapter 5. For a conclave session you need to identify the downside risks that may cause the designs to fail—typically items that one or more executives cannot accept—and move the group to the decisions that yield the greatest good for the most people.

Day one needs to end with a discussion about the three dimensions of reward strategy—money, mix, and messages—to begin to build architecture and philosophy. To facilitate this discussion and collect the initial insights of the executives about these dimensions, use the exercises on the CD-ROM (Phase III, steps 1, 2, and 3).

At the end of day one, the group will have all the information it needs to write the reward philosophy and Reward Architecture. It is inefficient, however, to have a group of executives do this task. Accordingly, creating these materials is generally done by the conclave's facilitators/sponsors based on the executive input. This work is done after day one but before day two—in fact, a week typically separates the two facilitated sessions to allow time for the writing of these materials. A suggested work plan for the interim period between the two sessions is provided in the next section.

### Step Three: Interim Work

The week separating the two sessions is used to write the first draft of the reward philosophy and Reward Architecture and to ensure that any open items remaining from day one are cleared before proceeding to day two. The team is assigned work between sessions that includes processing and organizing the information about the company and its environment (from day one) and turning that input into a cogent philosophy. The information is then organized and consolidated so that day two's facilitation will flow more easily. The interim work should provide the team with a much-needed jump-start on the second session. This is generally accomplished through follow-up conversations by the facilitators/sponsors with any executive who requires "extra assistance." The executive conclave agenda does not allow for wasted time. If a participant needs to provide additional information or receive further knowledge about a particular concept, the facilitators should work with that executive as part of the interim work between the sessions.

The process facilitators should use this interim time to:

- Draft the reward strategy using the insights from the money, mix, and messages discussion. The process steps for authoring Total Rewards Strategy (described in Chapter 5 and the corresponding tools in the CD-ROM) can be used to aid this process.

- Develop the initial design recommendations.
- Initiate the business case for change. Much of day two will be spent in this realm, so it is helpful to establish the foundation.

## Step Four: Day Two

Day two is structured to organize and convert the information from all prior work (i.e., prework, day one, interim work) into a tight statement of reward strategy. The agenda for day two contains practical exercises for the team to participate in to define critical factors of the business strategy that need to be addressed in a strategic reward plan. In addition, day two maps out upside/downside contingencies of potential strategies. Remember, Total Rewards Strategy design is a fact-based art. Prework was designed to collect facts. On day one, a scientific approach is utilized to organize and interpret the facts in a focused manner. On day two, a reward strategy philosophy is articulated that will provide the basis for all current and future rewards programs; this application of the facts is the art. Accordingly, skilled facilitation is needed to get the group through these steps because of the potential for competing agendas on the part of the various participants. One of the most valuable aspects of the conclave process is that executives share in how the issues that influence the design of reward plans drive design decisions. It may be that the influences affect different executives differently. Accordingly, a component of day two is identifying when and where to compromise; the process facilitators should strive for consensus, but given the time constraints of this process, agreement to move forward is acceptable. As your group moves through the process, the participants should identify showstoppers and hold them in a "parking lot," where they'll be addressed later. It is important to continue to move forward.

The most critical aspect of reward strategy implementation is to gain management's support. The facilitation of executives, and their direct involvement in the process, goes a long way toward building that support. The closer you can move the group toward consensus and resolve blockages to implementation, the more likely you are that the plans will ultimately be adopted. Ensure that you spend the time necessary to address the concerns of the various participants to get as close to a satisfactory resolution as possible.

## Step Five: Finalize Money, Mix, and Messages

Money, mix, and messages are used as the basis of Total Rewards Strategy. Developing the insights from day one into a Reward Architecture, in order to define what's needed from the reward programs to accomplish business objectives, is the team's focus for day two. The first job is to approximate the total amount of reward resources you have to allocate to deliver those messages. Then, establish the mix of programs to deliver those messages through rewards as efficiently as possible. The mix is intended to allocate rewards in a manner that effectively communicates key messages. Key messages can be communicated through every reward type, both extrinsic and intrinsic.

In little more than two days of the executives' time, spanned typically over a two-week period, the organization has articulated a plan that will move it toward effectively allocating reward resources. This plan provides a screen through which programs can be evaluated in regard to their fit in the company's overall scheme. Individual program merits are no longer measured in a vacuum, but are measured based on the effectiveness of the overall reward strategy.

The conclave approach should assist management in creating an effective strategy as quickly as possible. Using this approach, however, may result in the omission of certain important aspects of a reward strategy (such as employee input, the cornerstone of the Employee Engagement Process). Expediency necessarily sacrifices some degree of accuracy. This is a 70/30 approach that leaves some issues on the table and unresolved. The question that must be asked is: "During the pre- and interim work periods, what elements of the 30 percent that was overlooked do I need to address in order for our strategy to be successful?" The issues that may need to be addressed outside the scope of the conclave, or as part of the pre- or between-session work, typically include:

- *A Market Competitiveness Assessment of Total Remuneration.* This approach does not include the completion of an analysis of the competitiveness of existing plans, but as a diagnostic tool it is helpful—almost required—in determining what changes should be addressed and in what order.

- *Employee Input on Existing Plans to Determine the Extent to Which They May Be Emulated.* Employee input is a cornerstone of the Employee Engagement Process because of the power that rewards have in defining the compact between the employee and employer. Since the conclave approach focuses executives on the development of strategy, and since employees are not involved in the meetings, this issue must be resolved either in the prework or the between-session periods. Employee focus groups or attitude survey information can be brought into the session to engage employee opinions, and consequently gain employee acceptance more easily upon implementation.

■ *Communication to the Organization at Large.* These sessions are not intended to be secretive. However, they do occur over a condensed period of time. Because the approach, by its design, completes a three-month process in the space of one to two weeks, a concerted effort needs to be considered for communicating the team's activities to the organization at large. Consider this communication issue at the end of day one.

The conclave approach to Total Rewards Strategy is an excellent methodology for moving the team through the process of architecture and philosophy development. It can be used as a methodology in and of itself, or as a means to jump-start the design process. The conclave approach allows executives to work with one another, in a facilitated format and to see how rewards impact their part of the business, other parts of the business, and the business as a whole. It provides them with the framework for making informed decisions and building a Total Rewards model that works throughout the organization. And it is fast. Whether your organization requires the speed to achieve its business objectives or your executives don't have the time to offer to the development of a more involved TRS process, speed is an advantage.

## The Expert Panel/Ivory Tower Approach to Total Reward Strategy Development

This approach streamlines the development process by using a panel of subject matter experts to develop a "money, mix, and message" straw model for the organization. It is noninvasive, so it does not involve employees throughout the organization (which is a potential shortfall); like the conclave approach, though, it allows designers to jump-start the effort even before it is broadly known to be under way. Because of the informality of the process, the designers require fewer up-front materials—so more time can be focused on analyzing background information and agreeing on the strategy. Experts match their knowledge of the company with reward design alternatives for fast response. In essence, this approach puts the same structure and analytical tools used in the conclave approach into the hands of content experts, allowing them to do the design.

Having the appropriate participants is critical to the success of this approach. Tools are provided on the CD-ROM for Phase I of the Employee Engagement Process, under Project Planning, to assess both numbers and requirements for design team participation; use them to identify subject matter experts for this expert panel. The executive sponsor will be able to provide assistance in this regard; she should be considered for potential participation, too. If properly facilitated and focused, the panel of subject matter experts should be able to do its work in one day.

It is important to keep in mind that in shortcutting the Employee Engagement Process, this approach does not collect employee input. All of the data gathering is research based. The designers may choose to use a challenge team approach (described in Chapter 5) to test the designs with employees before moving forward.

On the CD-ROM, too, there are tools for articulating a Total Rewards Strategy through the development of money, mix, and messages. The panel should use these tools, along with a streamlined agenda that mirrors the conclave agenda, to work through the day.

Once again, speed is the advantage with this approach, but the challenge comes in achieving buy-in. Remember, employee input into the designs has been minimal at best. One way to overcome this shortfall is to focus on a more robust, detailed design. Chapter 6 illustrated that the greatest leverage comes from the development of the detailed designs and the organization's ability to link employees to business outcomes through rewards. Accordingly, use the expert panel to accelerate the strategy articulation process if executives do not have the attention span for a conclave. Then, through tools like SWOT and gap analysis, identify high-priority designs focusing the organization's attentions and efforts on the specific details of those programs.

The final step for the expert panel before handing its Total Rewards Strategy to the plan design team (which will ultimately develop the details) is to gain executive approval. Because the company's detailed reward plan designs will flow from the strategy, it is crucial that executives both understand and approve its content. The executive sponsor should be the team's point person in this regard.

As the expert panel is only commissioned to articulate the strategy, most of the work still needs to occur to make the strategy come alive in the details. The tools and processes described on the CD-ROM can be used to effectively take the articulated strategy and, through the Employee Engagement Process, design reward programs.

## The Upstream and Downstream Reward Strategy Audits

A methodology for simply assessing Total Rewards Strategy is the Rewards Strategy Audit. This, too, is a noninvasive approach that assesses the fit between Total Rewards Strategy and either business strategy (upstream) or reward plans (downstream), or both. As illustrated in Figure 3.1, the company's Total Rewards Strategy sits between the business strategy (at the top of the stream) and the reward programs (at the bottom of the stream). Accordingly, from the vantage point of Total Rewards Strategy, these two approaches provide effective methodologies for diagnosing problems and miscommunications that exist because of a lack of linkage between business strategy and rewards strategy and/or rewards strategy and plan designs. The most common problem is the delivery of mixed messages caused by the poor alignment of reward programs. Although the audits do not lead to a design, they can be used exclusively or as part of a design process.

Like the expert panel approach, the Rewards Strategy Audit requires industry and corporate knowledge, awareness of how to decode strategy and set metrics, and the insight to determine whether reward plans and strategy meet stated objectives. However, unlike the expert panel approach, where the goal is to articulate a strategy, the effort here is on assessing an existing strategy. Although it is fast and effective, affecting change may require additional effort to gain support. Let's explore the two versions of this approach.

### Upstream Reward Strategy Audit

The Upstream Reward Strategy Audit reviews the fit between Total Rewards Strategy and business strategy. In Chapter 3, you explored the factors that most dramatically impact Total Rewards Strategy design; the upstream audit process looks at what impacts the connection between business and rewards strategies. This audit can be used effectively when organizational changes drive a new business strategy to assess the existing Total Rewards Strategy. It requires:

- A complete review of the articulated Total Rewards Strategy.
- Assessment of the people-strategy dimensions of structure, process, and culture.

- A clear understanding of the business strategy, typically through a consensus-building or decoding process (tools for which are provided on the CD-ROM as well as in Chapter 5 of this book).
- Analysis of the external and internal influences on business success.

The key to the upstream audit is to assess the degree to which the organization's Total Rewards Strategy supports the people and business strategies and is aligned with the reward design influences. The team uses these inputs to determine the degree to which:

- The reward offerings—the money—"pay" for the right things. Those behaviors and outcomes, which are dictated in the business strategy that drives the right behaviors, enforce the right organizational structure model and lead the company to the right cultural paradigm.
- The mix of reward elements is appropriate. This mix drives the desired results and outcomes.
- The messages—messages about what the company is attempting to accomplish and what it means to work in this company—are deliberate and focused on those metrics that make the company successful.

### Downstream Reward Strategy Audit

The Downstream Reward Strategy Audit measures the degree to which the articulated strategy has been actualized through the deployment of reward programs. In Chapter 2 a methodology was provided to inventory current reward plans; this is an effective tool as you look downstream from strategy to the plans themselves. Inventorying involves:

1. Measuring the various reward elements against the organization's stated compensation philosophy for:
   - Appropriateness of the markets and the correctness of the competitive level (money)
   - Proper mix of reward elements
2. Assessing the degree to which employees understand and are committed to the various program designs:
   - Do employees know the plan's key messages?
   - Are employees taking actions toward desired outcomes?

The downstream audit is used when you know the strategy is correct and you want to ensure that it is being actualized through plans and programs. It requires that plans and programs be inventoried and then tested against the Total Rewards Strategy. It typically involves collecting employee input through focus groups.

The fundamental advantage to the upstream and downstream audits is that they allow the user to assess the area of greatest organizational pain, without disruption of the organization. This effort can be undertaken as a standard human resources intervention or as a means for collecting, organizing, and evaluating information to make design decisions.

Every organization has its own level of tolerance for process, and strategy development is clearly a process. This book as a whole is designed to give you the tools to navigate the course of your own design efforts—it supplies the compass, the map, and the expeditionary expertise that is required. In this chapter, it also provides some shortcuts to condensing the Employee Engagement Process and/or jump-starting design. Just bear in mind that shortcuts have their peril, and as a designer you never want to lose sight of them.

# Notes

## Preface

1. *2001 Business, People, and Total Reward Strategy Alignment Questionnaire* (New York: Andersen 2001).

## Chapter 1

1. *2001 Business, People, and Total Reward Strategy Alignment Questionnaire.*
2. Richard E. S. Boulton, Barry D. Libert, and Steve M. Samek (Andersen), *Cracking the Value Code* (New York: HarperBusiness, 2000), pp. 17–18.
3. James L. Haskett, W. Earl Sasser, and Leonard A. Schlesinger, *The Service Profit Chain* (New York: The Free Press, 1997), pp. 256–257.
4. "Beyond the Eleventh: How Employers Are Responding to the September 11th Terrorist Attacks" (New York: Buck Consultants, October 2001), p. 2.
5. *2001 Business, People, and Total Reward Strategy Alignment Questionnaire.*

## Chapter 2

1. *2001 Business, People, and Total Reward Strategy Alignment Questionnaire.*
2. Ibid.
3. Robert Kaplan and David Norton, *The Strategy Focused Organization* (Boston, MA: Harvard Business School Press, 2001), pp. 12–13.
4. *2001 Business, People, and Total Reward Strategy Alignment Questionnaire.*

## Chapter 3

1. Michael E. Porter, *Competitive Advantage* (New York: Free Press, 1985), p. 11.
2. Robert S. Kaplan and David P. Norton, *The Balanced Scorecard: Translating Strategy into Action* (Boston: Harvard Business School Press, 1996).
3. Todd Manas, "Making the Balanced Scorecard Approach Payoff," *The American Compensation Association Journal* (Second Quarter 1999), pp. 13–21.

4. Henry Mintzberg, *The Structuring of Organizations* (Upper Saddle River, N.J.: Prentice-Hall, Inc., 1979).

5. Jacalyn Serriton and James L. Stern, *Corporate Culture/Team Culture* (New York: AMACOM, 1997), pp. 26–27.

6. Richard E. S. Boulton, Barry D. Libert, and Steve M. Samek, *Cracking the Value Code* (New York: HarperBusiness, 2000), p. 135.

7. James R. Detert, Roger G. Schroeder, and John J. Mauriel, "A Framework for Linking Culture and Improvement Initiatives in Organizations," *Academy of Management Review,* Vol. 25, No. 4 (2000), pp. 850–863.

8. Daniel R. Denison, *Corporate Culture and Organizational Effectiveness* (New York: John Wiley & Sons, Inc., 1990).

9. Edgar H. Schein, *Organizational Culture and Leadership* (New York: Jossey-Bass, 1992).

10. Thomas P. Flannery, David A. Hofrichter, and Paul E. Platten, *People, Performance, and Pay* (New York: Free Press, 1996), pp. 29–40.

11. Ibid, p. 30.

12. Ibid, p. 32.

13. Ibid, pp. 37–38.

14. Ibid, pp. 38–39.

## Chapter 4

1. *2001 Business, People, and Total Reward Strategy Alignment Questionnaire.*

2. Ibid.

3. Ibid.

## Chapter 5

1. Todd Manas, "The Compensation Carpenter," *Workspan* (September 2001), p. 6.

## Chapter 6

1. *2001 Business, People, and Total Reward Strategy Alignment Questionnaire.*

2. Ted Buyniski and Brett Harsen, "2002: An Equity Forecast" (San Francisco: iQuantic Buck, 2002), pp. 1–6.

3. Todd Manas, "Rewarding Through Recognition: Learning from the Military," *ACANEWS,* October 1998, pp. 23–26.

4. *2000/2001 Compensation Budget and Planning Survey* (Secaucus, New Jersey: Buck Consultants, 2000), p. 20.

## Chapter 8

1. Robert S. Kaplan and David P. Norton, *The Strategy Focused Organization* (Boston, MA: Harvard Business School Press, 2001), pp. 69–70.

# Bibliography

"Beyond the Eleventh: How Employers Are Responding to the September 11th Terrorist Attacks." New York: Buck Consultants, October 2001.

Boulton, Richard E. S., Barry D. Libert, and Steve M. Samek. *Cracking the Value Code*. New York: HarperBusiness, 2000.

Buyniski Ted and Brett Harsen. "2002: An Equity Forecast." San Francisco: iQuantic Buck, 2002.

Denison, Daniel R. *Corporate Culture and Organizational Effectiveness*. New York: John Wiley & Sons, Inc., 1990.

Detert, James R., Roger G. Schroeder, and John J. Mauriel, "A Framework for Linking Culture and Improvement Initiatives in Organizations." *Academy of Management Review,* Vol. 25, No. 4 (2000).

Flannery, Thomas P., David A. Hofrichter, and Paul E. Platten. *People, Performance, and Pay*. New York: Free Press, 1996.

Haskett, James L., W. Earl Sasser, and Leonard A. Schlesinger. *The Service Profit Chain*. New York: The Free Press, 1997.

Kaplan Robert S. and David P. Norton. *The Balanced Scorecard: Translating Strategy into Action*. Boston: Harvard Business School Press, 1996.

Kaplan, Robert S., and David P. Norton. *The Strategy Focused Organization*. Boston: Harvard Business School Press, 2001.

Manas, Todd. "Making the Balanced Scorecard Approach Payoff." *The American Compensation Association Journal* (Second Quarter 1999).

———. "Rewarding Through Recognition: Learning from the Military." *ACANEWS* (October 1998).

———. "The Compensation Carpenter." *Workspan* (September 2001).

Mintzberg, Henry. *The Structuring of Organizations*. Upper Saddle River, N.J.: Prentice-Hall, Inc., 1979.

Porter, Michael E. *Competitive Advantage*. New York: Free Press, 1985.

Schein, Edgar H. *Organizational Culture and Leadership*. New York: Jossey-Bass, 1992.

Sherriton, Jacalyn and James L. Stern. *Corporate Culture/Team Culture.* New York:
    AMACOM, 1997.
*2000/2001 Compensation Budget and Planning Survey.* Secaucus, N.J.: Buck Con-
    sultants, 2000.
*2001 Business, People, and Total Reward Strategy Alignment Questionnaire.* New
    York: Andersen 2001.

# Index

accidents, 221
adaptability, and organizational culture, 79
administration
   of base pay, 203
   and impact testing, 241
   of variable rewards, 216, 218
advertising, 129
affected parties (in project planning), 31
affiliation
   as noncash reward, 5
   as recruitment incentive, 98–100
agendas, 35, 282
aggregate compensation costs, 242, 245
airline industry, 105
"all and only," 205
analysis
   of employees, 197–198
   of readiness for change, 166
   for Reward Architecture, 129, 162–167
   *see also* gap analysis; SWOT analysis; work analysis
architecture, reward, *see* Reward Architecture
assessment
   of need to update TRS, xviii–xx
   of plan effectiveness, 269, 271–272
   with Rewards Strategy Audits, 290–292
audience, 37
audits, 290–292

Baby Bells
   commitment at, 257
   gap analysis of, 134, 136
   people strategy at, 84
balanced approach to business measurement, 121, 122, 272–274
balanced scorecard (BSC), 54, 56–65, 274
bankruptcy, 43–44
barrier(s) to success, 250–259
   communication as, 253–259
   implementation as, 253
base pay, 190–203
   and administration, 203
   delivery of, 199–203
   foregoing increases in, 212–213
   freezing of, 245, 246
   and people analysis, 197–198
   and work analysis, 190, 192–197
"because" statements, 160–161, 247, 249
behavior change, 120
benefits, 3
"best-of-each" option, 205
"bigger than Bob," 46
Bloomberg news service, 128

boards of directors, 132
bonuses, 44, 203
Bossidy, Lawrence A., on organizational culture, 73
Brandon, Rhonda, on motivating talent, 98
Browne, David, on role redesign and behavior change, 120
BSC, *see* balanced scorecard
Buck Consultants, 233
"buckets o'cash," 200
budgets, 200, 213
Building Know-How (Phase I of TR Development Process), 8, 10, 13–37
   and communication, 32–37
   and creating a business case, 18–22, 24–25
   gap analysis for, 25–26
   and ownership of TR strategy process, 15–17
   and project planning, 30–32
   role of project team in, 22, 23, 26–30
Busang, Kristen, on line of sight, 244
Bushley, David, on ownership changes, 90
*Business, People, and Total Reward Strategy Alignment Questionnaire,* 59–64, 73–78, 130, 261
business case, 18–22, 24–25
business strategy, 41, 48–55
   and building know-how, 48–55
   knowledge levels of, 139–143
   levels of, xxi
   making, operational, 137–154
   objectives linked with, 155–157
   plan fit with, 272–274

caps, pay, 215
career advancement, 198–199
cash
   as compensation, 3
   and performance plans, 219, 220
casual dress, 232, 233
CEO (chief executive officer), 282
champions, process, 15, 18
change management, 73, 78, 262
change(s)
   in ownership, 90
   plan, 274–275, 277
   readiness for, 166
   responsibility for, 277
   timing of, 250–251
Chapter 11 bankruptcy, 43–44
chief executive officer (CEO), 282
choice, power of, 116
*City Slickers* (film), 161
Coca-Cola Company, 47
Colonial Pipeline Company, 98–100

combined performance metric (CPM), 213–214
commitment
    company, 257
    employee, 269, 271, 272
communication
    amount of, 258–259
    as barrier to success, 253–255
    case study illustrating, 255–256
    delivery methods of, 257
    with employees, 31, 131
    frequency of, 259
    of mission/objective, 172, 174
    to organization at large, 288
    of personal impact, 254–255
    of revisions, 275, 277
    in Reward Architecture, 136–137
    within team, 33, 35, 37
    and transfer of know-how, 32–37
communications and contacts process, 71, 76
"Communists and cowboys" tool, 208–210
community, 129, 131–132
compact, employment, 3
company cars, 227
company history, 129
compensation
    aggregate costs of, 242, 245
    and balanced scorecard, 58
    business integration driven by, 109–110
    cash, 3
    as communication tool, 32–33
    impact testing of, 243
    over-/under-, 243
    values-based, 101–102
    see also indirect compensation; pay; rewards
compensation-driven business integration, 109–110
competency anchor, 190, 192
competition
    influence of, 43, 91
    levels of, 171–173
competitiveness
    market, 287
    program, 129
conclave approach to TRS development, 281–288
    day one stage of, 283–285
    day two stage of, 286
    interim work stage of, 285–286
    money, mix, and messages finalization stage of,
        286–288
    prework stage of, 282–283
confidentiality, 131
consensus, 33, 35
consistency, and organizational culture, 79
constituency review, 181–182
consultants, 24, 30
contribute, opportunity to, 4
control, 79
coordination, 79
core values, 48, 101–102
Corporate Culture and Organization Effectiveness
    (Daniel R. Denison), 79
corporate planes, 227
cost advantage, 49–51, 140, 142, 143
cost/benefit modeling, 24–25
costs
    impact testing of, 242, 245
    plan, 25, 26
counseling services, 227
CPM, see combined performance metric
credibility, management, 275
culture, see organizational culture
culture and effectiveness model, 79
Curly (fictional character), 161, 181
customers
    and organizational capabilities, 59, 60
    Reward Architecture input from, 131–132
    as stakeholders, 24, 46, 93–95
customer service, 4

database, notes, 35
data collection
    for analysis, 128–132
    for effectiveness assessment, 268–270
"deadwood," 83
decision making, 71, 75
defined benefit programs, 223
defined contribution plans, 223
deliverables (in project planning), 31
delivery, pay, 199–203
Deming, Charles, on "deadwood," 83
Deming, W. Edwards, 104
demographics (of labor force), 265
Denison, Daniel R., 79
design, program, 187–238
    base pay principles of, 190–203
    case study illustrating, 233–235
    indirect compensation principles of, 221–233
    and long-term incentive plans, 218–221
    standard reward principles of, 187–190
    variable reward principles of, 203–218
design process (in project planning), 31–32
design teams, 17–18, 26–30, 256–259
detailed plans, 134
development, see training and development
development rewards, 229–232
diagnosis (of business case), 22
differentiators, 49–51
distribution, award, 215–216
document review, 128–130
Downstream Reward Strategy Audit, 274, 291–292

easy wins, 250, 251
economic value added (EVA), 82
effectiveness, sustaining, see Sustaining Plan
    Effectiveness
efficiency, 124, 125
elder/dependent care days, 232
"elevator ride," 157
eligibility, plan, 25, 205–206
e-mails, 35
employee assistance programs, 232
employee Engagement Process, 8–10, 13–15
employees
    analysis of, 197–198
    architecture review by, 182–183
    commitment of, 269, 271, 272
    communicating with, 31, 131, 136
    conclave approach input from, 287–288
    on design teams, 26–30
    eligibility of, 25, 205–206
    involvement of, 13–16, 280–281
    knowledge requirements of, 119
    line vs. staff, 66, 67, 69
    motivation of, 8, 11, 130
    and organizational capabilities, 63
    perceptions of, 130–131
    plan as understood by, 291
    on project team, 24
    recruitment of, 8, 42, 201–202, 218
    retention of, 3–4, 8, 43–44
    Reward Architecture input from, 130–131
    as stakeholders, 45
    TRS involvement of, 15–18
employee stay bonus, 44
employment compact, 3
"employment for as long as it makes sense," 159–160
entitlement mentality, 83, 222
equity plans, 219
EVA (economic value added), 82
excellence, affiliation with, 98–100
executive committees, 26, 27
executives, 22
    communicating with, 136
    conclave approach participation of, 281–282
    fears of, 28
    interviewing, 130, 131

executive sponsors, 281, 289
expectations, company, 157
expert facilitators, 30
expert panel approach to TRS development, 288–289
"expert witnesses," 30
external environment, 40, 41
 and building know-how, 42–44
 and industry profile, 91
 key stakeholder considerations in, 90–96
 and leading hallmarks, 91
external stakeholder(s), 29
 competition as, 91
 customers as, 93–95
 government as, 95, 96
 suppliers as, 93, 94

facilitators
 in conclave approach, 281–288
 expert, 30
 for focus groups, 131, 132
 process, 15, 18
feasibility matrix, 168, 170, 171
feedback loops, 33
field testing, 182–183
financial analysis, 242, 243, 245, 246
Fine, Howard, on entitlement mentality, 222
flexibility, 93
flexible benefits plan, 222, 223
flexible rewards, 117
flexible work schedules, 232, 233
focus
 and mix determination, 174
 and organizational culture, 79
focus groups, 130–132
focus strategy, 49–51, 140
foregone base pay increases, 212–213
formulas, funding, 213–214
freedom, degrees of, 176
functional culture, 80
funding, 212–214
future financial security programs, 222, 224, 226

gap analysis, 18, 162, 163
 for building know-how, 25–26
 reverse, 247
 and "therefore" statements, 134, 136
gap fillers, 232
general business strategy (GBS), xxi, 49, 102–104
General Motors paradigm, 242–243
geographic considerations (in project planning), 31
Girl Scouts of the USA, 47
Glantz, Martha, on timing of changes, 250–251
goals, 206–208
government
 base pay mandates from, 202–203
 indirect compensation statutes from, 222–223
 influence of, 42–43, 95, 96
growth strategy, 54

hallmarks, leading, 91
Hamel, Gary, 139
Hammer, Michael, on "being on the train," 268
historical payout, 25
holidays, 222
Horowitz, Mary, on communication of personal
 impact, 254–255
human resources (HR), 15
 and base pay design, 203
 conclave approach facilitated by, 281
 and impact testing, 241
 materials available from, 183–185
 and variable rewards design, 216, 218

identity, company, 157
illness, 221
impact testing, 241–243, 245–250
 of administration/human resources, 241

of compensation, 243
of costs, 242, 245
and financial analysis, 242, 243, 245, 246
of plan objectives, 245, 247–250
of variable rewards, 245, 246
implementation
 as barrier to success, 253
 of business strategy, 137–154
 of plan, 33
incentives
 long-term, 3, 180, 203, 218–221
 maximum, 215
 target, 215
 team-based, 205–206
income protection programs, 221, 223, 226
income replacement programs, 221–223, 226
indirect compensation, 221–233
 future financial security programs as, 222, 224, 226
 income protection programs as, 221, 223, 226
 income replacement programs as, 221–223, 226
 long-term disability coverage as, 221
 noncash rewards as, 229–233
 pay for time not worked as, 222, 226
 perquisites as, 225, 228–229
 short-term disability coverage as, 221
 sick pay as, 221
 statutory requirements for, 222–223
 workers' compensation as, 221
industry history, 129
industry profiles, 91
information
 analysis of, 162–167
 collection of, 128–132, 268–270
 team, 35
infrastructure, 203
injuries, 221
interviews, 130, 131, 283
involvement
 in business case, 22–24
 of employees, 13–16, 26–30, 280–281
 and organizational culture, 79
iQuantic Buck, 219
issue resolution, 21
ivory tower approach to TRS development, 288

Jackson, Toni, on line of sight, 244
job analysis, 193, 194
job description, 190, 192
job sharing, 232, 233
job valuation, 193, 195

Kaplan, Robert, 56, 59, 121, 122, 206, 272
key message(s), 6–8, 37, 88, 93
 and "because" statements, 160–161
 communication of, 33
 in conclave approach, 287
 Curly's "one thing" as, 161
 examples of, 157–159
 in expert panel approach, 288
 and general business strategy, 102
 importance of clear, 258
 for linking of objectives with business strategy,
  155–157
 and organizational capabilities, 104
 and people strategy, 115
 and PSCSFS, 121, 123
 reinforcement of, 265, 266
 and Rewards Strategy Audits, 291
 and value chain strategy, 105
 and vision, mission, and values, 100
key stakeholders, 45–46, 90–96
know-how
 building, see Building Know-How
 leveraging, see Leveraging Know-How for Success
 linking employees to, see Linking Employees to
  Know-How
 transferring, see Transferring Know-How

knowledge and innovation management, 71, 74
knowledge of organization strategy, 139–143
knowledge requirements, 119
knowledge transfer, 136–138, *see also* Transferring Know-How

labor market, 4, 201–202, 265
Leach, David, on compensation-driven business integration, 109–110
leading hallmarks, 91
learning map, 208
legal compliance, 202–203
legend makers, 232
level descriptor, 190, 192
Leveraging Know-How for Success (Phase IV of TR Development Process), 10, 127–185, 239–259
   and analysis of information, 162–167
   and data collection for analysis, 128–132
   and human resources, 183–185
   and impact testing, 241–243, 245–250
   and key messages, 155–161
   and knowledge transfer, 136–138
   and making business strategy operational, 137–154
   and mix determination, 174–176
   money dimension in, 167–174
   and organization of information, 132–136
   plan effectiveness of, 274
   and review of objectives, 177–183
   and SWOT analysis, 152, 155–156
lifestyle rewards, 230, 232–233
line managers, 8, 24
line of sight, 208, 244
Linking Employees to Know-How (Phase III of TR Development Process), 10, 87–125
   and general business strategy (GBS), 102–104
   and key stakeholders, 90–96
   with mission and objectives, 155–161
   and organization capabilities, 104–105
   and people strategy, 112–118
   plan effectiveness of, 274
   and priority setting, 123–125
   and PSCSFs, 117, 119–123
   and specific business strategy, 109–112
   and value chain strategy, 105–109
   with vision, mission, and values, 95, 97–102
location, 255
long-term disability coverage, 221
long-term incentives (LTI), 3, 180, 203, 218–221
low-cost providers, 49–51
LTI, *see* long-term incentives

macrotesting, 241
maintenance/reduction strategy, 54
management
   communicating with, 136
   credibility of, 275
   interviews of, 130
   levels of, 66–68
   and organizational capabilities, 62
   and people strategy, 66, 71–78, 114–115
Manas, Todd M., on perspective, 167
market
   competitiveness of, 287
   labor, 4, 201–202, 265
market share, 129
Martha Stewart Living Omnimedia (MSLO), 48
maximum incentive rewards, 215
McKinsey & Company, 157
medium, message, 37
messages, key, *see* key message(s)
metrics, 56, 59, 65
   and goal evaluation, 206–208
   and value proposition, 144, 145, 152–154
microtesting, 241
Miller, Jeff, on performance-based culture, 275–277
Mintzberg, Henry, 71

mission, 41
   articulation of, 172, 174
   and building know-how, 47, 48
   and organizational culture, 79
   TRS considerations in, 95, 97–102
mix, 6, 7, 88
   in conclave approach, 287
   determination of, 174–176
   in expert panel approach, 288
   and general business strategy, 104
   and organizational capabilities, 104
   and people strategy, 115, 117
   and PSCSFs, 121
   and Rewards Strategy Audits, 291
   and value chain strategy, 105
   and vision, mission, and values, 101
money, 6, 7, 88
   in conclave approach, 286–287
   in expert panel approach, 288
   and general business strategy, 102, 104
   and organizational capabilities, 104
   and people strategy, 114–115
   and PSCSFs, 121
   in Reward Architecture, 167–174
   as reward element, 168, 170–173
   and Rewards Strategy Audits, 291
   and value chain strategy, 105
   and vision, mission, and values, 101
   *see also* cash
motivation
   employee, 8, 11, 130
   and organizational culture, 79
MSLO (Martha Stewart Living Omnimedia), 48

name, plan, 25
network culture, 82
noncash rewards, 3–6, 229–233
Nordstrom, 107, 108
Norton, David, 56, 59, 121, 122, 206, 272
notes database, 35
not-for-profit organizations, 101–102, 250–251

objectives, plan, 13, 25
   articulation of, 172, 174
   of business case, 21
   business strategy linked with, 155–157
   confirmation of, 177–183
   impact testing of, 245, 247–250
   for teams, 30
one-percent assumption, 28
"one thing" technique, 161, 181
organization
   of information, 132–136
   of work, 193, 196, 197
organizational culture, 73, 79–83, 115, 117, 118
   focus on, 262, 264, 265
   overcoming boundaries of, 19
   performance-based, 275–277
*Organizational Culture and Leadership* (Edgar H. Schein), 79
organizational level of measure, 208–210
organizational structure, 65–70, 113
organization capabilities, 41
   and building know-how, 54, 56–65
   TRS considerations in, 104–105
orientation toward work, 79
overcompensation, 243
ownership
   changes in, 90
   public vs. private, 91, 92
   of TR strategy process, 15–18
owner stakeholders, 45, 131–132
*Ozzie and Harriet*, 224

parking perquisites, 229
partnership (with customers), 93

partner stakeholders, 45
Patton, George S., on execution of plan, 33
pay
  base, *see* base pay
  caps on, 215
  company history of, 25
  delivery of, 199–203
  and performance, 210–212
  sick, 221
  for time not worked, 222, 226
pay-decision system, 276–277
pay-for-performance orientation, 222, 244
*People, Performance, and Pay* (Flannery, Hofrichter, and Platten), 80, 82
people markets, 171, 173
people strategy, 41, 65–84
  and building know-how, 65–84
  case study illustrating, 84
  critical factors in success of, 82–83
  and management processes, 66, 71–78
  and organizational culture, 73, 79–83
  and organizational structure, 65–70
  TRS considerations in, 112–118
people strategy critical success factors (PSCSFs), 41, 83, 117, 119–123
  and key messages, 121, 123
  and mix, 121
  and money, 121
  for value proposition, 144, 149–151
perceptions
  employee, 130–131
  stakeholder, 132, 133
performance
  evaluation of, 202
  and payout, 210–212
performance-based culture, 275–277
performance unit plans, 219, 220
perquisites, 225, 228–229
personal impact, 254–255
personality conundrum, 174, 175
Petrucci, Antoinette, on employee involvement, 280–281
phantom equity plans, 219
Phillip Morris, 47
plan effectiveness, sustaining, *see* Sustaining Plan Effectiveness
planning, project, 30–32
Porter, Michael, xxi, 49, 50, 52, 139–140
power of choice, 116
PP&E (property plant and equipment), 17
priorities, setting, 123–125
process champions, 15, 18, 26
process culture, 80, 82
process facilitators, 15, 18
process optimization strategy, 54
process owners, 15, 18
productivity, 242
products and services
  customer influence on, 93
  and organizational capabilities, 61
product/service differentiator, 49–51, 140, 142, 143
profiles, industry, 91
project planning, 30–32
project teams, 22, 23, 26–30
property plant and equipment (PP&E), 17
purpose, 37

quality of work and life (as noncash reward), 5
questionnaire, rewards, xix, xxi–xxiii

rationality, 79
recognition awards, 230, 232
recruitment
  factors in, 42
  with long-term incentives, 218
  of new employees, 8
  with reward design, 201–202

regulation, *see* government
reorganization, 261, 263
resource planning, allocation, and monitoring process, 71
retail industry, 107, 108
retention, employee, 3–4, 8, 10–11, 43–44
retirement programs, 180, 223–224
return on plan investment (ROPI), 25–26
reverse gap analysis, 247
review(s)
  architecture, 182–183
  constituency, 181–182
  document, 128–130
  objective, 177–183
  plan, 26
Reward Architecture, 127–128, 134
reward programs
  knowledge of, 284
  outdated, xvii, 265, 267, 268
  recruitment with, 201–202
rewards
  development, 229–232
  flexible, 117
  incentive, 215
  lifestyle, 230, 232–233
  noncash, 3–6, 229–233
  short-term, 203, 204
  standard, 187–190
  variable, 203–218
  work balance, 230, 232–233
Rewards Strategy Audits, 290–292
role descriptor, 190, 192
role redesign, 120
ROPI, *see* return on plan investment

sabbaticals, 222
salary, 242
sales force, 205, 244
SBS, *see* specific business strategy
Scannella, James, on negotiating chapter 11 bankruptcy, 43–44
schedule, team, 35
Schein, Edgar H., on organizational culture, 79–80
scope, project, 24
self-directed learning and career pathing (SDLCP), 199
self-funding, 212
September 11, 2001 terrorist attacks, 4, 167
Sherriton, Jacalyn, on organizational culture, 73
short-term disability coverage, 221
short-term rewards, 203, 204
sick pay, 221
size, company, 113
skills, 201
SMEs, *see* subject matter experts
Smith, Roger, on salary-productivity relationship, 242
Social Security, 223, 224
Southwest Airlines, 105
special facilities perquisites, 227, 228
special risk perquisites, 227, 228
specific business strategy (SBS), xxi, 49, 53–55
  examples of, 110, 112
  TRS considerations in, 109, 111
sphere of influence, 210
sponsors, executive, 281, 289
stability, 79
stakeholders, 24, 41
  as affected parties, 31
  architecture review by, 181–182
  key, 45–46, 90–96
  and plan effectiveness, 269
  Reward Architecture input from, 130–132
Standard & Poor's, 128
standard rewards, 187–190
Starzmann, Gary, on affiliation with excellence, 98–100
steering committee, 26, 27
Stern, James L., on organizational culture, 73

Stern Stewart, Inc., 139
*The Strategy Focused Organization* (Robert Kaplan and David Norton), 272
subject matter experts (SMEs), 29, 30, 206, 289
success, barriers to, *see* barrier(s) to success
supervision process, 71, 77
supplier stakeholders, 24, 45–46, 93, 94, 132
"surfing the wave," 250, 252, 253
Sustaining Plan Effectiveness (Phase V of TR Development Process), 10, 25, 261–278
    assessment of, 269, 271–272
    and communication, 275, 277
    considerations for, 261–268
    and data collection, 268–270
    and fit with business strategy, 272–274
    and linkage/leverage, 274
    and need to adjust, 274–275, 277
SWOT analysis, 152, 155–156, 162, 164–166

talent, 4
target incentive rewards, 215
Taylor, Fredrick, 139
TCC (Total Cash Compensation), 3
TDC (Total Direct Cash), 3
team-based incentives, 205–206
teams
    design, 17–18, 26–30, 256–259
    objectives of, 30
    project, 22, 23, 26–30
technology, 64
Telecommunications Act of 1996, 134
telecommunications industry, 84
telecommuting, 232, 233
tenure, 180
terrorism, 4
testing, impact, 241–243, 245–250
"therefore" statement analysis, 134–136, 247
threshold incentive rewards, 215
time-based culture, 82
time off, 222, 226
time/timing
    of business case, 22
    of changes, 250–251
    and communication, 255
    of messages, 37
    and organizational culture, 79
    of plan implementation, 31
    of reward payouts, 216, 217
Total Cash Compensation (TCC), 3
Total Direct Cash (TDC), 3
Total Remuneration (TR), 1, 3, 4
Total Rewards Strategy (TRS), 1–3
    assessing need to update, xviii–xx
    defining dimensions of, 6–8
    definition of, 134
    and determination of appropriate mix, 174–176
    elements of, 187–190
    failure of conventional, xvii
    identification of alternatives in, 89
    prerequisites for creating successful, xvii–xviii
TR, *see* Total Remuneration
training and development, 229–232
    case study illustrating, 231–232
    as investment, 65
    of managers, 276–277
    as noncash reward, 5, 176
Transferring Know-How (Phase II of TR Development Process), 10, 39–86
    and business strategy, 48–55
    and core values, 48
    and defining critical factors, 39–42
    and external environment, 42–44

and leveraging know-how for success, 136–138
    and mission, 47, 48
    and organization capabilities, 54, 56–65
    and people strategy, 65–84
    and vision, 47
transportation perquisites, 227, 228
TRS, *see* Total Rewards Strategy
truth, 79
turnover, causes of, 10–11, *see also* retention, employee
*2000/2001 Compensation Budget and Planning Survey* (Buck Consultants), 233
Tyler, Cotton, on variable pay, 203
type, plan, 25

undercompensation, 243
unions, 44, 205, 227
Upstream Reward Strategy Audit, 290–291
U.S. military, 176

vacations, 222
valuation, job, 193, 195
value chain strategy (VCS), xxi, 49, 52, 53
    behavioral analysis using, 140–142
    examples of, 107–109
    and organizational capabilities, 59, 65
    TRS considerations in, 105–106
Value Line, 128
value proposition, 142, 144–148
value(s), 41
    compensation based on, 101–102
    core, 48, 101–102
    creating, 3–4
    TRS considerations in, 95, 97–102
value tree, 208
variable rewards, 203–218
    administration of, 216, 218
    amounts of, 212
    case study illustrating, 214
    distribution of, 215–216
    eligibility for, 205–206
    funding of, 212–214
    goals of, 206–208
    impact testing of, 245, 246
    and line of sight, 208
    maximum incentive rewards as, 215
    and performance-payout relationship, 210–212
    short-term, 203, 204
    and sphere of influence, 210
    target incentive rewards as, 215
    threshold incentive rewards as, 215
    timing of, 216, 217
VCS, *see* value chain strategy
vision, mission, and values (VMV), 41
    and building know-how, 47
    TRS considerations in, 95, 97–102

Wal-Mart, 107, 108
web sites
    company information on, 128–129
    team, 35
White, Scott, on recruitment with reward design, 201–202
wireless industry, 84
"wish lists," 134
work analysis, 190, 192–197
    and job analysis, 193, 194
    of job documentation, 190, 192
    and job valuation, 193, 195
    and organization of work, 193, 196, 197
work assurance perquisites, 227, 228
work balance rewards, 230, 232–233
workers' compensation, 221

# About the Authors

**Todd Manas** is a principal and is the Regional Practice Leader for compensation in the New York office of Buck Consultants. He has twenty years of combined line management, human resources practitioner, and consulting experience. Prior to joining Buck, Todd worked for several world-class organizations, including The Hay Group, Towers Perrin, and Philip Morris. His deep expertise is in developing Total Rewards Strategy and broad-based employee metrics and variable pay plans. He is expert in broad-based compensation plan design, management, and administration and has worked with many clients in developing Balanced Scorecard–based designs.

In addition to his consulting, Todd serves the professional community as lead faculty adviser for The WorldatWork's (formerly the ACA) broad-based variable pay course; a professional reviewer for its *Journal*; and a faculty member for its course on performance management. He is also adjunct professor, College of Labor and Industrial Relations, New York Institute of Technology.

Todd's human resources practitioner experiences are in the areas of compensation, benefits, and organization development. He served on active duty as an officer in the U.S. Navy and currently holds a commission as commander in the Naval Reserve.

Todd has an APC/Management from the New York University Stern School of Business, a Master of Business Administration from the New York Institute of Technology, a Bachelor of Science in Social Science from Michigan State University, and is a Certified Compensation Professional.

**Michael Dennis Graham** is a senior vice president in Clark/Bardes Consulting. In industry, he was Worldwide Director of Compensation & Benefits for both Albany International Corporation and Bausch and Lomb for ten years. Prior to joining the Clark/Bardes, he worked as a consultant and practice director with four major human resources consulting firms (Andersen Worldwide, Hay Group, Towers Perrin, and Watson Wyatt). He has led engagement teams in over 300 different organizations in the past eighteen years. His clients include organizations in all industries and countries.

Michael is a frequent speaker on such topics as Total Reward Strategy, people strategy, organization design, and retaining key talent with unique incentive programs.

He received a Master of Business Administration from Rensselaer Polytechnic Institute and a Bachelor of Science in Engineering from Worcester Polytechnic Institute.